Science with Storytelling

Science with Storytelling

Strategies for the K–5 Classroom

Edited by JANE STENSON,
SHERRY NORFOLK *and* LYNETTE J. FORD

McFarland & Company, Inc., Publishers
Jefferson, North Carolina

LIBRARY OF CONGRESS CATALOGUING-IN-PUBLICATION DATA

Names: Stenson, Jane, 1941– editor. | Norfolk, Sherry, 1952– editor. | Ford, Lyn, 1951– editor.
Title: Science with storytelling : strategies for the K-5 classroom / edited by Jane Stenson, Sherry Norfolk and Lynette J. Ford.
Description: Jefferson, North Carolina : McFarland & Company, Inc., Publishers, 2017] | Includes bibliographical references and index.
Identifiers: LCCN 2016049662 | ISBN 9780786498185 (softcover : acid free paper) ∞
Subjects: LCSH: Science—Study and teaching (Elementary) | Storytelling in education.
Classification: LCC LB1532 .S36 2016 | DDC 372.35/044—dc23
LC record available at https://lccn.loc.gov/2016049662

BRITISH LIBRARY CATALOGUING DATA ARE AVAILABLE

ISBN (print) 978-0-7864-9818-5
ISBN (ebook) 978-1-4766-2354-2

© 2017 Jane Stenson, Sherry Norfolk and Lynette J. Ford. All rights reserved

No part of this book may be reproduced or transmitted in any form or by any means, electronic or mechanical, including photocopying or recording, or by any information storage and retrieval system, without permission in writing from the publisher.

Front cover images of science students © 2017 ArtMarie/BraunS/iStock; Sherry Norfolk telling stories to a fourth grade class (author collection)

Printed in the United States of America

McFarland & Company, Inc., Publishers
Box 611, Jefferson, North Carolina 28640
www.mcfarlandpub.com

To the teachers and storytellers
whose curiosity, creativity, courage,
and love of story bring real advances
to the science classroom

and

in loving memory of Syd Lieberman (1944–2015), whose love of life and family translated into stories that made us care. Syd made science facts meaningful and history memorable, because they were so skillfully embedded in stories about people, and as he often said, "People care about people." Syd's work touched all of us as storytellers, teachers, parents, and partners in humanity. Syd's advice: "Follow what interests you, because you and the audience are the same. Ask questions."

"To raise new questions, new possibilities, to regard old problems from a new angle, requires creative imagination and marks real advance in science."—Albert Einstein

Table of Contents

Acknowledgments — xi

Preface — 1

Introduction
    Jane Stenson — 3

Science Is a Story
    Vito M. DiPinto — 11

Thinking Like a Scientist: How Do Scientists Figure Things Out?
    Mary Hamilton *and* Charles Wright — 13

Part One. Early Childhood: Pre-Kindergarten through Second Grade — 17

Introduction: "Eensy Weensy" First Steps into Scientific Inquiry
    Lynette J. Ford — 18

Physical Science

"Sody Sallyratus": States of Matter
    Sherry Norfolk *and* Jane Stenson — 22

"Anansi and Turtle Go to Dinner": Sink and Float
    Jane Stenson *with* Sherry Norfolk *and* Bobby Norfolk — 29

"How the Rainbow Was Made": Liquid Rainbow and the Density of Liquids
    Dana Allande O'Brien — 35

"The Lady Who Put Salt in Her Coffee"
    Vito M. DiPinto — 40

"Prairie Dogs in the Rain": Solving Problems with Simple Machines
SHERRY NORFOLK 46

Life Science

Creating a Pourquoi ("How and Why") Story
KATIE KNUTSON 52

Caterpillar to Butterfly: The Process of Metamorphosis
LYNETTE J. FORD 59

Caterpillar to Butterfly: Thoughts on Science and Storytelling
JUDITH BLACK 66

Hatching Chicks in the Kindergarten Classroom
TRACY DRUMMER AIDEN *and* ELIZABETH BARLOCK 75

"Tops and Bottoms": What Goes Up? What Goes Down?
JANE STENSON 80

"Why Mosquitoes Buzz in People's Ears": Pourquoi Stories and Mosquitoes
JOYCE H. GEARY 84

Stellaluna: Comparing and Contrasting Animal Needs
LINDSEY COHN 90

Earth and Space Science

"Rabbit's Tale": A Paiute Indian Nature Myth
LYNN RUBRIGHT 98

The Big Dipper: Patterns, Inspiration and Multicultural Stories
LYNETTE J. FORD 106

"Un Lazo a la Luna" and Other Tales: Observing the Moon
JANE STENSON 116

"Old Man Coyote and the Rock": The Rock Cycle
JANE STENSON 120

Part Two. Upper Elementary: Grades Three through Six 125

Introduction
SHERRY NORFOLK 126

Physical Science

"Turtle Wants to Fly": Gravity, Force, Thrust and Failure
LYNETTE J. FORD 130

Table of Contents ix

"Paddy the Bricklayer": Working and Playing with Pulleys
JANE STENSON ... 136

"The Lady Who Put Salt in Her Coffee": Life Science, Chemistry and Problem Solving Strategies
VITO M. DIPINTO ... 141

A Folktale Puppet Opportunity: Lights and Shadows
JANE STENSON *with* JULIE TUBBS ... 148

Life Science

"All Things Are Connected": Interdependence
SHERRY NORFOLK ... 155

Insects and Plants: Finding the Food Connection
MARY HAMILTON *and* CHARLES WRIGHT ... 160

"The Knee-High Man": Adding Science to Your Animal Stories
KEVIN STRAUSS ... 170

Developing Effective Animal Characters
KEVIN STRAUSS ... 175

An Adventure Through a Cell: Using Plant and Animal Cells to Create an Adventure Story
JENNY MCCRERY ... 180

George Washington Carver: The Argument for Crop Rotation
BOBBY NORFOLK *with* SHERRY NORFOLK ... 184

"Monkey and Buzzard": Animal Adaptations
FRAN STALLINGS *with* SHERRY NORFOLK ... 191

"Sausage Nose": Food Spoilage and Preservation
GEORDAN STENSON *with* CY ASHLEY WEBB ... 199

Nimrod and His Animal Teeth: Exploring Physical Structures, Functions, Life Cycles and Connections
INGRID NIXON ... 206

Earth and Space

"The Wave": Tsunamis
ANNE SHIMOJIMA *and* SHERI LUCTERHAND ... 215

"The Making of Whirlwind": The Cyclone Applied to a Dyson Vacuum Cleaner
JANE STENSON ... 220

x Table of Contents

Embodied Storytelling: Using Voice, Body, Visual Images
and Writing to Clarify a Pattern or Process
    ARIANNA ROSS   225

"How Dragon Lost His Tail": Shaping Landforms
    SHERRY NORFOLK   234

Pele, or a Volcanic Trip: Tectonic Plates, Sulfur Gases,
the Rock Cycle and Art
    JEFF GERE   239

To See Below the Surface: A Story of Folklore and Fossils
    DARLENE J. NEUMANN *and* LARRY C. NEUMANN   246

"Skunny Wundy and the Stone Giant": Crystallization
    MARILYN A. KINSELLA *and* LARRY KINSELLA   254

**Part Three. Conclusions and Possibilities: Storytelling
and the National Aeronautic and Space Administration**   260

An Interview with Beth Horner   261

An Interview with Jay O'Callahan   267

Science and Storytelling Online Resources
    Compiled by KAREN CHACE   273

Bibliography   281
    Compiled by LYNETTE J. FORD, SHERRY NORFOLK *and*
    JANE STENSON

About the Contributors   285

Index   295

Acknowledgments

Amazing and necessary advice came from a former university colleague and science educator Vito Dipinto, without whose help this book would not have been created.

Karen Chace was a huge help in gathering online resources for the bibliography. Thank you!

Our contributors worked miracles and continue to work miracles with children every day. We are indebted to you for your brilliance and your dedication and your ability to think critically, ask questions, and pursue what is curious to you.

*"A word is intrinsically powerful.
If you believe in the power of words,
you can bring about physical change in the universe."*
—N. Scott Momaday in *Ancestral Voice*

*"Words are intrinsically powerful. They are magical. By
means of words can one ... quiet the raging weather, bring
forth the harvest, ward off evil, rid the body of sickness and
pain, subdue an enemy, capture the heart of a lover, live in
the proper way, and venture beyond death."*
—N. Scott Momaday, "The Native Voice"
in *Columbia Literary History of the United States*

Preface

This is a book for curious people—for people who observe and experiment and ask questions, who are never really satisfied that they have the "right" answers, but who rigorously seek to "get it right." This is a book for story tellers, story listeners and story creators who tell the truth ... but not always factually.

Legend has it that scientists are exclusive, logical, and cold—"just stick to the facts"—linear people, while artists are expressive, emotional and not so sequential in how they approach life. Scientists live on genius and artists on epiphanies. Both are prejudices, and erroneous assumptions. Scientists are some of the most passionate people we know—but we have to learn to speak the same language. And artists, particularly storytelling artists, are some of the most accurate, logical thinkers we know ... but we cannot leap to unfounded conclusions. Rather, we can challenge ourselves to synthesize the combined strengths, ideas and knowledge presented by the disciplines of science and storytelling to inform and enhance both.

Every object in our life however old or new, however apparently humble or simple, holds the stories, thoughts and courage of thousands of people, some living, most dead—the accumulated new of fifty thousand years. Our tools and art are our humanity, our inheritance, the everlasting legacy of our ancestors. The things we make are the speech of our species: stories of triumph, courage, and creation, of optimism, adaptation, and hope; tales not of one person here and there, but of one people everywhere, written in a common language, not African, American, Asian or European but human.[1]

The present work synthesizes the values of the old tales with the educational demands for STEM topics—science, technology, engineering and math. The pendulum has swung toward innovation and the technologies that support what is new and toward active learning where students' natural curiosity allows them to pursue and develop scientific understanding through their experiences. Yet it is the old stories, told orally, that contain the wisdom of a culture, and the relational, told stories have always been the most powerful means of relating new technologies and humane values.

There is no magic to the ordinary hard work of creating just the right story or just the right chemical compound or useful tool. And so it is that we have noticed schools avoiding folktales because they are "soft." Folktales seem to be understood as no longer current or relevant in this STEM world. And, curiously, we have noticed that science is not—Congress passed the America COMPETES Act in 2007—getting *its* stories told (NASA being a notable exception). Elementary school science teaching is woefully underdeveloped; even teacher preparation emphasizes literacy and math at the expense of the sciences.

We (the authors/editors) are storytellers, teaching artists, and education practitioners, and we asked our friends and colleagues—some scientists, some storytellers, some storytelling teaching artists—to provide examples that will be useful to those who work with kindergarten through grade six children where story, particularly storytelling, and science activity can compatibly live together in order to lead to understanding. Our colleagues offer many fine ideas and examples of witty, wordy folktales coupled with rigorous science activity for primary classrooms in Part One, and for upper elementary classes in Part Two.

This is a book for storytellers and science/classroom teachers—those who recognize and accept the challenge of making science learning deep, relevant and meaningful! and for those who recognize that science is a story that WILL be told!

NOTE

1. Kevin Ashton. *How to Fly a Horse: The Secret History of Creation, Invention, and Discovery.* New York: Doubleday, 2015.

Introduction

JANE STENSON

How does the power of storytelling and story listening
demonstrate the various technologies of our culture?

How do narrative and science intersect?

How many ways are there to know something?

How is it that all knowledge can be taught and learned in
so many different domains, particularly in the arts?

How is science best taught and learned?

Why doesn't this model work?
What should I change to make it work?

Looking out my kitchen window onto snow-laden earth here in Southwest Wisconsin, I am reminded of various sciences that are truly awesome, and yet I observe them without truly seeing them. I take them for granted—the workings of my eyes, the heat in my house, the beep of my computer, the frosted windows, the birds and the feeders, animal tracks in the snow, windswept places, dormant plants, traffic at the bottom of the large hill where a neighbor's car is skidding. Oh, and the gray sky and the sun—is that sun really east or has it moved south? What is it that I see? And what can I discover? Physical Sciences, Earth & Space Sciences, and Life Sciences present in obvious ways, yet … and yet. Pushing them aside, I work on a story to tell, more comfortable with metaphor. I swing from factual elemental sightings and decide I will think critically about only the *big* ideas in my story—and run into the same situation: These days the world seems more interested in exploring the central role of science and technology in shaping human life, civilization and thought, and yet, I am largely unaware of the "science" that surrounds me. Give me a story to tell and to hear!

4   Introduction by Jane Stenson

It is a dual focus that Lynette J. Ford, Sherry Norfolk and I wish to pursue … how can, and how does, storytelling convey information about the various technologies of a culture? How can storytelling and science enliven each other? What are the interesting stories of science and technology that we should be telling and hearing? What does it mean to think critically about engines and pulleys, the sun and the moon, the rocks and the trees? Why embed science in a narrative format? Why tell science as a story? Why enliven and bring to the fore the science information embedded in the wise old stories? How relevant are the stories we tell to what are considered the "big ideas" of today?

As storytellers and storytelling teaching artists, the information we want to share is contained in a narrative, not a list of facts. Therefore, if I want to learn about and teach others about the parts of a plant, I go to the folktale "Tops and Bottoms" which has versions in several storytelling traditions. The folktale offers a witty, language-laden experience in which to frame the factual information. In the classroom a schematic of a plant structure plus lots of active experiences reinforce in a linear way what that folktale has presented. How will children likely remember the facts—through the story of a lazy bear and a hard-working, quick thinking hare *and* the linear list of the plants' components and functions? Yes! Storytelling and science are complementary, and allow us to exercise both sides of the brain in a unified pursuit.

Our brains leap to finding and interpreting patterns, so we must slow down to closely observe what we see versus what we wish we were seeing. This is the beginning of looking for the tools and technologies that shape our lives, which is just as important as the stories that govern our lives. Often the old stories are about the dream life (imagined equipment or special tool) of the folk and those dreams ultimately—through the decades—lead to scientific inventions and creations. For example, in the Russian tale "The Fool of the World and the Flying Machine":

> The ancient one says to the Fool, "Listen to me. Off you go into the forest. Go up to the first big tree you see. Make a sacred sign before it. Strike it a blow with your little hatchet. Fall backwards on the ground, and lay there, full length on your back, until somebody wakes you up. Then you will find the ship made, all ready to fly. Sit you down in it, and fly off whither you want to go. But be sure on the way to give a lift to everyone you meet."[1]

Of course this is magic … and a precursor to the technology that permits and allows the creation of an airplane. But dreams are not creative acts; rather, developing a product—execution—is the creative act. Think how many attempted flight, and synthesized other scientific knowledge into their models (people studying birds, Lilienthal's bat glider, the Wright brothers and their adaptation of the bicycle to the problem of equilibrium, etc.) before we arrived at today's complicated technology. The story of flight is the accumulation of activity and associated thinking over time layered with technical language and continually asking, "Why doesn't it work?"—from dreams of what might be, through documented layers of "failures" to a collaboration of activity over time. We do well to consider that the true story of scientific discovery is so awesome and exciting that it is important enough for storytelling—you can't make these things up.

As Anthony Fredericks writes, "For children, science can and should become a dynamic and interactive discipline. It should allow children to examine new ideas, play around with concepts and precepts, and discover that there is no such thing as a body of finite knowledge. What does this mean for teachers? It means children must be given a multitude of opportunities to probe, poke, and peek into the mysteries of the universe—whether that universe is their own backyard or a galaxy far away."[2]

Let's entertain the idea that storytelling and science share many strengths. Close observation of the tools and the stories of every culture make us realize that the scientific method, folktale structure and the engineering process are similar—similar enough to encourage all of us to slow down, pay attention and determine how to effect a needed change in science and in storytelling pedagogy (making both meaningful, creative and full of real-world problem solving). (See chart following the introduction.) Our brains are designed to remember best what is presented in story[3] and to detect patterns and make interpretations.[4] Layering language onto observations and moving that language into a story—whether of a character's dilemma or of how the tools are used—synthesizes what we as humans do best.

Expressing what one sees and feels is challenging ... and language isn't easily available. How often even we adults stutter and speak in fragments and get our sentences out of order. We read about the word gap of too many kindergarten children and know these children will struggle with school requirements and skills, as well as interaction experiences, their entire lives.[5] Where is the interactive basket of words that expands understanding, develops humor and love and humane development? That basket is story—the told story carrying vocabulary and meaning and comprehension and communication.

We know schools concentrate on the acquisition of measurable skills and knowledge in order to meet testing requirements. We know schools concentrate on completing work in a prescribed time period (covering the curriculum) and aim for deeper understanding. Hence storytelling!

But even classroom activity does not guarantee understanding when what must also happen is reflection, or *think time*. Authentic intellectual activity means observation, solving problems, making decisions and developing understanding using the tools and methods of the discipline, layered with descriptive, definitive, domain-appropriate language. Again, hence storytelling!

The language and structure of folktales and myth overarch the daily nature of our lives ... the observable and commonplace realities of life science, earth and space science and physical science. The tales present the lives of the folk and as such are cultural offerings ... more than "just" entertainment, yet even here the science is so embedded that it might seem to be missing. The artistic and scientific creativity involved in bringing these tales to life inspires and challenges us.

And the goal? That children's curiosity is so sparked by the story that scientific development becomes, "What questions do you find here in this awesome world?"

The present work begins with messages from two scientists; one asks that we think of science as a story while the other asks that we recognize what it means to think like a scientist; these are not mutually exclusive ideas! "Part One: Pre-Kindergarten through Second Grade," delves into the Life Sciences, Earth and Space Sciences, and Physics as the broad spectrum of science taught in schools. Part Two addresses the same topics for Upper Elementary students. The third part presents conclusions, and interviews with two renowned storytellers who have been tapped by NASA for their unique services, demonstrating the clear link between science, education and storytelling. Next follows a list of resources, compiled for the benefit of educators who wish to further explore working storytelling into their curriculum.

Beginning each lesson plan in a similar way tells you we are looking at the science and the story as an integrated unit, a metacognitive, integrated arts approach.

- The TITLE includes the story title and the science to be taught, along with the contributor's name.
- The CCC or Crosscutting Concepts and the POSE or Practices of Scientists and Engineers speak to the integrated science activity (discussed below).
- The story—either the full text or a synopsis—follows with its source.

Then we get specific with the "how-to" section of each article, providing:

- The Next Generation Science Standards (NGSS) covered.
- The Common Core State Standards (CCSS) covered.
- The relevant Artistic Processes of the National Core Arts Standards (see discussion below).

Next follows the Instructional Plan, which consists of a rationale, preparation, objectives, materials, activities, and assessment. It delineates how the story and science mesh and elaborate upon each other. Note that the objectives are measurable, that is, the student says "I can" accomplish the science, language arts, and art activities. There is a direct relationship between the objectives and assessment, helping form a progressive, metacognitive approach to teaching and learning.

And we have included a multitude of educational standards. We also have very high standards for ourselves and our work, and we have high ideals about how children can be encouraged to think critically about the world of people and the world of science. We want life to go "right" for children. When standards are established as an ideal rather than as a judgment, we (scientists, storytellers, educators) can work together and achieve our goals. It is our hope that by pursuing storytelling in the science domain and science in the storytelling domain we will provide a portal for deeper understanding and expression. Essentially, this book is about the intersection of language arts and science, integrating the arts and the sciences to create holistic learning opportunities; therefore, each of the lesson plans authentically addresses science, language arts, and fine arts standards.

Common Core State Standards (CCSS) are a set of "college-and-career-ready standards" in English-language arts, literacy, and mathematics for students in kindergarten through 12th grade; additionally, now available are language arts standards in science and in history. The National Governors' Association Center, after an independent, non-partisan research organization report issued in 2008, recommended that states upgrade their standards "by adopting a common core of internationally benchmarked standards in math and language arts for grades K–12." Forty-two states, Puerto Rico, the Virgin Islands, and District of Columbia accepted the CCSS. The curriculum and supportive materials for implementation and teaching of the Common Core are in the hands of leaders at the state and local levels. The purpose of a common core of standards is to equip students with the knowledge and skills that will prepare them for introductory courses in two- or four-year college programs, or to be "globally competitive" in the world's workforce. Those skills include more than straightforward language arts and math skills, including critical thinking, problem solving, communication and analytical ability. More information is available at the Common Core State Standards Initiative website: http://www.corestandards.org/.[6]

The Next Generation Science Standards (NGSS) (http://www.nextgenscience.org/) were developed because of major advances in science itself and in the understanding of how students learn. These advances were not reflected in the traditional state standards, established more than two decades ago; NGSS standards were developed by teams from twenty-six states under the direction of an independent science organization and then were reviewed by the National Research Council of the National Academy of Sciences. Quality science education for the twenty-first century needed to align with standards that reflect current content and practice in curricula, pedagogy, assessment, and up-to-date teacher preparation and development, as well as research on science and science learning. Completed in 2013, they address core ideas in science topic disciplines and performance criteria in the physical sciences, earth and space sciences, and the life sciences. The state adoption process is still occurring.[7]

The National Core Arts Standards (NCAS) were developed by a coalition of 10 national organizations plus the Kennedy Center and the Lincoln Center (as a group, called the National Coalition for Core Arts Standards), and are

> new voluntary arts standards designed to guide the delivery of arts education in the classroom with new ways of thinking, learning, and creating. The standards inform policy-makers about implementation of arts programs for the traditional and emerging models and structures of education. As with other subject areas, a commitment to quality education, equitable opportunities, and comprehensive expectations is embedded within the new arts standards. The standards and their accompanying documents outline the philosophy, primary goals, dynamic processes, structures, and outcomes that shape student learning and achievement in dance, media arts, music, theatre, and visual arts, as articulated in the National Core Arts Standards.[8]

The NCAS were introduced in 2014; scrutiny and adoption by states is ongoing. To learn more about the National Core Arts Standards go to www.nationalartsstandards.org. For the purposes of this book, we cited only the relevant Artistic Processes. This decision was made because while all of our instructional ideas involve storytelling (which is included in the NCAS under Theatre), many also include other disciplines. The four Artistic Processes are shared among the five arts disciplines, and are over-arching "big buckets":

Creating: Conceiving and developing new artistic ideas and work.

Performing/Presenting/Producing: Realizing artistic ideas and work through interpretation and presentation.

Responding: Understanding and evaluating how the arts convey meaning.

Connecting: Relating artistic ideas and work with personal meaning and external context.[9]

NOTES

1. Andrew Lang, *Yellow Fairy Book*. London: Dover Press, 1894.

2. Anthony Fredericks, "Evaluating and Using Nonfiction Literature in the Science Curriculum," *Making Facts Come Alive: Choosing and Using Nonfiction Literature K–8*, Rosemary A. Bamford and Janice V. Kristo, eds. Norwood, Massachusetts: Christopher-Gordon Publishers, 2003.

3. Kendall Haven, *Story Proof: The Science Behind the Startling Power of Story*. Westport, Connecticut: Libraries Unlimited, 2007.

4. David Sousa and Tom Pilecki, *From STEM to STEAM: Using Brain-Compatible Strategies to Integrate the Arts*. Thousand Oaks, California: Corwin, 2013.

5. Betty Hart and T.R. Riesley, "The Early Catastrophe: The 30 Million Word

Gap by Age 3," *American Educator* (Spring 2003), pp. 4–9. http://www.aft.org//sites/default/files/periodicals/TheEarlyCatastrophe.

6. Any publication or public display of the Common Core State Standards shall include the following notice: "© Copyright 2010. National Governors Association Center for Best Practices and Council of Chief State School Officers. All rights reserved."

7. The suggested citation for publication in printed format from the Next Generation Science Standards is: NGSS Lead States. 2013. *Next Generation Science Standards: For States, By States*. Washington, D.C.: The National Academies Press.

8. National Art Standards. http://www.nationalartsstandards.org.

9. National Coalition for Core Arts Standards. *National Core Arts Standards: A Conceptual Framework for Arts Learning*, p. 11. http://www.nationalartsstandards.org/sites/default/files/NCCAS%20%20Conceptual%20Framework_0.pdf.

Similarities of Folktales, Science and Engineering

Folktale Structure	*Scientific Method*	*Engineering Design Process*
1. **Who is the main character and what is the setting?** Be certain to include sensory descriptors of the character and the setting. AND this needs to be addressed in narrative.	1. **Ask a question.** What are you curious about; what do you want to know?	1. **Define the Problem**
		2. **Do Background Research**
	2. **Do Background Research.** Follow your curiosities and get a sense of each piece of the problem.	3. **Specify Requirements**
		4. **Brainstorm Solutions**
		5. **Choose the Best Solution**
2. **What is the question of the STORY?** This is the dilemma that the theme of the story pursues ... the character tries to solve puzzle/question/problem/conflict.	3. **Construct a Hypothesis.** Place the main character in a situation and ask questions about the character and about the situation.	6. **Do Development Work**
		7. **Build a Prototype**
		8. **Test and Redesign**
3. **Sure enough, the problem gets worse**—more complicated, seemingly more difficult to solve. The main character should have a real dilemma, as in "life can be really messy."	4. **Test Your Hypothesis by Doing an Experiment.** What solutions did you attempt?	
	5. **Analyze Your Data and Draw a Conclusion.** Answer the question the (science) story asked.	
4. **What are some attempts to answer the question and solve the problem?** In some cultures three is the number of challenges and in others four. (This section can be extended to form a strong arc to the story.)	6. **Communicate Your Results.** A coda? Denouement? Tell the observed truth.	

10   Introduction by Jane Stenson

Folktale Structure

5. Answer the question.
Solve the problem; reach a resolution.

6. The calming down of the story. Communicate the importance of the story. Tell the emotional truth.

Scientific Method

Engineering Design Process

@JStenson2014

Science Is a Story

Vito M. DiPinto

What if science was conceptualized as a story? Story has been the primary means by which human beings have communicated and passed down information and culture from generation to generation. Oral tradition gave way to written narratives; during our lifetimes, written narrative evolved from various analog formats to digital presentations. However, these stories still rely upon text or language. Pictures, ideas, and concepts are painted in words. Words inherently require language. Pictures, illustration, and visual images are ways to transcend the limitations of text.

What if science was conceptualized as a story? Imagine your child's science textbook is a story you tell around a metaphoric campfire. Or imagine that your child's science textbook is a chapter book that your child reads throughout his/her K–8 learning experience adding to the on-going science story each school year.

What if science was conceptualized as a story? What story does science tell? Brian Swimme describes the short version as: You take hydrogen atoms and leave them alone for 10 billion years and you get roses, giraffes and us! This is a remarkable intriguing story; yet, it is never told in your child's science textbook. Using picture storybooks and children literature is one way not only to tell this story but also to engage the scientific imaginings of your child(ren).

Here is some wisdom from children's literature.

> "Think left and think right
> And think low and think high.
> Oh, the THINKS you can think up
> If you only try!"
> Dr. Seuss, *Oh, the THINKS you can think!*

"When your head's full of pictures, they have to come out."—
Bill Maynard, *Incredible Ned.*

"The whole world is full of things, and somebody has to look for them."—Astrid Lindgren, *Pippi Longstocking*.

"You must always take risks when experimenting."—Tove Jansson, *Fin Family Moomintroll*.

"Anyone can fly. All you need is somewhere to go that you can't get to any other way. The next thing you know, you're flying among the stars."—Faith Ringgold, *Tar Beach*.

Finally, let us consider the following model, to which we will return later in the text.

The "I Wonder" Model of Science Teaching and Learning

"I Wonder"
I wonder
I explore
I question
I investigate
I analyze
I interpret
I share
I act
I inspire
I wonder…

Thinking Like a Scientist
How Do Scientists Figure Things Out?
MARY HAMILTON *and* CHARLES WRIGHT

Pose topic: "Distinguish among facts, reasoned judgment based on research findings, and speculation in an explanation."
CCC topic: "Science theories are based on a body of evidence and many tests."; "Science explanations describe the mechanisms for natural events."

This story also appears in Mary and Charles' article Insects & Plants in Part II. This first-person anecdote is a true story retelling an incident experienced by Mary and is followed by a conversation with her husband Charles and can be successfully used with their science activity, as well as a stand-alone lesson.

One day I was carrying bags of groceries into my house, and I saw a blue-black wasp caught in a spider's web near the front door. "Uh oh," I thought, "that wasp is going to be a spider's dinner." But then I noticed that only two of the wasp's six legs were touching the web. "Wait just a minute," I said to myself, "I've seen moths with more legs caught escape from spider webs. Something's up. I wonder what?" So, I set my groceries down, and I watched.

The wasp shook the web and shook the web, as if struggling to escape. The spider ran toward the wasp, then stopped, and ran away. Again, the wasp shook the web, as if to say, "Help! Help! I'm caught!" Again the spider ran toward it, but once again it stopped and ran away. The wasp shook the web even more. This time, when the spider ran toward the wasp, it did not stop.

I expected the spider to grab the wasp. Instead, the wasp grabbed the spider. Then the wasp flew over to a window shutter and crawled behind it while still holding the spider. From behind the shutter I heard a high pitched whine. After that, I picked up my grocery bags and carried them inside.

Later my husband Charles came home. I said, "Charles, today I saw a blue-black wasp catch a spider! It took it back behind the shutter, and I heard it eat it!"

Charles is an amateur entomologist so he's been learning about insects for years. He said, "I don't believe you heard the wasp eat the spider. I think you saw a kind of wasp called a mud dauber. Some mud daubers are blue-black and they build their nests in sheltered places, like behind our shutter.

"When a mud dauber catches a spider it doesn't eat it. Instead, it stings the spider to paralyze it, not kill it. Then, the mud dauber carries the spider to its nest, stuffs it in and lays an egg on it. When the mud dauber egg hatches, the larva eats the spider."

"Oh my," I gasped, "that's amazing!"

"But that's not all. If a small bright blue cuckoo wasp happened to be nearby, it would wait for the mud dauber to leave the newly made nest. Then the cuckoo wasp would fly in, and lay its egg on the spider. Because its egg would hatch first, the cuckoo wasp larva would have both mud dauber egg and spider to eat."

Wow! I thought spiders were creatures that ate insects, but on that day, I learned spiders can become insect larva food instead.

Objectives

Fifth Grade students will be able to say...

- I can identify when characters in a story are thinking like scientists. (Basic lesson)

A more advanced lesson would include the following:

- I can propose *questions* scientists would have needed to answer to find out about the relationship between mud daubers, spiders, and cuckoo wasps.
- I can suggest studies (*observations, experiments*) scientists might have conducted to find answers to their questions about the relationship between mud daubers and spiders.

First Objective

Mary Hamilton's thoughts on what the story shows about scientific thinking.

In the personal anecdote, I am thinking like a scientist at first. (I notice an insect caught in a spider's web. I use past experience with spider's webs

16   Thinking Like a Scientist

The answers to such questions will prompt students to think about what scientists observe that prompt them to ask questions and what sort of scientific tests/experiments scientists might have conducted to learn what they know today about mud daubers catching spiders to feed their larva, and cuckoo wasps laying their eggs in mud dauber nests.

This example of "Thinking Like a Scientist" is applicable to all science and to storytelling.

to anticipate it will become the spider's dinner; however, when I notice only two legs are caught, I call upon past experience of watching moths escape spider webs and decide to observe to see what it really happening.) As I watch the spider, I am thinking like a scientist—observing and noticing what I am seeing.

But then, when Charles comes home, I completely mess up on thinking like a scientist when I tell Charles I heard the wasp eat the spider. I did not see it, and I had no past research through study or reading and no past experience with spider-eating wasps to back up that conclusion. However, I have a good imagination; scientists may have good imaginations too, but they don't announce their ideas until they can back them up with evidence.

Charles, however, has lots of past studying and reading of research on insects. He shows scientific thinking when he connects the "blue black wasp" with the sheltered nest location and suggests I saw a mud dauber. He then tells me what he knows likely happened behind the shutter based on his past reading about mud dauber behavior.

His additional information on cuckoo wasp behavior also comes from his reading—*he's not making anything up!*

So, a basic lesson on thinking like a scientist would be using the story to demonstrate where thinking can fall short of scientific standards (leaping to conclusions instead of basing information on evidence or research findings). So, in discussing a story's characters to decide who is thinking like a scientist, ask follow-up questions: "What makes you say that?" "What evidence from the story or text do you have?"

Second and Third Objectives

You can also use the personal anecdote to promote scientific thinking by asking students to consider what questions scientists might have asked and what studies scientists might have conducted to answer their questions about the relationship between mud daubers, spiders, and cuckoo wasps.

Examples:

A scientist might have asked, "Why did the mud dauber catch a spider?"

How could scientists have learned the mud dauber did not eat the spider?

Once scientists learned the spider had not been eaten, how could they have learned why the mud dauber put the spider in the nest?

How could they have learned the spider was paralyzed and not dead?
How could they have learned what happened to the paralyzed spider?
How would they have known to investigate cuckoo wasp behavior?
How could they have figured out what the cuckoo wasp was doing?

PART ONE

Early Childhood
Pre-Kindergarten through Second Grade

Introduction
"Eensy Weensy" First Steps Into Scientific Inquiry

Lynette J. Ford

"Science and stories are not only compatible, they're inseparable."—Roald Hoffmann, 2005

> The eensy weensy spider went up the water spout.
> Down came the rain and washed the spider out.
> Out came the sun and dried up all the rain, so the
> Eensy weensy spider went up the spout again.

"How big is an 'eensy weensy' spider? Does anyone know another word that means 'eensy weensy'? Yes, 'little,' 'tiny,' *very* tiny.... Let's gather some information on eensy weensy spiders...."

Long, long ago, in my preschool-teaching days, the inquiry into the lives and behaviors of spiders, the introduction of new vocabulary, a simple study of information on weather concepts, and transcultural storytelling began with a creepy-crawly adventure and a fingerplay. Movement and rhyming words and a simple tune distracted from the protagonist of the piece—a spider. That song's cute little spider hardly resembled the eight-legged monster who had prompted our teachable moment; a huge, black and yellow spider had managed to follow the children from the playground into the classroom. Panic ensued, with high-pitched screams and rampaging little bodies searching for large toys and books to throw at an unsuspecting garden arachnid simply taking a stroll on a warm summer's day.

Although I am not a fan of spiders, I managed to capture the thing under a cup. I slid a piece of cardboard beneath the cup, lifted cup and cardboard and my catch, and carried it back to the playground, where my assistant teacher and our students waited with a small aquarium. I dropped everything into the aquarium, retrieved the cup and cardboard, and began to sing: "The eensy weensy spider…" Whereupon my assistant said, "That is *not* an eensy weensy spider." She slid a fine-meshed screen over the top of the aquarium, and weighted the screen with a rock. My assistant teacher was not a fan of spiders, either.

The spider was named "Big Boo."

Research began. What kind of spider was this? What would it eat? What else might it need to survive? Should we keep it in the aquarium to show parents (one child wanted to scare his big sister, of course), or would it be better for the spider if we immediately let it go? In the days before easy Internet access and Googled encyclopedic information, we pulled out the childcare center's encyclopedias and every book we could find that had any details about spiders. And we sang "Eensy Weensy Spider," replete with gestures and emphasis on the directional statements "up," "down," and "out," again and again.

After my shift had ended that day, I stopped at our local public library and gathered more books for the children, nonfiction picture books about spiders, easy readers about spiders, books the big folks would have to read and share about spiders. And I thought about some confusing actions and words in the nursery rhyme's fictional spider journey, and the factual spider journey our students were trekking thanks to Big Boo.

We had made a word list: "spider"; "spout"; "up"; "down"; "rain"; "sun." The children's self-created definitions were added, with room for more. There was some confusion about the meaning of an adjectival phrase, for the quoted fingerplay made no distinction between the spider's size (eensy weensy) and the finger movements that denoted the spider's actions. Some of our four-year-old students mistook that descriptive phrase representing the spider's size for the movements of fingers, twisting back and forth and rising on something that could have been a small swirl or potentially dangerous roil of oceanic water.

The water spout (two words) mentioned in the nursery rhyme is a pipe for carrying rainwater from a building's gutters. We added the word "gutter" to the word list.

But a waterspout (one word) could have meant something far more dangerous. In this era of easily accessible information, on the page, "What is a waterspout?" on the website of the National Oceanic and Atmospheric Administration, one finds the following definition:

> A water spout is a whirling column of air and water mist…. Tornadic waterspouts are tornadoes that form over water, or move from land to water. They have the same characteristics as a land tornado. They are associated with severe thunderstorms, and are often accompanied by high winds and seas, large hail, and frequent dangerous lightning…. Fair weather waterspouts form in light wind conditions so they normally move very little….

> Typically, fair weather waterspouts dissipate rapidly when they make landfall, and rarely penetrate far inland.[1]

This talk of oceans and spiders encouraged us to cross the waters from the United States to the West Coast of Africa, and the Akan tales of the trickster-hero, Anansi the Spider (see "Anansi and Turtle" in the Physical Science section of this part).

The word list grew: "creeping" and "eensy weensy" were now clarified and made distinctive with visual and physical imagery as the children danced. And we spent some time listing the differences and similarities between the facts of Big Boo and the fictions of Anansi: real spiders don't talk like people; real spiders can live in houses as Anansi does, but real spiders don't cook or dance like Anansi.

What happened to Big Boo? After about an hour's worth of observation and speculation, documented on large pieces of white paper and illustrations created by the children, Mrs. Big Boo (for the children had determined this must be "a girl spider" because she was so big, and the entry in the encyclopedia stated that many female spiders are larger than the males) was released into the wild far from the doors of the childcare center. The decision was one that came from the children, with the remarks, "Take her picture and let her go. If we keep her, somebody has to feed her. What if she dies? And what if we come back in the morning, and she's *gone*?!?"

The study of Mrs. Big Boo (albeit in absentia) went on for more than a week, and included illustrated stories of the day we found her, the way "we" captured her, the knowledge we gained from her, and the happy moment when we said goodbye to her.

I was excited to discern the wisdom of young scientists who had utilized logical, critical thinking, and knowledge based in research and scientific study. I could imagine how well these students might do in and beyond their kindergarten classrooms.

I was also relieved. What if we had come back in the morning, and Mrs. Big Boo *was* gone? That was a question I would not have wanted to answer.

What's the big picture we can appreciate in all of this? Our students, some of whom would soon attend public and private schools, had experienced the following cross-curricular events:

- using English Language Arts skills in intonation, rhythm, rhyme, and the use of descriptive words and phrases and action verbs, as well as researching and sharing both fictional and nonfictional narratives in visual and oral formats;
- practicing scientific research, and formulating questions and conclusions;

- enriching self-initiated studies with music, movement, song, illustrations, folktales and stories transcribed for them to keep.

All that from a not-so-eensy-weensy spider.

In Part One, we offer similar steps toward scientific inquiry, research, and conclusion, through the use of multicultural folk tales and pourquoi (how and why) tales, and the instructional plans that accompany them. The chapter is specific to educational planning for kindergarten through second grades. The structure of these lesson plans corresponds to the Next Generations Science Standard's "call to action that the education system meets the learning needs of the nation's increasingly diverse student population."[2] "Thus, students develop mastery of crosscutting concepts through repeated and contrastive experiences across school curricula."[3] The first steps toward such mastery can begin with a well-told, well-heard, well-experienced story, even one that is as simple as a fingerplay.

NOTES

1. Quoted from "What is a water spout?," http://oceanservice.noaa/gov/facts.waterspout.html. the website of the National Oceanic and Atmospheric Administration of the United States Department of Commerce.

2. Appendix D—"All Standards, All Students": Making the Next Generation Science Standards Accessible to All Students, p. 1.

3. *Ibid.*, p. 3.

"Sody Sallyratus"
States of Matter
SHERRY NORFOLK *and* JANE STENSON

CCC topic: Patterns, cause and effect, energy and matter
POSE topic: Asking questions (science) and defining problems (engineering)

The Story

Sody Sallyratus

Source: Margaret Read MacDonald in *Twenty Tellable Tales*,
retold, with science additions, by Jane Stenson

One time there was an Old Man, and Old Woman, a Little Boy, a Little Girl, and a Pet Squirrel up on the mantelpiece. Ran back and forth, back and forth, and he chattered.

One day the Old Woman went to the cupboard to get the ingredients to make some biscuits, and she didn't have any Sody Sallyratus. That's baking soda, you know, to make the biscuits rise.

So, she called Little Boy. Says, "You go on down to the grocery store and git some Sody Sallyratus."

Little Boy went out and toward the grocery store. He went walking down the road ... and walking down the road ... singing, "Sody, Sody, Sody Sallyratus!" And walking across the bridge.... Went on down to the store and bought some Sody Sallyratus. Put it loose in a brown paper bag.

Came on walking back up the road.... Starting walking across that bridge ... and an old bear stuck his head out from under the bridge.

"Who's that walking over my bridge?"

"Just me, Little Boy, me and my Sody Sallyratus!"

"Well—ell-ell-ell, I'm going to eat-you-up! You and your Sody Sallyratus too!"

And sure enough that old bear swallowed that Little Boy down. GLUMP ... GLUMP.... Just like that! Little Boy didn't come home.

So the Old Woman called Little Girl, "Little Girl, run on down to the grocery store. See what's keeping Little Boy. He should have been home by now."

Little Girl started out. She went walking down the road ... and walking down the road ... singing "Sody, Sody, Sody Sallyratus!" Started walking across that bridge.

And big Old Bear stuck his head out from under the bridge!

"Who's that walking across my bridge?????"

"Just me, Little Girl."

"Well—ell—ell, I ate the Little Boy, Him and his Sody Sallyratus too, and I reckon I'll eat you up."

And big Old Bear swallowed up Little Girl. GLUMP ... GLUMP.... Just like that!

The Old Woman waited and waited.... Little Girl didn't come home. So Old Woman called the Old Man: "Old Man, go on down to the grocery store and see why Little Boy and Little Girl don't come home." So, Old Man went on out. He went walking down the road ... and walking down the road ... singing, "Sody, Sody, Sody Sallyratus!" Started walking across that bridge.

And that huge Old Bear stuck his head out.

"Who's that walking across my bridge?" says Old Bear.

"Just me, (I'm) Old Man."

"Well-ell-ell, I ate Little Girl, and I ate Little Boy, him and his Sody Sallyratus. And I reckon I'm going to eat you too!" And that huge Old Bear swallowed the Old Man down. GLUMP ... GLUMP.... Just like that! Old Man didn't come home.

Old Woman waited and waited ... and finally she said, "I'm going to see what's keeping them." And she went walking down the road and walking down the road. Started walking across that bridge.

And Old Bear, who by this time was enormous, stuck his head out from under the bridge, "Who's that walking over my bridge?"

"Just me, Old Woman."

"WELL, -ell, -ell, -ell I ate the Old Man. And I ate the Little Girl. And I ate the Little Boy, him and his Sody Sallyratus. And I reckon I'm going to eat you too!" And he swallowed her down GLUMP ... GLUMP.... Just like that!

Well, who was left? The Pet Squirrel back home on the mantelpiece running back and forth, back and forth. He went running up and down the mantelpiece ... and running up and down the mantelpiece.... Said: "I'd better go see what's keeping those fool folks. They should have come home and baked my biscuits before now." And Pet Squirrel went skipping out the door ... skipping down the road ... skipping down the road ... started skipping across that bridge...

And the Old Bear stuck his head out from under the bridge and rose up full and fierce on his hind legs!

"Who's that skipping over my bridge???!"

"Just me, Little Squirrel."

"Well, -ell,-ell, I ate the Old Woman, and the Old Man. I ate the Little Girl and the Little Boy, him and his Sody Sallyratus. And I reckon I'm going to eat you too."

And Old Bear snapped at that Little Squirrel...

But Little Squirrel ran off that bridge and ran up the nearest tree! And turned to look at Bear. And he chattered at that bear. Old Bear was mad. He came a-climbing out from under the bridge and started climbing up the tree after Little Squirrel. Little Squirrel went higher and higher. Old Bear came higher and higher. Little Squirrel went higher ... and higher still.... Old Bear came higher ... and higher still.... Clear to the very tip-top of that tree. The tree swayed left and then leaned right, right then left.

Little Squirrel climbed out on a long limb.... Old Bear climbed right out after him. The limb sagged.

Little Squirrel looked around ... he was so frightened ... and he gave a great leap onto the next tree. Old Bear looked down at the ground.... He looked over to the next tree ... and Old Bear said: "HUMPF! If he can jump with those little stubby legs of his.... Why I can jump it with these Great Big Legs of Mine!"

And *he* jumped! And you know what happened to him.... He fell right down to the ground ... busted wide open.... And almost killed him dead ... but not quite....

And when he busted open ... why out came the Old Lady! And the Old Man! ... and the Little Girl ... and the Little Boy! And they weren't hurt at all. Because he'd swallowed them whole, you know....

And the Old Lady said, "Where's my Sody Sallyratus??"

And Little Boy said, "Here it is!" and he held up a wet, slimy paper bag that the bottom had been worn off ... and the Sody Sallyratus was long gone. He handed it to the Old Woman who nodded for Little Boy to go back to the store and buy more.

While he did that, she took out a needle and thread and stitched up Old Bear good as new.

She said, "Old Bear, You go away from these woods, and don't come back to these parts

No More! Not ever again!" Old Bear got to his feet. He said, "HUMPF!!!" And he walked off and never ever did come back no more.

When Little Boy got back from the store, they all walked home together—the Old Woman, the Old Man, the Little Girl and the Little Boy—him and his bag of Sody Sallyratus. Pet Squirrel scooted on ahead of them, climbed back on the mantelpiece, and curled his tail over his back, and watched the Old Woman until she took the biscuits out of the oven. They smelled delicious and raised right up just the way a biscuit is supposed to be. Old Woman broke him off a piece and blew it cool and handed it to him. Pet Squirrel took the biscuit in his forepaws and turned it over and nibbled on it—and when he finished it, he leaned down and chattered for more! He was so hungry, Old Woman had to hand him chunks till he eaten two whole biscuits!

(This telling leans heavily on Margaret Read MacDonald's version. I credit her when I tell it. Another version is by Richard Chase found in *Grandfather Tales*. The bear dies in that version.)

Standards

NGSS—Physical Science (Chemistry)

PS1.A: Structure and Properties of Matter

- Different kinds of matter exist and many of them can be either solid or liquid, depending on temperature. Matter can be described and classified by its observable properties. (2-PS1-1)
- Different properties are suited to different purposes. (2-PS1-2), (2-PS1-3)
- A great variety of objects can be built up from a small set of pieces. (2-PS1-3)

PS1.B: Chemical Reactions

- Heating or cooling a substance may cause changes that can be observed. Sometimes these changes are reversible, and sometimes they are not. (2-PS1-4)

CCSS-ELA—Writing, Speaking and Listening

W2.2. Write informative/explanatory texts in which they introduce a topic, use facts and definitions to develop points, and provide a concluding statement or section.

W.2.5. With guidance and support from adults and peers, focus on a topic and strengthen writing as needed by revising and editing.

Objectives

Kindergarten through Second Grade students will be able to say:

- I can explain that one thing can disappear into another, such as sugar into tea, smoke into air, baking soda into biscuit dough.
- I can document what happens in this experiment through scientific method, using pictures and text.
- I can tell the story of Sody Sallyratus and act it out with a group.

Materials

- small container of water
- small container of lemon juice
- small container of white vinegar
- balloon with wide mouth
- empty bottle (plastic)
- baking soda
- drawing paper
- colored pencils

Instructional Plan

Rationale

In a systematic way students can observe the experiment and use the "meta" understanding of the scientific method. This experiment supports that growth, particularly because it requires a structured documentation. The story encourages the Kindergarten–Second Grade student to think like a scientist.

Preparation

Prepare small containers of water, lemon juice, and white vinegar. Be certain students can see/observe what happens. Try the experiment outside of class beforehand as sometimes the balloon flies off (fun!) (oh well).... And the clean-up can be messy.

Activity

1. The story: Tell the story "Sody Sallyratus"; you may decide to tell the story *after* the experiment. I've done it both ways. Younger children

may need the experiment first and then the story in order to discuss and understand "what happens." Older children enjoy the experiment very much, especially if the balloon flies off.

2. Discussion: a. who are the characters and in what order do they appear?
    b. why does the Old Woman need sody sallyratus?
    c. what does it do when added to biscuit dough?
    d. what is the pattern/plot of the story?
    e. let's talk about Old Bear—what did he do to the people? why?
    f. how did Pet Squirrel trick Old Bear?
    g. how did the story end? Old Bear? Pet Squirrel?

3. The science: gather the containers of water, lemon juice and white vinegar, the empty bottle, balloon, and baking soda. Have paper and colored pencils available.

4. Ask students "Tell me what you know about these things." The scientific method shall have been taught prior to this activity; this is a review or application of the method.

5. Ask students, "What will happen if I put baking soda into the water?" Ask, "what is your HYPOTHESIS?" Add baking soda. OBSERVE and discuss what happened.

6. Ask students, "And, what will happen if I put baking soda into the lemon juice? What is your HYPOTHESIS?" Students will respond with what will happen and why they think this could be true. EXPERIMENT: Place the baking soda into the balloon and twist the top of the balloon before affixing balloon on the top of the bottle. Then raise the balloon and untwist so the baking soda falls into the lemon juice. OBSERVE: what happened? COLLECT DATA: "What happened?" ANALYZE DATA: "What is the difference between the water solution and the lemon juice solution?" FORMING A NEW HYPOTHESIS: Ask students, "What will happen if I put baking soda into the vinegar?" Repeat procedure. Follow the steps of the scientific method and FORMULATE A CONCLUSION: Discuss the differences between the reactions in water, lemon juice and vinegar. and wonder why this is so.

Student-generated questions are possible student questions or places of confusion or curiosity. Make a list and try hard to have <u>students</u>, not the teacher or teller, answer the questions, or leave some questions unanswered. Here are examples of student questions:

    a. Why did the bear rise higher and higher when each character stepped on the bridge? Do you think a bear's body will respond to sody sallyratus?
    b. Did the bear die when he fell? (Chase says YES and MRM has the old woman stitch bear up.) Both generate questions from students.

c. Why didn't the people die; how could they pop up whole and unharmed?

d. Why didn't the baking soda and lemon juice or the soda and vinegar form a vortex?

e. Did the baking soda cause the bear to become huge? Were the raised biscuits "normal" size?

Information can be added to the MRM's narrative without changing the substance of the story, while bringing out the science for discussion.

1. The Little Boy will carry the sody sallyratus from the store in a paper bag.

2. Show that the bear rises up successively higher from under the bridge with the eating of each character.

3. When the bear splits open and the people pop out whole, Little Boy offers the (wet) paper bag covered in bear slime with NO bottom to the bag. Then he goes back to the store for dry sody sallyratus.

4. Old Woman bakes the biscuits which rise and rise; they all enjoy the hot biscuits.

Assessment

1. The documentation (in text and drawing) of the science methods is crucial to this discussion; has the student been accurate in the use of the scientific method and accurate in the delineation of the science observed and experienced? Note what knowledge was factual and what was assumed.

2. Has the student demonstrated strong informative writing skills? Informative/explanatory texts include introducing a topic, using facts and definitions to develop points, and providing a concluding statement or section. The student should include examples of cause and effect, and energy and matter. In the write-up, the student should include questions about the relationship of the story and the science as well as defining the problems presented in the story and science experiment.

RESOURCES

Appalachian History: Stories, Quotes and Anecdotes: Sody Sallyratus. http://www.appalachianhistory.net/2012/08/sody-sallyratus.html.

MacDonald, Margaret Read. *Twenty Tellable Tales: Audience Participation Folktales for the Beginning Storyteller.* New York: H. W. Wilson, 1986.

Sloat, Teri. *Sody Sallyratus.* New York: Dutton Junior, 1997.

"Sody Sallyratus," told by Richard Chase. https://archive.org/details/richardchase-sodysallyratus 1977.

"Anansi and Turtle Go to Dinner"
Sink and Float

Jane Stenson *with* Sherry Norfolk *and* Bobby Norfolk

CCC topic: Patterns, Cause and effect, Stability and change
POSE topic: Asking questions (science) and defining problems (engineering), Planning and carrying out investigations

The Story

"Anansi and Turtle Go to Dinner"
retold by Sherry and Bobby Norfolk

One evening, Anansi was sitting down to dinner when Turtle came to his door. Anansi knew the law of the jungle: If you have company, and you have food, you must share the food with your company.

"Come in, Turtle. You're just in time for dinner!" Anansi sighed.

Turtle sat down. "Thanks, Anansi. How are you?"

Turtle reached for a bowl of yams.

"I'm fine," answered Anansi, "but Turtle, your hands are very dirty. You know you can't sit down to dinner with dirty hands. Please go wash them before you eat."

Turtle looked sadly at his hands. They had gotten very dirty on the long walk to Anansi's house. "Oh! You're right, Anansi. I'm sorry. I'll be right back."

Turtle slowly crawled off to wash his hands.

As soon as Turtle was out of sight, Anansi ate as fast as he could! He ate peanut soup, rice and beans and meat. *Slurp, slurp, gobble-gobble, munch-crunch, BURP!*

When Turtle got back, the bowls and plates were nearly empty.

"Anansi, you've been eating all of the food!" Turtle said unhappily.

"Well, Turtle, you are very slow. I had to eat it before it got cold. But there's plenty left—help yourself," said Anansi.

"Thanks, Anansi. I'm really hungry."

Turtle reached for the bowl of rice.

"Wait!" cried Anansi. "Your hands are still dirty, Turtle!"

Turtle looked at his hands. Yes, they were dirty again, because he had crawled back to the table across Anansi's dirty, unswept floors.

"Oh! Sorry, Anansi, I'll be right back."

Turtle crept back to wash again. Then he searched through his shell and found some nice, soft slippers to keep his hands and feet clean.

Then he started back as fast as he could go.

But as soon as he was gone, Anansi had stuffed the rest of the food into his mouth. *Slurp, slurp, gobble-gobble, munch-crunch, BURP!*

When Turtle saw the empty table, he cried, "Anansi, you have eaten everything!"

"Turtle, I could not wait any longer. The food was getting very cold. Maybe next time you come to dinner, you'll wash your hands and get to the table on time!"

Turtle nodded slowly and left with an empty tummy. As he walked, his hungry tummy growled and his hungry mind began to work.

"Hmmm! Anansi tricked me! He got me to wash my hands twice while he gobbled up all the food. It's time to teach Anansi a very important lesson!" Turtle reached home, ate his dinner, and began to plan.

The next day, Anansi found an invitation in his mailbox to go to Turtle's house for dinner.

"All right!" he cheered. "Turtle is a great cook!

Anansi put on his best jacket and went to the edge of the pond. He saw Turtle down at the bottom of the pond, setting the table.

"I'm here, Turtle! I'm here for dinner!" he called.

"Come on down, Anansi! Your dinner is almost ready!" answered Turtle.

Anansi jumped into the water—*Splash!* But he didn't sink to the bottom! He just floated on the top of the water.

Anansi kicked all eight legs and bounced as hard as he could, but he could not make himself sink.

"Hurry, Anansi! Dinner is getting cold!" grinned Turtle as he watched Anansi splashing above him.

Anansi climbed out and tried again, and again, and again! *Splish, splash, splish, splash, SPLASH!* He could NOT sink to the bottom.

Anansi thought.

"Aha! I know what to do. I have big pockets in this jacket. I'll put heavy rocks in the pockets and I'll drop right down to Turtle's house!"

Anansi gathered big rocks and filled his pockets.

Then *Ker-SPLASH!* He jumped into the pond.

Glub, glub, glub! He went down, down, down to the bottom of the pond, where Turtle had set out a feast.

"This sure does look good!" said Anansi as he reached for a bowl of food.

"Wait, Anansi!" Turtle cried. "You know you can't sit down to dinner with your jacket on! Please take off your jacket."

"But, Turtle, if I take off my jacket—"

"You MUST take it off if you want to eat," said Turtle.

Anansi slowly took off his jacket and hung it on the back of his chair. He popped right back up to the top of the water!

Anansi floated and watched as Turtle ate every bite of the feast. He had plenty of time to think while he watched.

Finally he climbed out of the water and started back home.

"Turtle tricked me out of a meal just like I tricked him! I guess my mama was right: What goes around, comes around!" And that's the end of that.

Standards

NGSS—Physical Science

K-PS2-1. Plan and conduct an investigation to compare the effects of different strengths or different directions of pushes and pulls on the motion of an object.

CCSS-ELA—Reading, Writing, Speaking, Listening

ELA/Literacy—RI.K.1. With prompting and support, ask and answer questions about key details.

ELA/Literacy—W.K.7. Participate in shared research and writing projects.

ELA/Literacy—SL.K.3. Ask and answer questions in order to seek help, get information, or clarify something that is not understood.

Objectives

Kindergarten students will be able to say:

- I can make predictions about what will or will not float and explain why.

- I can tell what happens to the water when items are placed in it.
- I can document what happens with drawings and words, to create a SINK & FLOAT book.

Materials

(And *you* can think of some interesting items to experiment with ... so can the children!)

- a farm style metal washtub, four feet wide by three feet high
- tap water
- Week One: variety of shaped corks
- Week Two: natural sponges
- Week Three: watermelon—be sure to eat it after the experiment
- Week Four: log shaped wood—vertical or horizontal—predict and WHY?
- Week Five: a wood shingle and a (waterproof) tar paper shingle
- Week Six: a very big chunk of ice (isn't this ice made from water?)
- Week Seven: a very big pumpkin (let it roll in and splash)

Instructional Plan

Rationale

Kindergarten children have prior knowledge to help them with this experiment, and that must be pointed out to the children. They know rocks will sink in water and they may know that a watermelon will float ... and that experience as part of science thinking needs to be recognized as we proceed. These "experiments" occur once a week during the fall in order to elicit and build "prior knowledge" and encourage children to think critically/scientifically in a patterned way. Further, students are encouraged to accurately document what they see in words and pictures.

Preparation

Teacher purchases a large farm-style metal tub, about four feet wide and three feet deep. About four inches from the top place a line (black) that will not wash off. That is the water-fill line. Prior to each experiment fill the tub with water. Have the object to be tested that week available for observation. Teacher generated discussion shall always include the nature of what happens to the object *and* what happens to the water ... that is, what force does the object employ on the water and what force does the water employ on the object. Note how deep/high the object floats. Children should be encouraged to consider why something floats or doesn't float in the water.... Offer alternate examples such as an ocean liner, a truck, a person, a dolphin, a mosquito, a rock (consider the shape of the rock), a mountain; why can rocks skip across the surface of water? Offer alternate liquid substances to water, such as cola or dish soap.

Activity

Tell the really fun story of "Anansi and Turtle" and ask children why Anansi had so much trouble eating dinner at Turtle's house. You may wish to tell the story again later in the unit.

Over the next seven weeks the teacher will organize sink and float activities in a predictable pattern: Show the object to be placed in the tub of water. Make predictions as to whether it will sink or float ... and WHY do you think that is true. The second question always is, "What makes you say that?" Then children draw what happened and teachers scribe their thoughts. Their drawings go into a folder to save (sometimes difficult for kindergarten children).

1. Fill tub with water to the black line.
2. Show the object to be placed in the water to assembled children.
3. Make predictions and explain why you think as you do.
4. Teacher places object in water (a little roughly) and children watch.
5. Children's language bubbles up at this point!
6. Take the paper and colored pencils and draw what happened/the result of what happened. "Draw what you see." Ask a teacher to scribe your thinking on the paper. Put your name on the paper.
7. Collect the drawings and save them.

Assessment

Children's articulation of their thinking about "sink & floats" and well as their drawings are important to document. Children will save their drawings every week in order to compile/create a SINK & FLOAT book: make a cover and place each drawing in order by the date observed. Savoring the book and the children's growth in the expression of their understanding is one of the joys of working with young children.

Resources

Anansi and the Turtle (BBC). https://vimeo.com/4076703

34   Part One. Early Childhood (PHYSICAL SCIENCE)

Refugee Week. "Anansi and the Turtle: A Story from Nigeria." http://www.refugeeweek.org.uk/Resources/Refugee%20Week/Simple%20Acts%20Text/Story_Anansi%20and%20Turtle%20-%20Nigeria.pdf

Weingarten Design. "Anansi and Turtle's Feast: a West African Tale." http://www.weingartdesign.com/TMaS/Stories/tmas1-Anansi.html

Richard Young and Judy Dockrey. "Anansi and Turtle." *African American Folktales for Young Readers.* Little Rock, AR: August House, 1993.

"How the Rainbow Was Made"
Liquid Rainbow and the Density of Liquids

Dana Allande O'Brien

CCC topic: Cause and effect, Systems and system energy
POSE topic: Asking questions (science) and defining problems (engineering), Developing and using models

The Story

"How the Rainbow Was Made": A Creation Tale from the Ojibwe Nation

Long, long ago, when the rivers were chocolate brown and the days were full of wonder, Nanabozho looked at his surroundings and realized that everything was the same color. The flowers were white. The trees were white. The river was white. What else do you think was white? (take time to get answers from children) How boring! He decided he wanted things to be more interesting. So he decided he would do some painting. He collected his paints and his paintbrushes.

Nanabozho stood in the meadow of tall grass near the river and looked around. He could hear the birds chirping (children make the sound); he needed to shade his eyes from the bright light of the sun (pause to let children do this). And then, after setting up his supplies, he began to paint. He poured orange onto all the flowers and painted orange stripes onto birds (add honey to the cylinder). He poured red paint onto the roses and other flowers full of passion (pour syrup into cylinder). He poured blue paint into the sky and all the rivers (add dish soap to cylinder), and green paint into the grass, the leaves and the plants (pour water into the cylinder). Then he poured yellow into the daffodils, sunflowers and sun (pour vegetable oil into cylinder). He poured touches of purple into all the flowers and birds (add rubbing alcohol to cylinder). Nanabozho continued all day happily adding color to his day.

The animals became increasingly happy and inspired as they saw brilliant colors added to their day. They began to zip and buzz here and there. Soon wonderful colors and sweet sounds filled the air.

The birds and bees began to enjoy chasing one another through the air and would zip this way and that way. Occasionally they would get too close to the pots of paint and their wings would be filled with colors. Nanabozho shooed them away from his place of work. Reluctantly, the birds and bees flew away and again began enjoying the chase. As they flew back and forth through the sky, the mist of the rushing waterfall sprayed their wings. Each wing left different, bright colors across the sky as the chase continued. As the sun shone on these stripes, Nanabozho could see the stripes of the colors—the orange, red, green, blue, and purple. "You have made a rainbow!" He loved the arch of colors so much that he decided to leave the rainbow there in the sky for all to enjoy.

From that day forward, whenever the sun shines through the rain or the mist, a wonderful rainbow forms. It is a reflection of the everlasting rainbow that stands over the waterfall at Nanabozho's house.

Source: americanfolklore.net

Standards

NGSS–Physical Science

2-PS1-2 Plan and conduct an investigation to describe and classify different kinds of materials by their observable properties.

2-PS1-4 Construct an argument with evidence that some changes caused by heating or cooling can be reversed and some cannot.

CCSS-ELA—Reading, Writing, Speaking, Listening

RL.2.2 Recount stories, including fables and folktales from diverse cultures, and determine their central message, lesson, or moral.

RL.2.3 Describe how characters in a story respond to major events and challenges.

W.2.8 Recall information from experiences or gather information from provided sources to answer a question.

SL.2.1.a. Follow agreed-upon rules for discussions (e.g., gaining the floor in respectful ways, listening to others with care, speaking one at a time about the topics and texts under discussion).

SL2.2.1.b. Build on others' talk in conversations by linking their comments to the remarks of others.

SL2.1.c. Ask for clarification and further explanation as needed about the topics and texts under discussion.

SL.2.2 Recount or describe key ideas or details from a text read aloud or information presented orally or through other media.

SL.2.3 Ask and answer questions about what a speaker says in order to clarify comprehension, gather additional information, or deepen understanding of a topic or issue.

SL.2.4 Tell a story or recount an experience with appropriate facts and relevant, descriptive details, speaking audibly in coherent sentences.

SL2.5 Create audio recordings of stories or poems; add drawings or other visual displays to stories or recounts of experiences when appropriate to clarify ideas, thoughts, and feelings.

SL 2.6 Produce complete sentences when appropriate to task and situation in order to provide requested detail or clarification.

Objectives

Second grade students will be able to say:

- I can compare the liquids in the cylinder by observing the model.
- I can determine the heaviest liquids by observing the model.
- I can compare the weight of tiny objects added to the cylinder and make predictions about which ones will sink or float.
- I can retell a story that I have heard using a visual to assist me.

Materials

- clear cylinder—500 mL or 1000 mL graduated cylinders work well
- 50–100 mL Honey
- 50–100 mL Corn Syrup
- 50–100 mL Vegetable Oil
- 50–100 mL Dish Soap
- 50–100 mL Water
- 50–100 mL Rubbing Alcohol
- Food coloring
- Tiny items (for example: washer, grape, seed, bottle caps, game pieces or die, beads, etc.)

Instructional Plan

Rationale

This is a lesson on floating and sinking of liquids. The liquids, when added in the correct order, will begin to "float" on top of each other, but not mix. To further the exploration of density, by adding the tiny objects, the children will witness which small objects are denser or less dense than water.

Preparation

Prior to the experiment, we have discussed and experimented with mixing liquids like water and oil or milk, food coloring and soap. The children have made predictions, observations and investigated reasons for why water and oil do not mix or why the colors swirl when mixed in milk and soap. The properties of a liquid have been researched and observed and the children now have enough background information to begin to make predictions as to what will happen when we mix some different types of liquids. We will have also reflected on past lessons revolving around the concept of "sink or float?" Looking at the small items gathered, children will begin to think about whether the items will sink or float in the different liquids before them.

Activity

The lesson will begin with the children looking at the various liquids and describing them verbally. Once they have compared and contrasted the liquids, the story will begin. The story shown above will be told and the liquids will be added (preferably with a turkey baster in the order they are listed—try not to allow the liquids to touch the sides of the cylinder) to the cylinder as indicated in each spot. After the liquids have been added discussion can now begin as to the scientific properties of the liquids. Suggested questions are:

- Which of the liquids is the most dense? What does "dense" mean scientifically?
- Why do you think it is the most dense? Answers to both questions can be written on large chart paper or white board.
- How many liquids in the cylinder are less dense than water? (discuss reasons)
- What do you think would happen if you doubled the amount of any of the liquids?

The students will now look at all of the small objects that you have collected. We will make a class prediction chart as to what objects will sink and

"How the Rainbow Was Made" (O'Brien)   39

which ones will float (and where they will float). After dropping each of the objects, the class may discuss the results. Once every object has been added, we can discuss what this activity can tell us about the liquids and about the objects. Finally, the students will be asked to retell the story using story box paper (comic book template follows) with both words and illustrations. The cylinder will remain in clear sight so the students can us it as reference. Then, using these story boxes, the students will retell the story to someone at home.

comic book template: storybook paper

Assessment

Through classroom discussion and the students' active participation in the discussion, the teachers will be able to assess how much the students understand about liquid density and object weight vs. liquid density. By the final written project and the retelling at home, teachers will be able to determine how much of the story the students are understanding and how much they understand about sequencing.

Resources
Comic Book Template: storybox paper
"How the Rainbow Was Made: A Creation Tale from the Ojibwe Nation." www.amer
    icanfolklore.net

"The Lady Who Put Salt in Her Coffee"

VITO M. DIPINTO

CCC topic: Cause and effect, Structure and function.
POSE topics: Explanations and designing solutions; Engaging in argument from evidence; Obtaining, evaluating and communicating information.

The Story

The Lady Who Put Salt in Her Coffee
retold by Vito M. Dipinto

Mrs. Peterson got up in the morning and needed a cup of coffee to begin her day. She made a fresh pot of coffee, poured a cup, and put what she thought is sugar into it. She took a sip. YUCK!! There was salt instead of sugar in her coffee. What was she to do? Having no solution, she sat down to ponder her situation.

Soon Mr. Peterson came downstairs for breakfast. Seeing his wife obviously distressed, he asked, "What is the problem?"

Mrs. Peterson explained about *how she got up in the morning and needed a cup of coffee to begin her day, made a fresh pot of coffee, poured a cup, and put what she thought was sugar into it, took a sip, and YUCK!! There was salt instead of sugar in her coffee*, and perhaps he had a solution.

Mr. Peterson had no solution. Fairly soon, all the Peterson children came into the kitchen and saw their mother and father obviously distressed. They asked, "What is the problem?"

Mr. Peterson explained about how (*refrain*) *Mrs. Peterson got up in the morning and needed a cup of coffee to begin her day, made a fresh pot of coffee,* poured a cup, and put what she thought was sugar into it, took a sip, and YUCK!! There was salt instead of sugar in her coffee, and perhaps they had a solution.

The children had no solution so it became a family crisis. They adjourned to their family crisis room: the dining room. They thought and thought and finally Agamemnon, who had gone to college, remembered that there was a chemist who lived down the street. Perhaps he could help. Mr. Peterson said, "Oh, well" and Mrs. Person said, "Oh, my." All the Peterson children jumped for joy, put on their red India rubber boots, and went over to the chemist's house. The chemist was definitely weird. He had this idea: He thought he could turn ordinary things into precious metals. Unfortunately, he had used all the precious metals in house except his wife's wedding ring. He had been on his knees for hours begging, pleading, and cajoling his wife to donate the ring to the cause of science. This time the experiment was sure to be a successful and they would be rich beyond imagining. She was just about to acquiesce when in tromped the Peterson children. The chemist's wife left. The chemist was mightily miffed. However, he put on his best professional face and asked, "May I help you?" Agamemnon explained about how

refrain

The chemist was about to kick them out on their proverbials when Agamemnon said they could pay in gold. He gathered all sort of chemicals and chemical paraphernalia. He went over to the Peterson's house. He picked up the cup of coffee, looked at it, smelled it, and tasted it, and YUCK!! It had salt instead of sugar in it. He began to work a bit of chemical magic. But everything he added, although it made the salted coffee taste interesting, did not make it taste precisely like coffee. He threw up his hands in despair saying, "The theory was correct but the experiment was a failure. Pay up!"

They returned to the dining room where they all pondered the situation more. Finally Solomon John remembered there was an herb lady who lived at the other end of the street. Mr. Peterson said, "Oh, well" and Mrs. Person said, "Oh, my." All the Peterson children jumped for joy, put on their red India rubber boots, and headed over to the herb lady's house. Now the herb lady's house was a wondrous place filled with plants and plant stuff. Solomon John explained about how

refrain

and that the chemist had made it quite worse, and could she help? She agreed and gathered all sort of plants and plant stuff. She went to the Peterson household, picked up the cup of coffee, looked at it, smelled, tasted it and YUCK!! It had salt instead sugar in it. She began to work a bit of botanical magic. Everything she added made the cup of coffee taste worse and worse.

Finally she held up her hands in despair saying that the coffee was bewitched. After Solomon John paid an honorarium for her troubles, she left.

It was getting dark and Mrs. Peterson still had not begun her day. Finally Elizabeth Eliza remembered that the lady from Philadelphia was in town and she had a reputation for wisdom. Perhaps she could help. Mr. Peterson said, "Oh, well" and Mrs. Person said, "Oh, my." Elizabeth Eliza jumped for joy, put on her red India rubber boots, and headed over to the lady from Philadelphia's house. Now the lady from Philadelphia got her reputation for wisdom for two reasons. One, like all of you, she was a good listener and two, she could ask good questions. So when Elizabeth Eliza explained about how

refrain

and the chemist and the herb lady had made it quite worse, could she help? The lady from Philadelphia listened carefully to Elizabeth's words, asked her a few questions, and pondered the responses. Then she said, "Elizabeth, go home. Tell your mother to throw out that cup of coffee. Make a new pot. Pour a fresh cup and taste the sugar before putting it in." Elizabeth Eliza went home and told her mother the advice from the lady from Philadelphia. Mrs. Peterson made herself a fresh pot of coffee, poured herself a steaming hot cup, and put sugar (for sure) into her cup. She drank the cup and she and the family immediately went to bed.

Source: Based on *The Peterkin Papers* by Lucretia P. Hale. Boston and New York: Houghton Mifflin, 1886, 1914; A. Schwartz, The lady who put salt in her coffee. New York: Harcourt Brace Jovanovich, 1989.

Editor's note: The author used this story for second, fifth, and eighth grades. The second-grade activity is here and the fifth grade activity is in Part 2.

Standards

NGSS—Physical (chemistry) science, Life science

2-PS1-1: Plan and conduct an investigation to describe and classify different kinds of materials by their observable patterns.

2-PS1-2: Analyze data obtained from testing different materials to determine which materials have the properties that are best suited for an intended purpose.

LS2.A: Independent Relationships in Ecosystems—plants depend on water and light to grow.

2-LS2-1: Plan and conduct an investigation collaboratively to produce data to serve as the basis for evidence to answer a question; designs can be conveyed through sketches, drawings, or physical models

CCSS-ELA—Reading, Writing, Speaking and Listening

RL.2.4: Describe how words and phrases (e.g., regular beats, alliteration, rhymes, repeated lines) supply rhythm and meaning in a story, poem, or song.

RL.2.5: Describe the overall structure of a story, including describing how the beginning introduces the story and the ending concludes the action.

RL.2.6: Acknowledge differences in the points of view of characters, including by speaking in a different voice for each character when reading dialogue aloud.

W.2.7: Participate in shared research and writing projects (e.g., read a number of books on a single topic to produce a report; record science observations).

W.2.8: Recall information from experiences or gather information from provided sources to answer a question.

SL.2. Tell a story or recount an experience with appropriate facts and relevant, descriptive details, speaking audibly in coherent sentences.

Objectives

Second Grade students will be able to say:

- I can transplant herbs and keep them growing.
- I can work collaboratively on a science project to determine the scope of the experiment, document changes along the way, and reach conclusions (new hypotheses).
- I can retell the story and the science behind the story.

Materials

- The video https://www.youtube.com/watch?v=Y8Y8CfoHvQc
- planting containers
- soils
- water source, light source
- herbs and spices such as basil, mint, and fennel
- other herbs and spices to create (fill out) tongue maps
- drawing paper
- colored pencils

Instructional Plan

Rationale

1. General Science: The nature of science and empirical data go hand-in-hand. But we have discovered more information than our brains can remember. How can scientists make sense of all this data? How can second grade students make any sense of it? They both search for patterns. Using the patterns they design classification systems in order to sort this vast amount of data into categories. This story, like all good stories, has patterns in its language: Mrs. Peterson gets up in the morning. She needs her cup of coffee to begin her day. Accidentally, she puts salt instead of sugar in her coffee. What is she to do? In the telling of the story there are other kinds of patterns. Each of these phrases is always said to the same student each time they are repeated. The storyteller (teacher) selects students scanning from left to right from his/her class. In addition, all the chemist information takes place on the storyteller's right side, the herb lady on the left side and the lady from Philadelphia is in the middle. These patterns are a way to introduce all the standard categorization and classification activities that are usually done in second grade.

2. Chemistry: People have been using herbs and spices to flavor their food for as long as there have been people. These herbs and spices come from plants. The flavors are chemicals. The students start by learning the names of the plants and the chemicals responsible for the distinctive flavor. For instance, benzaldehyde is the chemical that gives almonds their characteristic flavor. (By the way, the benzaldehyde made by the almond tree and the benzaldehyde made by the chemist in the lab are indistinguishable. This idea that there is a difference between naturally occurring compounds and those synthesized in the lab is a major misconception in chemistry.) Citric acid is the chemical that gives fruits like lemons their sour flavor. Of course, you are not expecting your second grade students to have any idea about how these names are connected to chemical formula and structures. But they learn the names! **Vocabulary precedes concept development in science.** Also when young children know "big words" it empowers them, making them members of a very select group of adults.

Preparation

Gather basil, mint, and fennel plants for students to grow. Establish planting containers, soils, light sources for students to conduct their experiment.

Gather herbs from a grocery store to compare and/or enlarge the study.

Activity

- Using the "I Wonder" Model, found in "Science Is a Story" earlier in the book, students plan and execute a study of the plants from which the herbs and spices are derived.
- They examine and document the plants' physical characteristics. The students grow some of the plants in the classroom trying to determine what are the best conditions to produce basil, mint, and fennel plants indoors ... and document their observations. This is an introduction to dependent and independent variables (and you get to eat the results).
- Students begin to identify unknown samples by comparing a set of unknowns to known ones (easily obtainable in grocery stores). This introduces second grade students to the idea of qualitative analysis.
- Another idea to introduce is the concept that flavor is taste plus odor. This gives you the chemical basis to map the tongue (fun!) and explore the sense of smell.

Assessment

- Documentation of the physical characteristics of studied plants in both drawing and text.
- Commentary should include the dependent and independent variables and resulting plant growth.
- Student documentation should include a map of the tongue!

Resources

Although the following began as a high school activity, it is great resource for the second grade teacher for some ideas on designing the herb and spice lab and assessing it.
   http://www.stoughton.k12.wi.us/HighSchool.cfm?subpage=1463751

This site has all kinds of fun and intriguing activities using herbs with kids, from "Fennel Babies on Fennel Day" to "Playing with Peppermint."
   http://mamarosemary.com/herbs-for-kids/

This site is from the McCormick Science Institute and contains good scientific information on what parts of the plants are used for herbs and spices and the difference between an herb and a spice.
   http://www.mccormickscienceinstitute.com/Spice-Landing/Culinary-Herbs-and-Spices.aspx

"Prairie Dogs in the Rain"
Solving Problems with Simple Machines

SHERRY NORFOLK

CCC topics: Structure and function, Stability and change
POSE topics: Asking questions and defining problems, Constructing explanations and designing solutions

The Story

"Prairie Dogs in the Rain"
adapted by Sherry Norfolk
Based on *Heart Full of Turquoise*, 1988.
Original source can be found at
www.drarcheology.com/texts/zunifolktales/zft2t.htm

One day, all of the prairie dogs were out eating grass as usual. The guard prairie dog was watching for danger.

"Ooooh!" He saw a great big cloud moving towards Prairie Dog Village, so he watched. The cloud got closer and closer and bigger and bigger, and suddenly the lightening flashed and the thunder crashed—BOOM!

"Arf, arf, arf!" Whoosh! The prairie dogs went down in their holes in the ground.

"Hee, hee, hee, hee, hee! That was a close one. We almost got wet! Boy, do we hate getting wet!" And they all snuggled down nice and warm and safe and dry in their holes in the ground.

Outside, the rain began to fall. It rained and it rained and it rained, and the rain began to fill up those holes in the ground.

"Oh, no! Look at that! Our little prairie dog toes are getting wet!"
It rained and it rained and it rained…
"Yuck! Look at that! Our little prairie dog ankles are getting wet!"
It rained and it rained and it rained…
"Blah! Look at that! Our little prairie dog knees are getting wet!"
It rained and it rained and it rained…
"Argh! Look at that! Our little prairie dog belly buttons are getting wet!"
It rained and it rained and it rained…
"EEEEK! Look at that! It's up to our little prairie dog chins! HEEEEEE-EEELP!"

The prairie dog mayor said, "I know what to do. I'll go talk to the burrowing owl. He's the smartest guy out here on the prairie. He'll know what we should do."

So the mayor came up out of the hole in the ground, ran across the desert, and dove down into the hole where the burrowing owl lived.

"We have problem," cried the mayor. "The rain is filling up our little holes in the ground, and it's up to our chins, and we don't know how to swim. We're gonna drown. HEEEEELP!"

"Whoooooooooo! I can tell you what to do, but you won't like it," answered the owl.

"Oh, yeah, we'll like it. If it'll keep us from drowning we'll like it a lot. What do we do?"

"All right, here's what to do: Tell all of the prairie dogs to get bags, and to fill their bags with stink bugs."

"Wait a minute … did you say stink bugs? Pe-eeeeuew!"

"I tooooold you that you wouldn't like it!" hooted Owl.

"All right, we'll do it."

Burrowing Owl and Prairie Dog Mayor went back to Prairie Dog Village, and by this time the rain was all the way up to the little prairie dog noses.

"Help! Blu-blu-blub! Help! Blu-blu-blub! Help!"

The mayor said, "It's all right. I know what to do. Everyone get a bag."
All of the prairie dogs got bags.

"Now fill your bags with stink bugs."

"WHAT?"

"Just do it!"

So they filled their bags with stink bugs. "Now what do we do?"

"Find a big rock and a piece of long, flat wood. Put the wood across the rock, half on one side, half on the other."

The prairie dogs scurried around in the rain, following Burrowing Owl's instructions. "Now what?"

"Now twist your bags shut, and then go shake, shake, shake—shake, shake, shake—shake, shake, shake, shake, shake, shake. Put all of the bags on one end of the wood. Now, you all climb up the mesa and jump off onto the other side of the wood."

The prairie dogs twisted the bags shut, and they went shake, shake, shake—shake, shake, shake—shake, shake, shake, shake, shake, shake, shake. They stacked the bags on one side of the piece of wood. They climbed up the mesa and ... "One, Two, Three—JUMP!" they all landed on the other side of the piece of wood.

The bags flew up into the clouds, opening as they went. The smell went up to the sky and the clouds said, "EEEEEEEUW!"

And the clouds moved a so far away that the rain stopped.

Now ever since that day, the clouds don't hang around that prairie dog village very much, because they remember the smell of those stink bugs.

"PEEEEEE-EUW!"

Standards

NGSS—Physical Science

ETS1-1. Ask questions, make observations, and gather information about a situation people want to change to define a simple problem that can be resolved through the development of a new or improved tool.

ETS1-2. Develop a simple sketch, drawing or physical model to illustrate how the shape of an object helps it function as needed to solve a given problem.

ETS1-3. Analyze data from tests of two objects designed to solve the same problem to compare the strengths and weaknesses of how each performs.

CCSS-ELA—Writing, Speaking, Listening

W.2.3 Write narratives in which they recount a well-elaborated event or short sequence of events, include details to describe actions, thoughts, and feelings, use temporal words to signal event order, and provide a sense of closure.

SL.2.4 Tell a story or recount an experience with appropriate facts and relevant, descriptive details, speaking audibly in coherent sentences.

Fine Arts Anchor standards—Create, Respond, Perform, Connect

Objectives

Second Grade Students will be able to say:

- I can write a story about a community that solves a problem with a simple machine.
- I can create a model of a simple machine.
- I can describe the machine with appropriate details.
- I can tell the story coherently.

Materials

- "The Prairie Dogs Chase the Clouds Away," in Hayes, Joe. *A Heart Full of Turquoise: Pueblo Indian Tales.* St. Paul, MN: Mariposa, 1988.
- Recycled materials for making models of simple machines: blocks, cardboard, sticks, shoeboxes, construction toys (such as Legos), string, etc.
- Paper and pencils

Instructional Plan

Rationale

In the process of writing their own stories, students create a situation the characters want to change, then resolve the problem through the development of a simple machine. Being allowed to follow through by making the machine that they imagined brings their story to life—and engages the students in deeper understanding.

Preparation

Simple machines are easy to understand. They are all around us. They are fun to build! They solve problems and make work easier.

After discussing what simple machines are and how they work, take a stroll around the school and ask students to identify the simple machines in their everyday life.

Take advantage of all of the wonderful books on simple machines that are now available—you might start with *Simple Machines* by Deborah Hodge (Toronto, ON: Kids Can Press, 1998), and read about a different machine every day for a week or so until the students have an idea of what a simple machine does. In addition, www.brainpop.com has a great lesson on simple machines with tutorials and games and all kind of things to teach the students in a fun way.

Send a note home to parents asking for recycled "things" to use in the classroom. Explain that they are going to build the simple machines described in the students' original stories.

Activity #1

Tell "The Prairie Dogs Chase the Clouds Away," in which the Prairie Dog Village is flooded by a heavy rainstorm. Prairie Dog Mayor goes to Burrowing Owl for advice. In Joe Hayes's version, the owl tells him that everyone must fill bags with stinkbugs, then twist the bags shut, shake the bags, hold them up and open them. After doing this three times, the clouds are driven away by the smell! I made one strategic change to the Burrowing Owl's plan in the text above: they use a fulcrum, creating a catapult to send the bags of stinkbugs up to the sky.

After the story has been told, discuss what the problem was and how it was solved. What kind of simple machine did they use to solve their problem? Were there other ways they could have used a simple machine to solve their problem?

Now discuss the pattern of the story:

- Who lives in the community?
- What is their problem? (Must be a problem common to all.)
- Who is the leader?
- Who is the Wise Person?
- What is the Wise Person's advice? (Problem must be solved with the use of a simple machine.)
- What is the result?

Together, generate a new story, answering the questions above. Focus on the simple machine and how it can solve the problem. *Note:* Don't accept the first answer, even if it's wonderful! Gather as many ideas as possible, encouraging kids to use their critical thinking skills to come up with solutions and to postulate possible outcomes of each idea. Let the class vote on the solution, then tell the resulting story to the class.

Next, provide forms with the same questions, asking students to create their own original answers. Upon completion of the outline, they will tell their stories to a partner before writing a rough draft.

Activity #2: Creating Simple Machines

Have the children design and draw a sample of their simple machines and ask them to write a paper describing how it works. They can work in teams or choose to do theirs individually.

After all the materials come in from home, they can start to pick the parts they need to make their machines. Some of the things they might choose are paper towel rolls or yarn, egg cartons or Styrofoam containers.

Once the machines are finished, return to the stories to revise the description of the simple machine and finish editing. Publish the final copies of the stories, accompanied by the paper describing how the machine works and a sketch or a photo of the completed machine.

Presentations

Students will be excited to share their stories and their simple machines! Provide plenty of time for them to rehearse the storytelling using voices, gestures, and sound effects along with demonstrating the use of the simple machine. Then, on with the show!

Assessment

Stories can be assessed on adherence to the framework, use of details that describe actions, thoughts, and feelings, use of temporal words to signal event order, and a sense of closure. The descriptive paragraph and image can be assessed on feasibility, clarity and contribution to the overall understanding of the text. Performances are assessed for ability to tell the story with appropriate facts and relevant, descriptive details, speaking audibly in coherent sentences.

LIFE SCIENCE

Creating a Pourquoi ("How and Why") Story
Katie Knutson

CCC topics: Cause and effect.
POSE topics: Asking questions & defining problems, Developing & using models, Planning & Carrying out investigations

The Stories

Pourquoi tales, stories that explain *how* or *why* things are the way they are, are the foundation of these lessons. You may use any Pourquoi stories you like for examples before the lessons, though I focus on stories about the origins of physical characteristics of animals. Some of my favorites include: "Why Bear Has a Stumpy Tail" (Norway), "Why Leopard Has Spots" (Liberia), "How Tiger Got His Stripes" (Vietnam), and "The Turtle Who Talked Too Much" (India). See the resources list for additional ideas.

Standards

NGSS—Life Science

K-LS-1. Use observations to describe patterns of what plants and animals (including humans) need to survive.

K-ESS-3. Use a model to represent the relationship between the needs of different plants and animals (including humans) and the places they live.

CCSS-ELA—Reading, Writing, Speaking & Listening

CCSS.ELA-LITERACY.RI.K.3. With prompting and support, describe the connection between two individuals, events, ideas, or pieces of information in a text.

CCSS.ELA-LITERACY.W.K.3. Use a combination of drawing, dictating, and writing to narrate a single event or several loosely linked events, tell about the events in the order in which they occurred, and provide a reaction to what happened.

CCSS.ELA-LITERACY.W.K.8. With guidance and support from adults, recall information from experiences or gather information from provided sources to answer a question.

CCSS.ELA-LITERACY.SL.K.1. Participate in collaborative conversations with diverse partners about *kindergarten topics and texts* with peers and adults in small and larger groups.

CCSS.ELA-LITERACY.SL.K.1.A. Follow agreed-upon rules for discussions (e.g., listening to others and taking turns speaking about the topics and texts under discussion).

CCSS.ELA-LITERACY.SL.K.6. Speak audibly and express thoughts, feelings, and ideas clearly.

CCSS.ELA-LITERACY.L.K.1.D. Understand and use question words (interrogatives) (e.g., *who, what, where, when, why, how*).

ARTS—STANDARDS:

TH:Cr1.1.Ka. With prompting and support, invent and inhabit an imaginary elsewhere in dramatic play or a guided drama experience (e.g., process drama, story drama, creative drama).

TH:Cr3.1.Ka. With prompting and support, ask and answer questions in dramatic play or a guided drama experience (e.g., process drama, story drama, creative drama).

TH:Re8.1.Kb. With prompting and support, name and describe settings in dramatic play or a guided drama experience (e.g., process drama, story drama, creative drama).

TH:Cn11.1.Ka. With prompting and support, identify skills and knowledge from other areas in dramatic play or a guided drama experience (e.g., process drama, story drama, creative drama).

Objectives

Kindergarten students will be able to say:

- I can research an animal and habitat and share what I have learned.
- I can ask and answer questions about an animal.
- I can imagine and explain how different actions would affect an animal (cause and effect).

- I can describe and draw the animal in my story with details about it, its habitat, and what it needs to survive.
- I can draw and retell my class's How or Why story.

Materials

- Day 1: One piece of paper for each student with a large blank space to draw and lines on the bottom. The top should be labeled "A (animal) lives in a (habitat/setting)." The bottom should say, "The (animal) eats _____. It drinks_____. It lives inside (shelter)."
- Day 2: Basic storyboard with 3 large boxes labeled Beginning, Middle, and End, and room to write below each picture. Alternately, you could provide 3 pieces of paper with a large blank space to draw and lines on the bottom, labeled with Beginning, Middle, and End.
- Pencils with erasers for each student.
- Crayons.

Instructional Plan—Day 1 (60 minutes)

Rationale

Pourquoi stories are some of the oldest forms of science we have; people observed the world around them and created hypotheses to make sense of it all. Today, many parts of science look differently, but we still rely heavily on observation and educated guesses. On the first day, we explore a habitat and what things might be in that habitat that an animal needs. These two days use multiple learning styles to teach and share information and ideas.

Preparation

Before this session, students should have a basic understanding of sequencing and story structure, including beginning, middle, and end. They should have read and acted out two Pourquoi stories, and clearly articulated what the animal/main character looked like at the beginning of the story, what changed in the middle, and how the animal looked at the end of the story. Students should have prior knowledge of at least one habitat, which could include their own backyards. Make sure you know which habitats they have been studying and do your own basic research on them.

Activities

- Review what animals need to survive (food, water, shelter). Ask, "What other things do some animals have that would help them survive?" (Camouflage, claws, specific skills, etc.)
- Choose a habitat with which students are familiar. Collect information from the students about what you would see, hear, smell, touch, and maybe even taste in this setting, including the kinds of plants and animals that live there. (Write these things down so you can reference the list later.)
- Go on an imaginary journey to this habitat, starting with packing an imaginary backpack filled with the things you would need for the journey (e.g., sunscreen, a parka). Next, lead the students through the classroom, using their ideas of the things they could encounter in this place. Make sure to explore several options for food, water, and shelter for animals.
- Choose two animals that you saw on your journey. List the things that could have met their needs in that place; as a group, act out that animal eating/drinking/living in that thing. List the things that make each animal interesting (e.g., a thin tail, short legs, stripes). Students vote on their favorite animal for the class story.
- Demonstrate Day 1 handout, filling in the blanks with the students. They each draw a picture of the class animal in its setting, with all the things it needs to survive. If students finish early, have a few share their drawings with the whole class, then allow each student to turn and talk to the person next to them about their artwork.

Instructional Plan—Day 2 (60–90 minutes, can be broken up into two sessions)

Rationale

In the second day, students become writers, storytellers, and scientists as they share their research, brainstorm, and work together to create a story.

Preparation

Students should finish their drawings, read and act out another Pourquoi story, and research their class animal by reading informational texts or watching nonfiction videos as a group. Research the class animal yourself, and bring any interesting pictures with you. As a part of their research, students should brainstorm questions that start with How or Why and keep that list, which could be part of a KWHL chart. KWHL stands for what we *Know* already, what we *Want* to learn, *How* we will learn it, and what we have *Learned*. This chart can be used throughout their research to compile ideas, and is highly recommended, but not required.

Activities

- Review the class animal and what makes it unique. Share research findings (class shares first, then you).
- Mark the How or Why question(s) that were *not* answered by any of the research, and choose one question to be the basis of your story. This often relates to one of the unique characteristics of the animal.
- Brainstorm possible answers to the question. How or why *could* this thing have happened? What else is similar to this thing? Relate ideas directly to the setting (i.e., if a snake who lives in the jungle needs to get red on its body, a red flower or feather would be a better place to start than a can of red paint). How do these ideas relate to the animal's needs?
- Choose one option for how or why this thing happened. Act it out, getting the kids to tell you what would need to happen first, next, then, and last.
- Review the structure of a Pourquoi story.
- Sit down and create the story as a group, adding more details. Start with the beginning. Ask lots of questions to pull the story out of the students. Emphasize how the animal looks different in the beginning than in the end.
- Discuss Day 2 Handouts, starting with the beginning. Review how the animal looks in the beginning of the story, then have students draw that, adding description words on the bottom. Repeat with middle and end.
- Gather. Retell the class's story with vivid detail, giving them credit for writing that story. Have students turn to a partner and retell the story with their pictures. If time allows, invite students to share with the class.

Optional Follow-up Activities

- Record the voices of students telling the story. Type up their words, dividing the story into pieces based on the number of students in the class. Give each student a section, and have her/him draw the illustration for that section. Create a class book of the story.
- Scan their pictures and record their voices narrating the story. See examples at www.ripplingstories.com (click on videos).

- Make the story into a piece of Reader's Theatre or a play and perform it for other classes or parents.

Assessment

1. I can research an animal and habitat and share what I have learned.

Teacher pulls popsicle sticks with each student's name out of a container and records which students can share a piece of research or information about the class's animal or habitat.

2. I can ask and answer questions about an animal.

Teacher pulls popsicle sticks with each student's name out of a container and records which students can ask or answer a question about the class's animal.

3. I can imagine and explain how different actions would affect an animal (cause and effect).

While brainstorming potential answers to unanswered questions, have students brainstorm ideas, then turn and talk with a partner about how that would change the animal and what that animal would have looked like before this thing happened. Have some students share with the entire class. Record the number of students actively engaged in conversation and who can share relevant details.

4. I can describe and draw the animal in my story with details about it, its habitat, and what it needs to survive.

Assess work samples. Does the student list the name of the animal and habitat? Does she/he list/show the animal's needs? Does the picture represent some details about the animal?

5. I can draw and retell my class's How or Why story.

Assess work samples. Does the student have the beginning, middle, and end boxes filled in appropriately? Can that student retell the story to a partner, the teacher, or the whole class?

Note: This lesson may be adapted to fit other areas of science by using different Pourquoi stories (e.g., "One Day, One Night," a Native North American Story, can be used to talk about space and the earth's movement through it).

Optional Follow-up Activities in Action

As an extension of this lesson, I recorded the students' words as they told the story. Then, I typed up their words, dividing the story into pieces based on the number of students in the class and the flow of the story. After a few brief drawing lessons and conversations about pictures in books, I gave each student a section of the story to illustrate.

Then, after a brief coaching session with each student on reading with expression and using character voices, I recorded them reading their sections of the story using Garage Band. I scanned all their drawings, and edited the pictures and voices together with iMovie. To watch the digital stories, visit www.ripplingstories.com, and click on videos.

I returned the students' drawings to them as a class book, with their words glued to each page.

Resources

Hamilton, Martha and Mitch Weiss. *How and Why Stories: World Tales Kids Can Read and Tell.* Little Rock, AR: August House, 2000.

Holt, David and Bill Mooney, Ed. *More Ready-to-Tell Tales from Around the World.* Little Rock, AR: August House, 2000.

Kraus, Anne Marie. *Folktale Themes and Activities for Children, Volume 1: Pourquoi Tales.* N.p.: Libraries Unlimited, 1998.

McCarthy, Tara. *Multicultural Fables and Fairy Tales: Stories and Activities to Promote Literacy and Cultural Awareness.* New York: Scholastic, 1994.

Caterpillar to Butterfly
The Process of Metamorphosis

Lynette J. Ford

CCC topics: Patterns, Systems and system models, Structure and processes

POSE topics: Asking questions and defining problems, Planning and carrying out investigations

The Story

Caterpillar to Butterfly
(West African oral traditions)
retold by Lynette J. Ford

Two caterpillars make their way through a garden. They see something, yellow and beautiful, settle on a blade of grass, then flutter into the sunlight. One caterpillar says, "Did you see that? You wouldn't catch me trying to do anything like that. I'll never try to fly. I'll just stay like this, here on the ground."

The other caterpillar knows what that "something" is. She says, "Not me. Someday I'll fly. Someday I'll be a butterfly."

The first caterpillar doesn't eat, because he doesn't want to grow or change. One day, he just isn't around anymore.

The other caterpillar eats what she needs and grows, sometimes eating so much that she outgrows her skin and has to come out of it. Soon, she feels like it's time to change and become that "something." She climbs up the branches of a bush, hides herself under a leaf, and wraps herself in the chrysalis of her dreams. She rests there, until she feels it's time to stretch. She stretches right out of the chrysalis, and spreads her wings so that they can dry. Then she flutters and soars up into the sunlight, for she is a butterfly.

Moral (for students who are ready for higher-level critical thinking and discussion): When we are willing to change and grow, to stretch ourselves and spread our wings, we can fly, and soar like a butterfly.

Standards

NGSS—Life Science

K-LS1-1. From Molecules to Organisms: Structures and Processes: Use observations to describe patterns of what plants and animals (including humans) need to survive. [Clarification Statement: Examples of patterns could include that animals need to take in food but plants do not; the different kinds of food needed by different types of animals; the requirement of plants to have light; and, that all living things need water.

1-LS3-1 Read texts and use media to determine patterns in behavior or make observations to construct an evidence-based account that young plants and animals are like, but not exactly like their parents.

2-LS4-1 Biological Evolution: Unity and Diversity: Make observations of plants and animals to compare the diversity of life in different habitats.

3-LS3-1 Develop models to describe that organisms have unique and diverse life cycles but all have in common birth, growth, reproduction, and death.

CCSS—Reading Informational Text, Writing and Research

W.K.7 Participate in shared research and writing projects (e.g., explore a number of books by a favorite author and express opinions about them). (K-LS1-1)

RI.1.1 Ask and answer questions about key details in a text.

RI.1.2 Identify the main topic and retell key details of a text.

RI.1.10 With prompting and support, read informational texts appropriately complex for grade.

ARTSAnchor topics: Responding, Presenting

Objectives

Children in Grades K–2 will be able to say:

- I can explain that every living thing goes through life stages.
- I can tell the different stages of a butterfly's life cycle (egg, caterpillar, or larvae, chrysalis, butterfly).
- I can compare the eating habits of a caterpillar and a butterfly.

Materials

- a painted lady box and larvae for observation;
- writing surface such as whiteboard, chalkboard, or poster board, on which to keep two lists for the duration of this lesson's activities;
- torn spinach or romaine lettuce leaves for children to chew in their caterpillar stage;
- a flashlight to use as a signal for adult butterflies to emerge from the chrysalis;
- blankets or sheets in different colors, to use as imaginary flowers for butterflies to taste with their feet;
- one bendable straw per child, for use as a proboscis;
- juice (or plain cold water, if sugar is a problem) to imagine as nectar, and
- slightly salted water (or plain tepid water, if salt is a problem) to imagine as mud; two paper cups per child, one for "nectar" and one for "mud puddle";
- bubble wrap, cut into strips for children to use as nearsighted butterfly eyeballs, one strip per child;
- several different-colored pieces of construction paper;
- large sheets of white paper for drawing and writing;
- crayons or colored markers (depending on your students' skill level).

Instructional Plan

Rationale

Every healthy creature, including humans, eats, grows and changes; every animal and insect goes through the process of birth, growth, reproduction, and death. Caterpillars are excellent and unique examples of these processes, and their eating habits and movement can be compared and contrasted with the creature they become, the butterfly.

Preparation

- Set up the cardboard painted lady butterfly house. Place larvae inside as children watch. Discuss the handling/not of the house by children.
- Print out a copy of the life cycle of a butterfly from any of the numerous images available on the Internet; be certain that the printout has four stages: egg; caterpillar (larva); chrysalis (pupa), and butterfly. Copy this printout, one for each student.

- Create a list on your whiteboard, chalkboard, or poster board that includes the following information about caterpillars. Items to list are in italics, followed by details you can share:

1. *A caterpillar or larva hatches from its egg, then usually eats the eggshell.* Then the caterpillar feeds on the plant where the egg was laid. Caterpillars crawl along their host plant, and chew their food.

2. *A caterpillar eats until it is too big for its "skin," or cuticle.* Once it grows too big, it comes out of the skin, or molts. Sometimes it eats this cuticle or skin, a meal that gives the caterpillar healthy nutrients and proteins.

3. *A caterpillar or larva continues a cycle*—eat, poop, molt, eat, poop, molt—*until it is ready to create a chrysalis.* (A butterfly caterpillar makes a chrysalis; a moth caterpillar makes a cocoon).

4. *A caterpillar who is getting ready to create a chrysalis often leaves the host plant, the plants where it was born and where it had its first meals. It looks for a safe place for the next stage of its life.*

5. *Once this safe place is found, a caterpillar forms a thick, strong skin (pupa or chrysalis).* It stays here, changing into an adult butterfly until some effect—changes in light or temperature, chemical signals, or even hormonal triggers—causes the adult to leave its chrysalis.

- Create a list on your whiteboard, chalkboard, or poster board that includes the following information about butterflies. Items to list are in italics, followed by details you can share:

1. *Butterflies taste with their feet.* Taste receptors on a butterfly's feet help a mama butterfly to find the right plant on which to lay her eggs; she drums on the plant with her feet, so that the plant's juices start to ooze out, then she checks the ingredients in the juices, with spines (like sticks) on the back of her legs, for the chemicals her eggs will need. Taste receptors on a butterfly's feet help him to find needed sugary food sources, like rotting fruit.

2. *Butterflies drink all their food.* Butterflies can only eat liquids, like nectar from flowers. They can't chew, but they can drink; butterflies use a special tube called a proboscis to slurp up their meals. When a butterfly has just come from its chrysalis, the proboscis is in two parts. The butterfly's face works the two pieces together into one long, curled straw. Then the butterfly will curl and uncurl its proboscis, testing it to make sure it works.

3. *Butterflies drink from mud puddles.* A butterfly needs sugar and minerals. So nectar is important as a source of sugar, and mud puddles are important as a source of minerals and salts.

4. *Butterflies that have just come out of the chrysalis can't fly.* When

it breaks free from the chrysalis, a butterfly's wings are tiny and shriveled, like a ball of crumpled tissue. The butterfly immediately pumps the wings up and down to get body fluid through its wing veins. This makes the wings expand, or grow larger. Once the wings are the size they are supposed to be, the butterfly must rest for a few hours, while its body dries and hardens for its very first flight.

5. *Butterflies don't see well, but they can see and recognize a lot of colors.* Butterflies are near-sighted; anything beyond 10 to 12 feet is blurry for them. But they can see well enough to find other butterflies, and flowers on which to feed.

6. *The mature butterfly lays eggs which will become their next generation.* Having laid eggs, the butterfly dies.

Activity

1. Share the story. Ask students how they can tell that this is a fictional, make-believe story. List their responses.

2. Present information on the life cycle of the butterfly, first by sharing the printed handout on the life cycle of a butterfly, then by going over the lists of information on each. Number the stages of development, from egg to butterfly.

3. Ask students to number the stages of development on their own handouts. Then facilitate the students' recognition of each stage by calling out a number and asking them to point at it and tell what is happening.

4. Ask students to compare the facts about caterpillars and butterflies to what happens in the folktale. Reflection: Which parts of the story are based on facts about the life cycle of butterflies?

5. Compare the needs in the life cycle of a butterfly to the needs for the healthy growth of the students. Reflection: What do both caterpillars and people need to be healthy and grow?

6. Play with the process and cycle of development:
   a. Offer students leaves of spinach or romaine lettuce to chew as caterpillars do. Reflect on the diet of a caterpillar—eggshell, leaf or plant, skin—and how it is different from each student's lunch that day.
   b. In a large, open space, become crawling caterpillars by lying on bellies with arms at sides and trying to move forward. Reflect on the ease or difficulty of this movement.
   c. Curl up on the floor to pretend to be in a chrysalis. If music is available, use soft, gentle music to enhance the concept that the developing creature seems to be at rest.

d. Slowly uncurl to mimic the new butterfly's emergence from its chrysalis. Instruct students to lie on their backs and stretch their arms and legs out at their sides; as they continue to rest on the floor, tell them to slowly move their arms and legs back and forth and up and down. Then tell students to rise and stretch on their toes, and wave their arms as they slowly walk around the room, in semblance of the butterfly's first flight.

e. Read *The Very Hungry Caterpillar*. Ask students to consider the page where the butterfly emerges from—a cocoon. Is this correct? No! A moth comes from a cocoon. A butterfly emerges from a chrysalis. Ask students to rewrite (revise) that page of Eric Carle's book to reflect the facts about butterflies.

f. Spread the sheets or blankets on the floor as flowers or fermenting fruit. Remind students that butterflies find the sugary nutrition in nectar or rotting fruit, and also determine which plants would be good places to leave their eggs on the leaves, by drumming on them with their feet. Students remove their shoes and "taste" the flowers or fruit, determining for themselves what types of plants or fruits they have discovered.

g. Students tell and/or write about their tasting experience, and draw pictures of their discovered plants or fruits.

h. Pour juice (or cold water) into one cup, and lightly salted water (or tepid water) into a second cup, one of each per student. Give each student a bendable straw. Review the butterfly's liquid diet. Give students the opportunity to taste "nectar" and "mud puddle" with their straw proboscis. Reflection: Would you be content on a diet of nothing but liquids? Why or why not? What solid foods would you miss?

i. Reread The *Very Hungry Caterpillar*, emphasizing the foods the caterpillar eats. Encourage students to join in the narration as you show each food. Ask students which foods might a caterpillar really eat? Ask students to rewrite (revise) the food pages of Eric Carle's book to reflect the diet of a caterpillar.

j. Give each student a strip of bubble wrap, which is to be held over the eyes. Remind students that butterflies are nearsighted, but can see many colors. Hold up items in the classroom, and ask the students to look at them. Can they determine what you are holding? Hold up pieces of construction paper, one color at a time. Can students determine the colors? Reflection: How does this compare to the vision of a butterfly?

k. Facilitate more research about caterpillars, butterflies, and the life cycle of a butterfly, using the Internet if possible, as well as

any books in your school or public library and any printouts you have available.
1. Give each student a large sheet of white paper, and crayons or markers. Facilitate each student's drawing, writing, and telling the life cycle of a butterfly. Collect these drawings in a classroom book.
7. When the butterflies in the butterfly house are ready to be released, discuss with students where—outside—should we take them. Ask "'what habitat' will help the butterflies feed, fly, and reproduce. Think of something you might want to say or wish for the butterflies."

Assessments

1. Through movement, actions with props, and narrative, students will communicate information about and demonstrate their knowledge of the basic characteristics of a caterpillar and a butterfly.

2. Through narrative and numbering the stages in the life cycle of a butterfly, students will describe the pattern that is the life cycle of a butterfly.

3. Through illustration and written or spoken narrative, students will share a final project about the life cycle of a butterfly, for example, students can draw and dictate what they observe in a page by page rendering of the changes occurring in the butterfly house. Students can conclude their drawings with the release and "good wishes" for the butterflies. All drawings/dictations can be complied into a non-fiction book authored and illustrated by each student.

BIBLIOGRAPHY AND RESOURCES

Books

Carle, Eric. *The Very Hungry Caterpillar*. New York: World Publishing, 1969.
Ehlert, Louis. *Waiting for Wings*. Boston: Houghton Mifflin, 2001.
Heiligman, Deborah. *From Caterpillar to Butterfly* (Let's-Read-and-Find-Out Science, Stage 1). New York: HarperCollins, 1996.
Singer, Marilyn. *Caterpillars*. Waynesville, NC: Early Light, 2011.

Websites

www.butterflywonderland.com/curriculum/Butterfly,%20Butterfly,%20Butterfly%20Lesson%20Kinder.pdf
www.canteach.ca/elementary/songspoems26.html
http://creativeeducator.tech4learning.com/2013/lessons/Metamorph#ixzz353F7w8vt
www.enchantedlearning.com/crafts/butterfly/ (NOTE: site membership required for some information and printouts)

Caterpillar to Butterfly
Thoughts on Science and Storytelling

Judith Black

CCC topics: Patterns, Systems and system models
POSE topics: Asking questions & defining problems, Planning and carrying out investigations, Analyzing and interpreting data

A number of years ago I was hired as an artist-in-residence for a Massachusetts elementary school. The beleaguered 3rd grade teacher already had 8 armloads of teaching objectives she was required to cover, and did not look forward to an interloper stealing away her class time. I didn't look forward to an antithetical relationship and so asked: "What do you have to cover in the next few months?" When she came to the natural sciences and stated, "How caterpillars metamorphose into moths and butterflies, and the differences between them," I thought, "Bingo! This is a job for a good story." There is nothing that can't be taught more effectively through a narrative that engages the cognitive through the heart and imagination.[1]

You can always find a folktale that touches on the learning you hope to impart, but why not create a story that will perfectly address your objectives? It is not that difficult, and following is an outline and model of how to dot it.

    1. Articulate exactly what you want to teach. General ideas lend themselves to ineffectual generalized stories. For example:

General	Specific
I want to teach about the planetary system	I want to teach about the order of the planets in our solar system
	Or
	I want to teach about the effects of the sun's rays on the atmosphere of each planet.

Caterpillar to Butterfly: Science and Storytelling (Black)   67

General	Specific
	Or
	I want to teach about the gravitational pull that the sun exerts and how it keeps each planet moving in it's own orbit.
To teach about metamorphosis	To teach how mayflies develop from an aquatic nymph, into a winged, air bound insect
	Or
	To teach how some insects pass through a larval stage, then enter an inactive state called pupa, or chrysalis, and finally emerge as adults.
	Or
	To teach how both moths and butterflies emerge from caterpillars, and how to identify their similarities and differences

Trust that when you are creating a story, choosing specific teaching objective will enable you to shape a sharper and more engaging tale that will lead children to an authentic desire to learn more about the subject. The specific can lead to the general!

2. Research and record every fact that you want to teach. You may not be able to include them all, but have them available for your story making. If you don't know exactly what you want to teach, then chances are that little will be communicated!

I went to the school library, took out a few 3rd grade level books about moths and butterflies, checked with the teacher, and made a list of all the facts that the curriculum required. These included:

How to identify a caterpillar; how a caterpillar turns into a moth or butterfly; and the differences and similarities between butterflies and moths.

3. Create the world of your story. This is when you start to have fun. Since you have a teaching objective, use the reality of the environment you are exploring, but allow it to be big, vital, and filled with anthropomorphic details that will enable your listeners to identify with and enter it. Purists will claim that trees don't talk, and caterpillars don't have personalities. Much in same spirit that children understand that fairy tales are metaphors, wolfs don't don nightgowns, and birds cannot give you all you need for success at the ball, they understand that you are making art.

In the case of the caterpillar story, the woods are its setting.[2] (Other, more detailed, examples follow.)

The Story of Cynthia the Caterpillar

Deep in the woods, there lived two caterpillars, eating, eating eating,
    the leaves of trees and
Eating, eating, eating the leaves of flowers, and arguing!

What you do is take that natural environment and bring it into their realm of understanding for your specific listeners. The above works for third graders. If I was shaping the story for older students the ecology of the specific wooded area would come alive with the types of trees that grow there looking down on the creatures that dwell there, until we felt at home in that place.

    4. Create Your Primary Character/s. Here is when you, as an educator, have a huge advantage. You know your students. You know their cognitive, social/emotional, physical, and curricular strengths and challenges. With this information you have the unique opportunity to create characters they will identify with.[3] (More examples below.)

For my story I needed two characters (the eventual moth and butterfly), and wanted ones that would resonate for my 3rd grade target audience. I went and watched them during recess on a playground, and found the main players.

(Please feel free to make up tunes or rhythms for the two sung parts of this story. Cognitively, it is always useful to switch presentational modalities. They provide gentle jolts of engagement. Also, music travels through different neural pathways than the spoken word, and often children with spoken language challenges will be able to enter and hold on to a story or a lesson when even a part of it is offer through melody. It works well to break your group in half, teaching each one of the songs.)

The Story of Cynthia the Caterpillar

Deep in the woods, there lived two caterpillars, eating, eating eating,
    the leaves of trees and
Eating, eating, eating the leaves of flowers, and arguing!

    CYNTHIA: (*in character: Feminine and faux sophisticated, and rapturous*) Hello, my name is Cynthia and today I am a caterpillar. But I know my fate. I know my destiny. Some day I shall be a butterfly! You know, only 1 out of every 5 of we caterpillars become butterflies. Only 2 out of 10 ... only 10 out of ... oh never mind! Just look at them, out in the daylight, like all civilized creatures, with their stunning orange and yellow and gold and black wings. And they are so polite, always resting their wings demurely upon their backs when they land. They have those fashionable, long thin bodies

Caterpillar to Butterfly: Science and Storytelling (Black)   69

and pointed antenna. Ah, they are so smart looking. Yes, it is my fate. It is my destiny.

(Singing)

> I want to be a butterfly
> Soaring through the sun filled sky
> My wings perched neatly on my behind
> I want to be a butterfly.

CHUCK: (Think: Retired boxer from the South Bronx) Hey Cynthia! Cynthia! I's talkin' to yous.

CYNTHIA: Oh dear! That is Chuck caterpillar. He is a low grade, gross, and disgusting character. Pay him no mind.

CHUCK : Hey Cynthia, face it. Yous gonna be a moth. 4 outta every 5 of us'n caterpillars turn into moths. 8 out 10, 40 outta 50. Nothin' wrong with bein' a moth Cynthia. So what if their bodies are rounder and furrier, and their antennas is shorter and kinda fuzzy. I like that their wings are gray and black and gray and some white and gray and just hang out at their sides. No pretensions, ya know what I mean? And they live at night! Lot more fun at night Cynthia! Face it.

(Singing)

> Moth Moth you're gonna be a moth.
> Take your fight in the night (2 claps)
> Hang out by an open light.
> Moth moth you're gonna be a moth.

CYNTHIA : Chuck, you are disgusting!

4. Plot Development: The joy and ease of creating stories to teach the natural sciences is that the plot is given. It is the process you want your students to learn about.

In this case, the metamorphosis of a caterpillar. I want my listeners to learn how the larva grows, follows it's eventual journey into a chrysalis or cocoon, and it's emergence as a moth or butterfly, all the while reinforcing the basic differences between these two Lepidoptera. The fascinating cell reorganization, imaginal disks, and the transformative digestive process within the cocoon or chrysalis would have to wait for an adaptation for middle school students! Simply put, *you are hooking your listeners on characters, in which they can see themselves and pulling those characters through the facts and process you want to teach about.*

All day the butterflies would flutter from flower to puddle to old tossed away apples, their proboscises drinking in nectar. With their beautiful wings of orange and yellow and gold and black, delicately resting on the back of their long slim bodies. It was during their infrequent rests they would discuss the up-and-coming generation of caterpillars.

BERNICE BUTTERFLY: Oh dear, look at them. So many caterpillars, so few to join "our" ranks.

70   Part One. Early Childhood (Life Science)

BETTY BUTTERFLY: Who do you think deserves to be 1 out of 5, 2 out of 10, 12 out of 50?
BERNICE: That's 10 out 50 dear. Math isn't your subject is it? Those 10 will be blessed! With our elegant extended antennae, our diurnal habits, and just look at these long stunning bodies, we are the best. Which of them deserves to join the best? Let's hear it caterpillars!
CATERPILLARS: (singing)

> I want to be a butterfly
> Soaring through the sun filled sky
> My wings perched neatly on my behind
> I want to be a butterfly.

All night the moths would gather around the glowing light bulb at Joe's Bar and Grill, reviewing the next generation.

MORTIE MOTH: Hey, look at all of 'em! And almost every one of those lucky buggers gets to be one of us. 4 in 5, 8 in 10, 40 in 50. Math is my subject.
MACK MOTH: Hey nothing wrong with having a rounder furrier body. Keeps ya warmer. I like my short antennae. They don't get caught on stuff. The wings hangin at our sides...
MORTIE: Hey man, that just honest. You know like, here I am, all of me
MACK: Yeah and nocturnal insects know how to party! Ouch! I burnt my wing on that light bulb!
MORTIE: Hey, just saw someone hang up a cloth coat. I think it's dinnertime! How's a-bout our song before we go?
MOTHS: (singing)

> Moth Moth you're gonna be a moth.
> Take your fight in the night (2 claps)
> Hang out by an open light.
> Moth moth you're gonna be a moth.

(Now you can pick and choose from the facts and processes, turning those that work for this age group into part of the story.)
Every day Cynthia and Chuck would argue.

CYNTHIA: Chuck, I know my fate. I know my destiny. I will be 1 out of 5, 2 out of 10, 12 out of....
CHUCK: That's 10 outta 50. Math ain't your strong suit!
CYNTHI : No Chuck, beauty, grace, elegance. Those are my strong suits.
CHUC : Looks like you've eaten right through 2 or 3 of your strong suits already!
CYNTHIA: I don't understand it! I eat modestly....
CHUCK: But constantly.
CYNTHIA: And then at some point my leotard just slips off!
CHUCK: That's called molting.
CYNTHIA: That sounds disgusting.
CHUCK: We eat. We outgrow our skin. We shed our skinny skin, so we can grow a bigger one and eat even more! I think I'm on my 3rd or 4th. You like my new one?
CYNTHIA: Disgusting! Anyway, mine is much nicer! Look, I am striped!

CHUCK: So am I and so are convicts' clothes!
CYNTHIA: Well, look closely. I have 13 body segments!
CHUCK: So do I.
CYNTHIA: Well, I have 3 pairs of angled legs, and 5 pairs of straight ones!
CHUCK: So do I, and so do the Rocketts.
CYNTHIA: My caterpillar coat has a lovely soft fuzz to it!
CHUCK: Me too.
CYNTHIA: Oh Chuck! I know who I am meant to be. A long, lean, pointy antennae beauty with wings of gold and yellow and orange, and black which sits demurely behind me as I suck nectar from my proboscis....
CHUCK: Just face it Cynthia, you's gonna be one of the 4 outta 5, 8 outta 10, 40 outta 50.

There is no dishonor to bein' a:

(Singing)

> Moth Moth you're gonna be a moth.
> Take your fight in the night (2 claps)
> Hang out by an open light.
> Moth moth you're gonna be a moth.

CYNTHIA: NEVER!

Sometimes the creatures of the forest would come just to hear them argue. It was more fun than a water fight in the pond.

CYNTHIA: I know my fate. I know my destiny. Oh, just look at them dating.
CHUCK: Dating? You messin' with me?
CYNTHIA: Of course not! When a butterfly boy sees a beautifully colored butterfly girl he will do a dance to impress her, and if they like the aroma of one another....
CHUCK: Ach, the moth boy just (*sound like a big raspberry on someone's skin*) lets out a smell.

A moth girl shows up and if she digs the smell they do do that voodoo that they do so well!

CYNTHIA: Chuck, has anyone mentioned that you have no class at all?

(Singing)

> I want to be a butterfly
> Soaring through the sun filled sky
> My wings perched neatly on my behind
> I want to be a butterfly.

CHUCK: Face it baby:

(Singing)

> Moth Moth you're gonna be a moth.
> Take your fight in the night (2 claps)
> Hang out by an open light.
> Moth moth you're gonna be a moth.

5. Closing Your Tale: Once you have taken your characters through

the various processes or stages that you want to teach about, it is time to end the tale. For this, nature provides![4]

Here is what happens to Cynthia and Chuck:

Life moves on, and after constant fighting and eating, eating and fighting, Cynthia and Chuck left their many molted skins behind and started toward a tree. Of course they argued the entire time:

>CYNTHIA: I know my fate, I know my destiny. I will have a long lean body.
>CHUCK: You'll have a furry fat one!
>CYNTHIA: I will have lovely pointed antennae.
>CHUCK: Ha, they'll be short and featherlike!
>CYNTHIA: My stunning wings of gold and yellow and orange and black will perch delicately upon my back when I am drinking from my proboscis!
>CHUCK: Hey, you'll look great in big old wings of grey and brown. They'll help you blend in at night, when you'll be flyin!
>CYNTHIA: Never never! I will never be a nocturnal creature. I was born for the sun, the beauty, the glamour of Butterflydom. I shall be 1 out of 5, 2 out of 10, uh … how many out of 50?
>CHUCK: Ten Cynthia. You really should catch up on your math.
>CYNTHIA: I won't need it. I'll be beautiful!
>
>(Singing)
>
>>I want to be a butterfly
>>Soaring through the sun filled sky
>>My wings perched neatly on my behind
>>I want to be a butterfly.
>
>CHUCK: So sad! Oh well, see you in mothdom.

Now, if you looked closely you could see them making their way to a tree. One edged its way up the bark and wove its sleeping bag against the trunk, a cocoon. The other edged its way up the trunk and out to a branch where it wove its sleeping bag, a chrysalis. Then with the earth holding them safely in her protection, both caterpillars went to sleep. A loud snore coming from the cocoon and gentle breathing from the chrysalis until, wooooosh, they turned into something no one could recognize, a liquid that is reshaping, repurposing itself for a new life.[5] Even the colors of the cocoon and chrysalis changed in that week and a half, until one day you could see them trembling, shaking. Look at the cocoon. Breaking through it's sleeping bag is a strange folded, bent creature. It presses out it's proboscis and takes in a breath of life and with that pushes new liquids within it to … wooooo fill the rounded furry body. Woooosh, fill the gray, brown, black wings that hangs at it's side, woo, fill the short fluffy antennae.

>CYNTHIA: Oh dear. Short furry body, feathery antenna, uncomely wings of gray and brown and black, just hanging there. I guess Chuck was right. I am 4 out 5, 8 or 10, … how many out of 50? Maybe I should of paid better attention to the math. Well, it's daytime; I might as well go to sleep. (Snores)

In the meantime the chrysalis was also trembling and shaking. Breaking through its sleeping bag is a strange folded, bent creature. It presses out it's proboscis and takes in a breath of life and with that pushes new liquids within it to ... wooooo fill the long lean body. Woooo, fill the orange, yellow, and gold wings slowly, but clearly enlarging as they rest elegantly on the creature's back. Woosh, fill the long graceful, pointed, antennae.

> CHUCK : (Looking around) Hey Cindy, Cindy, guess what! Look at me! Long lean bod, pointed antenna; just take a gander at them pretty wings on my back! Cindy! (Looking down) Cindy (spies her) HA HA HA.

The moral of the story being that in this natural world, all things continue to change.
Let's all sing both of the songs:

(Singing)

> I want to be a butterfly
> Soaring through the sun filled sky
> My wings perched neatly on my behind
> I want to be a butterfly.

(Singing)

> Moth Moth you're gonna be a moth.
> Take your fight in the night (2 claps)
> Hang out by an open light.
> Moth moth you're gonna be a moth.

Enjoy story making, bring the natural sciences into the hearts and minds of your students!

NOTES

1. Yes, this is a generalization. If you are a fan of Gardner's learning modalities, you will note that children with strengths in logical, math/science approaches can flourish in a fact-filled curriculum. This approach is for all the rest.

2. You can see how any organic process you want to teach, from the vaporization of water, to photosynthesis could be a plot, and that the story could easily take place in the environment that hosts it. For vaporization you could choose a New Hampshire lake. For photosynthesis, that tale could take place within the cell structure of a leaf. These are dynamic places, and only require a human bridge to bring listeners into it.

Dewy drop was the 3076th child of his mother, Squam Lake. As you might guess, he was never lonely. Swimming along with so many brothers and sisters makes for a full life. On top of that, his mom was a gracious hostess to whitefish, yellow perch, slimy scupins and so many others. Dewy loved when they swam right by him. It tickled and he would rush away and then hope for it to happen again. (You start to see how the ecology of the area can be integrated easily.)

3. For instance, kindergarteners are still reaching for basic physical autonomy and independence. If you were teaching about mayflies, your main character might be Normy Nymph who everyone treats like a baby! He's only allowed to eat stuff that grows on the bottom of the rock where he lives, and he's not allowed to leave that

place! Your students will identify with and be deeply invested when Normy, for the first time, with great courage starts to crawl away from that rock on a warm spring day. Despite the warnings of other creatures, and his own fears, he is drawn toward the water's surface…

4. What happens to sad Dewy Drop once he has been evaporated into a cloud? Missing his water family he floats gently in another form. Airily he calls other lost drops to join him until there are so many that Precipitation occurs! Shocked by returning to his original form and finding himself and new friends sliding down a mountain, going faster and faster, you can imagine his joy and relief when he finds himself back in the lake he came from, reunited with family and friends!

You can do this with hundreds of organic cycles. Simply allow the authentic science to guide your plot, and have your characters, in the fullness of the personality you have developed, make the journey to its logical end.

5. There are fantastic videos available on the Internet of this process, as well as more detailed descriptions of what is occurring. Remember, this is the 3rd grade version!

Gorgeous video shows the entire life cycle of the Monarch: https://www.youtube.com/watch?v=7AUeM8MbaIk´

Great Pictures of process: http://lifecycle.onenessbecomesus.com/

Hatching Chicks in the Kindergarten Classroom

TRACY DRUMMER AIDEN *and*
ELIZABETH BARLOCK

CCC topics: Patterns, cause and effect, Stability and change
POSE topics: Asking questions and defining problems, Planning and carrying our investigations, Engage in argument from evidence

The Stories

This study is driven by dynamic science. The children are engaged. Their families often stop in to observe and comment. It takes over! As such, the folktales are important and broaden the science study in humane ways ... and it is not just one story that is the focus; these are literature based classrooms. *Chicken Little, The Little Red Hen, The King of the Birds, Cuckoo, The Quetzal,* etc., all in picture book formats, contribute to the integrated curriculum and encourage conversations about how we treat each other and care for our world.

Standards

NGSS—Life Science—life cycles

LS1.A: Structure and Function: All organisms have external parts. Different animals use their body parts in different ways to see, hear, grasp objects, protect themselves, move from place to place, and seek, find, and take in food, water and air.

LS1.B: Growth and Development of Organisms: Adult animals can have young. In many kinds of animals, parents and their offspring engage in behaviors that help the offspring themselves engage in behaviors that help the offspring survive.

LS1.D: Animals have body parts that capture and convey different kinds of information needed for growth and survival. Animals respond to these inputs with behaviors that help them survive.

CCSS—writing, listening, language

W.K.7 Participate in shared research and writing projects (e.g., explore a number of books by a favorite author and express opinions about them).

W.1.2 Write informative/explanatory texts in which they name a topic, supply some facts about the topic, and provide some sense of closure.

W.1.5 With guidance and support from adults, focus on a topic, respond to questions and suggestions from peers, and add details to strengthen writing as needed.

Objectives

Kindergarten students will be able to say:

- I can observe the developmental growth stages of an embryo.
- I can associate and measure the incubation time (21 days).
- I can notice changes during the incubation.
- I can sequence the growth changes in an embryo.
- I can begin to understand the anatomy of a chick.
- I can document thinking with writings and drawings.

Materials

- Fertilized eggs
- Incubator
- Thermometers
- Heat lamp
- Candling light
- Brood/home
- Water and appropriate water dispenser
- Food and chicken food dispenser
- Journals, paper, pencils
- Collection of fiction books

- Collection of nonfiction books
- Lifecycle materials/visuals/21-day countdown calendar

Instructional Plan

Rationale

There is such excitement in the classroom, the school, and in the homes of the kindergarteners when the eggs arrive in the spring. In the month that follows everyone "drops in" to the classrooms and talks about what's happening. Interest in the development of these eggs (chickens, ducks, and one year only, turkey eggs!) by these suburban children expands the concept of what it means to be alive. The activity described below is augmented by the reading and rereading favorite folktales and fiction.

Preparation

I have always done the hatching project with a private farmer and had a family take the chicks afterward. If we have too many hatch, I would give them back to the farmer or the parent would take them to the farmers' market.

Activity

1. Chick Journals: Daily documentation (21 days) of embryo growth, development and chick hatching. Documentation done by children through drawings and writing of embryo development, by observing scientific pictures, incubating eggs, and reading nonfiction literature.

2. Candling of Chick Eggs: Candling of eggs on days 10 and 16 to observe growth of embryos within the egg. Students will experience a scientific way of observing the development process of chick embryo growth. Through candling the children will begin to engage in conversations about life and death by witnessing movement and growth or lack of within the egg. Children will begin to:

- Make predictions about chick development and growth
- Observe anatomy of growing chicks.
- Compare between the collection of eggs
- Document thinking through writings and drawings.

3. Chick Hatching Process: Children will have the opportunity to observe the hatching of chicks in the classroom incubator. Children will begin to:

- Observe the hatching process of the chicks.
- Predict amount of time it will take from first crack to actual emerging of chick.
- Observe the rapid changes in growth of a baby chick.
- Document the first day of life through writing and drawings.

4. Caring for Baby Chicks: Children will have the opportunity to investigate what a chick needs to survive and ways in which to set up an appropriate habitat for the chicks. Children will begin to:

- Design a habitat set-up
- Learn to read temperatures and understand the correct temperatures that chicks need for proper health and development.
- Understand dietary needs of a chick.
- Understand health needs and concerns of chicks.
- Provide basic care to chicks.
- Document chick growth through drawings and writing.
- Discuss and understand the life cycle of a chick
- Observe the anatomy of a live chick.

Assessment

Student documentation of the science never fully defines student engagement in this project. The interest and care students develop mirrors the eggs' development in this 'mysterious' adventure.

BIBLIOGRAPHY

Dorros, Arthur. *City Chicken*. New York: HarperCollins Publishers, 2003.
Ehlert, Lois. *Cuckoo/Cucu*. New York: Harcourt, 1997.
Freedman, Deborah. *Blue Chicken*. New York: Viking, 2011.
Gibbons, Gail. *Chicks & Chickens*. New York: Holiday House, 2003.
Graves, Keith. *Chicken Big*. San Francisco: Chronicle Books, 2010.
Heller, Ruth. *Chickens Aren't the Only Ones*. New York: Grosset & Dunlap, 1981.
Kellogg, Steven. *Chicken Little*. New York: W. Morrow, 1985.
Legg, Gerald. *From Egg to Chicken*. New York: F. Watts, 1998.
Pinkney, Jerry. *The Little Red Hen*. New York: Dial Books for Young Readers, 2006.
Reynolds, Aaron. *Chicks and Salsa*. New York: Bloomsbury Children's Books, 2005.
Sklansky, Amy E. *Where Do Chicks Come From?* New York: HarperCollins Publishers, 2005.
Stein, David Ezra. *Interrupting Chicken*. Somerville, Mass.: Candlewick Press, 2010.

Stileman, Kali. *Roly-poly Egg*. Wilton, CT: Tiger Tales, 2011.
Thomson, Ruth. *The Life Cycle of a Chicken*. New York: PowerKids Press, 2007.
Ward, Helen. *The King of the Birds*. Ontario: Templar, 1997.
Ward, Jennifer. *What Will Hatch?* New York: Walker Books for Young Readers, 2013.

"Tops and Bottoms"
What Goes Up? What Goes Down?

JANE STENSON

CCC topic: Patterns, Systems and system energy, Structure and function

POSE topic: Asking questions (science) and defining problems(engineering), Developing and using models, Planning and carrying out investigations, Analyzing and interpreting data

Story Synopses

Tops and Bottoms—African American

Br'er Rabbit and Br'er Bear were neighbors. Br'er Rabbit and his family worked hard while Bear was very lazy. Br'er Rabbit offered to grow crops in Br'er Bear's field, asking "At harvest time do you want the tops or the bottoms of the plant?" In three growing seasons Br'er Rabbit grew crops whose "worth" was other than Br'er Bear declared, e.g., if Bear said tops, then Rabbit grew root vegetables.

Tops and Bottoms—Northhamptonshire

A farmer inherited four fields when his father died. Nothing had been grown in one of the fields for generations. But the soil was good and black. To clear the field and one spring the farmer brought his plow and horse and began to plow. POP! a foul, horrid goblin appeared stating he would take the entire crop. The farmer wagered that he would do all the work and that the goblin could have half of the crop—"Do you want the top half or the bottom half?" and the farmer planted crops whose worth was the other half. After several seasons the goblin declared the field would be planted in wheat and at the harvest they would have a mowing contest to determine who would win the crop. The farmer not only planted wheat, but also iron rods on the goblin's half of the field, winning the bet.

Standards

NGSS—Life Science—Plants

LS2.A: Interdependent Relationships in Ecosystems: Plants depend on water and light to grow.

LS4.D: Biodiversity and Humans: There are many different kinds of living things in any area, and they exist in different places on land and in water.

ETS1.B: Developing Possible Solutions: Designs can be conveyed through sketched, drawings, or physical models. These representations are useful in communicating ideas for a problem's solutions to other people.

CCSS-ELA—Reading, Writing, Speaking, Listening, Language

W.2.7. Participate in shared research and writing projects. W.2.8. Recall information from experiences and or gather information from provided sources to answer a question.

SL.2.5. Create audio recordings of stories or poems; add drawings or other visual displays to stories or recounts of experiences when appropriate to clarify ideas, thoughts, and feelings.

ARTS—Anchor topic: Creating, Presenting, Responding, Connecting

Objectives

Kindergarten—Second Grade students will be able to say:

- I can identify the parts of plants and their functions with the correct botanical vocabulary.
- I can care for a plant and identify/draw the stages of its life cycle.
- I can tell two stories where plants figure prominently in the plot.

Materials

- an amaryllis and planting medium and pot

82 Part One. Early Childhood (Life Science)

- one narcissus bulb for each child
- clear beer cups
- pebbles as medium for the narcissus
- white paper
- colored pencils

Instructional Plan

Rationale

Learning requires various ways to teach a topic, so the telling and listening to the story (fun), the availability of picture books, the experience of setting up a (fragile) narcissus and documenting its grow, and the class's observation of the splendid and showy amaryllis make many ways to experience and learn the parts of plants. Documentation subscribes to the idea that "if you can draw it, then you know it." Each child will create a plant book.

Preparation

Gather a variety of picture books—fiction and non-fiction—about plants to keep in the classroom.

Learn the Northhamptonshire story (Leslie Conger's adaptation) Tops and Bottoms or one of the variants to tell to the class. Purchase a "good" amaryllis (not one that has been sitting on the shelf for a long time); they often come with a pot and planting medium. Purchase the narcissus, clear beer cups and pebbles (which may need to be rinsed).

Activity

1. Setting up the narcissus: Each child places three inches of pebbles into the beer cup, gently places the basil plate of the narcissus on the gravel and fill in securely around the bulb. Water to the basil plate. Put in sunny window and draw Picture #1: Draw a picture of the bulb in the cup in the window using colored pencils.

2. Every other day or every three days each child creates a drawing, documenting the changes visually in his/her bulb. What parts have begun to grow? What does 'grow' mean? What color(s) do you find? Is the plant tipping toward the window? Label each drawing—DAY 1 or DAY 5, etc. Days later when the bulb dies back, be certain to draw the picture as the last page in the book. When complete, students will now fashion the pages

into a plant book and title it ("My Narcissus," for example). Also, some bulbs may not grow—if the basal plate is injured, it will not put out roots. That's nature.

3. Setting up the amaryllis: Following the packaging directions prepare the amaryllis in its pot and discuss throughout its splendid growth what is happening. The amaryllis is large enough that the pistil and stamen show easily. Use this flower to show the reproductive pieces of plant life. Children may wish to paint a picture of the flower.

4. Perhaps the third or fourth day of the narcissus growth is the optimum time to read Janet Stevens' adaptation of "Tops and Bottoms." Later in the activity cycle tell the Northhamptonshire "Tops and Bottoms." Compare and contrast these folktales, mentioning versions or variants of folktales.

Assessment

1. Completion of the Narcissus Book, noting the student's attitude and ability to care for the bulb as well as the visual and written/dictated documentation. Note the student's identification and use of the proper names for each part of the plant.

2. Can student tell one of the tops and bottoms stories in an abridged form, that is, can the student explain how the "lazy" character was tricked?

RESOURCES

Brown, Peter. *The Curious Garden*. New York: Little, Brown Books for Young Readers, 2009.
Bunting, Eve. *Flower Garden*. New York: HMH Books for Young Children, 1994.
Conger, Leslie. *Tops and Bottoms*. New York: Four Winds Press, 1970.
Cooney, Barbara. *Miss Rumphius*. New York: Puffin, 1982.
Demi. *The Empty Pot*. New York: Square Fish, 1990.
Ehlert, Lois. *Growing Vegetable Soup*. New York: HMH Books for Young Children, 1987.
_____. *Planting a Rainbow*. New York: HMH Books for Young Children, 1988.
Gibbons, Gail. *From Seed to Plant*. New York: Holiday House, 1993.
_____. *The Vegetables We Eat*. New York: Holiday House, 2008.
Jordan, Helene. *How a Seed Grows: Let's Read and Find Out Science 1*. New York: HarperCollins, 2000.
Schwartz, David M. *Stems and Roots*. Creative Teaching Press, 1998.
Stevens, Janet. *Tops and Bottoms*. New York: Harcourt Brace, 1995.
Stewart, Sarah. *The Gardener*. New York: Square Fish, 1997.
Uchida, Yoshiko. *The Fox and the Bear*. New York: Harcourt Brace, 1955.

"Why Mosquitoes Buzz in People's Ears"
Pourquoi Stories and Mosquitoes

Joyce H. Geary

CCC topics: Patterns, Cause and effect, Energy and matter
POSE topics: Asking questions and defining problems, Planning and carrying out investigations

The Story—Synopsis

"Why Mosquitoes Buzz in People's Ears": A West African Tale
retold by Verna Aardema

An iguana was taking a drink at a waterhole when a mosquito came by and said, "You won't believe what I saw yesterday!" and proceeded to tell the iguana a tale. "I saw," said the excited mosquito, " a farmer who was digging yams as big as I am!" "That's a ridiculous story," scoffed the iguana. "I really don't want to listen to such nonsense. I'd rather be deaf." And, with that, he put a stick in each ear and walked off grumbling and muttering to himself—"A yam the size of a mosquito—total nonsense!"

The rest of this cause and effect, pourquoi story shows what happens when the iguana ignores the python who then thinks that iguana is angry and plotting something bad against him. To escape iguana, the python slithers into rabbit's hole and a very frightened rabbit runs out his back door, causing crow to spread the alarm for danger and monkey, watching from the tree above, runs through the branches to warn the other animals. When a branch under monkey breaks off, falls, and kills an owlet, monkey is blamed for killing the baby owl. Mother Owl is devastated and fails to wake up the sun to start a new day.

Eventually King Lion calls a meeting of all of the animals to see what the animals know about the killing of the owlet. One by one each animal is called before the King from monkey back to iguana and mosquito. Each tells his story and why it's not his fault until the fault finally rests with mosquito and his ridiculous tale to iguana. All of the animals are angry with mosquito. "Punish the mosquito!" the animals yell. And the Mother Owl is satisfied and hoots " Hoooo! Hoooo!" and the sun finally wakes up so that a new day comes.

The mosquito hears all of this but keeps hiding, although she does have a guilty conscience and to this day she goes around whining in people's ears— "ZZZZZZZ—is everyone still angry at me?"

And she always gets a quick answer—SWAT! SPLAT!

Standards

NGSS—Structure and Function, Life Cycles

LS1.A: Structure and Function: All organisms have external parts. Different animals use their body parts in different ways to see, hear, grasp objects, protect themselves, move from place to place, and seek, find, and take in food, water and air.

LS.4.D: Biodiversity and Humans: There are many different kinds of living things in any area, and they exist in different places on land and in water.

ETS1.B: Designs can be conveyed through sketches, drawings, or physical models. These representations are useful in communicating ideas for a problem's solutions to other people.

CCSS for ELA—Reading, Writing, Speaking, Listening

RL 3.1 Ask and answer questions to demonstrate understanding of a text, referring explicitly to the text as the basis for the answers.

RL 3.2 Recount stories, including fables, folktales, and myths from diverse cultures; determine the central message, lesson, or moral and explain how it is conveyed through key details in the text.

RL 3.3 Describe the characters in a story (e.g., their traits, motivations, or feelings) and explain how their actions contribute to the sequence of events.

W 3.1 Write opinion pieces on topics or texts, supporting a point of view with reasons.

W 3.2 Write informative / explanatory texts to examine a topic and convey ideas and information clearly.

W 3.4 With guidance and support from adults, produce writing in which the development and organization are appropriate to task and purpose.

W 3.7 Conduct short research projects that build knowledge about a topic.

SL 3.4 Report on a topic or text, tell a story, or recount an experience with appropriate facts and relevant, descriptive details, speaking clearly at an understandable pace.

Objectives

Third Grade students will be able to say:

- I can understand the question and answer in a pourquoi story.
- I can understand "Cause and Effect" in a story and in scientific studies and research.
- I can identify the parts of a mosquito.
- I can recount the life cycle of a mosquito and how the natural water cycle affects the mosquito.
- I can ask questions about the mosquito, research the questions, and evaluate conflicting answers from different sources.
- I can share my research through writing or an oral report to others.

Materials

- Aardema, Verna. *Why Mosquitoes Buzz in People's Ears*. Illus. by Leo and Diane Dillon. New York: Dial Books for Young Readers, 1975.
- Map of West Africa.
- Chart paper to write questions created and drawings of Water Cycle and Life Cycle of a Mosquito.
- Materials to research questions chosen by individuals or groups—Google and other computer research sources.
- Books and/or magazine articles on mosquitoes.
- Computers to use in research and writing.

Instructional Plan

Rationale

Stories that ask "How and Why" (pourquoi stories) allow students to think about the answers to questions for which they have no answer—yet.

Stories that are cumulative, showing cause and effect of activities, serve to remind students that every action has a consequence whether it is in the listener's life or in the scientific questions of life. "How did the earth begin?" "How does electricity work?" "Why can't I breath under water like a fish does?" "Why does it rain? "Why do mosquitoes buzz in our ears?" Stories can ask and answer questions; research and experimentation can provide scientific answers to questions. We can ponder and come up with answers to our questions; we can complete experiments and research many resources on-line, in print, and through interviews with experts. We can then come to conclusions, and share our information with others.

And why study mosquitoes? Because they are a fact of our lives!

Preparation

Discussion in preparation for story: Do people always understand what they see or hear? What questions do the students have about things that they don't understand? Do they ever try to make up answers about "how" and "why" questions? Do adults ever make up those answers? (Write down questions.)

Activity

a. Tell the students that long ago in West Africa people wondered about many questions. Show a map of West Africa and find countries in that area. One question was about mosquitoes which were and are very prevalent in that area. It was "Why Do Mosquitoes Buzz in People's Ears?" Tell this story.

b. Have students discuss the story, characters, actions, the way each animal had a reason for what he did (cause) and how that made something else happen (effect). What was the story's answer to the question posed? Is this a logical answer? Why or why not?

c. Do the students know any other stories of cause and effect? Do they know any other pourquoi stories—stories that ask how and why something happens? (See bibliography.)

d. Can we find the scientific answer to the question "Why do mosquitoes buzz in people's ears?" Study and learn to identify the parts of a mosquito, remembering to understand the function of each part of the insect. Remember—a mosquito is an insect. What body parts are common to all insects? What is unique about a mosquito's body parts and uses of those parts? What is a mosquito's life cycle and how does the water cycle of evaporation and condensation affect the mosquito's life? Why do mosquitoes bite animals (people)?

e. Have students draw or show the water cycle of evaporation and condensation and the life cycle of a mosquito. In what ways do they intersect? How could this intersection reduce or eradicate mosquitoes and the diseases they carry to humans and animals? Is this scientific thinking? How?

f. What other questions would you like to ask about mosquitoes? (Some further questions might be as follows: What value is there in having mosquitoes? What difference would it make if they all disappeared? Is it possible to make them all disappear? When are mosquitoes present/not present? Why? Which mosquitoes bite us? Can they hurt us? Why did my husband and I, in a recent trip to El Salvador, have to learn about malaria, dengue fever and chikungunya? How do certain mosquitoes cause malaria and what happens in a person's body when they get malaria? Why is DEET considered an important repellant—specifically, why and how does it repel mosquitoes?) Make a list of the students' questions.

g. Assign individual students or small groups a question to research and take notes. Share whether all of their sources gave them the same facts. Evaluate which facts are most logical but share alternative answers. Can these ambiguities be resolved? Students (individuals or groups) will write a brief report to answer their question.

h. Prepare an oral report to share with the whole class.

i. This may be an extended one session lesson researching and answering only a few questions such as the mosquito's body parts, life cycle, how mosquitoes cause malaria, or how to prevent illnesses caused by mosquitoes. The science study can be expanded to cover more questions, depending on the time available.

Assessments

- Were the students able to respond to questions about the meaning of the story, actions of the characters, idea of cause and effect, and whether the stated question had a logical answer?
- Were they able to write and research questions about the mosquito?
- Were they able to think like a scientist?
- Were the students able to identify the body parts and the life cycle of a mosquito?
- Were they able to synthesize all of their research and prepare logical, understandable written reports to answer their questions?
- Were they able to share these reports orally with the class and to explain or resolve ambiguities in their research?

BIBLIOGRAPHY

Aardema, Verna. *Why Mosquitoes Buzz in People's Ears*. Illustrator Leo and Diane Dillon. 1975. New York: Dial Books for Young Readers.
Coughlan, Cheryl. *Mosquitoes*. Mankato, Minnesota: Pebble Books, 1999.
Emberley, Rebecca, and Ed Emberley. *Chicken Little*. New York: Roaring Book Press, 2009.
Litzinger, Rosanne. *The Old Woman and Her Pig: an Old English Tale*. San Diego: Harcourt, Brace, Jovanovich, 1993.
MacDonald, Margaret Read. *Old Woman and Her Pig: An Appalachian Folktale*. Illustrator John Kanzler. New York: HarperCollins, 2007.
Martin, Rafe. *Foolish Rabbit's Big Mistake*. Illustrator Ed Young. New York: G.P. Putnam's Sons, 1985.

Stellaluna
Comparing and Contrasting Animal Needs
Lindsey Cohn

CCC topics: Patterns
POSE topics: Asking questions and defining problems.

The Story (Synopsis)

Stellaluna
Synopsis by Lindsey Cohn

Stellaluna is the story of a young bat whose mother was attacked. She finds herself in the nest of a few birds and quite out of place. She is not sure she belongs anywhere, but later finds out who she really is as an animal.

Standards

NGSS—Life Science—birds and bats

K-ESS3-1 Use a model to represent the relationship between the needs of different plants and animals (including humans) and the places they live.

CCSS for ELA

RL 1.9 Compare and contrast the adventures and experiences of characters in stories.

NCAS—Connect, Perform

Objectives

First Grade Students will be able to say:

- I can list the needs of animals using a text.
- I can compare and contrast the needs animals.
- I can respond as an animal to a need using body, face, gestures, and voice.

Materials

- Cannon, Janell. *Stellaluna*. Boston: HMH Books for Young Readers, 1993.
- graphic organizers for listing animal needs and the Venn diagram
- sheet of animals and a duplicated set (cut out and folded)
- basket
- same and different cards (copied onto the back of compare/contrast cards)
- picture badges of bat and bird (if needed)
- writing assessment
- pictures of the different needs or "non-needs" of each animal

Instructional Plan

The students will be using the text of *Stellaluna* to gather information on the needs of birds and bats. They will then compare and contrast those needs. Their last activity is to use body and voice to respond to the needs or "non-needs" of that animal.

Rationale

The students need to know the different needs of various plants and animals. Using the skill of comparing and contrasting, the students will be able to differentiate their needs and find similarities between them. Using the theatre standard gives them even more ownership over the needs of each animal being studied.

Preparation

Students should have mastered the common core skill of using text and illustrations to gather key details from a story. They will use this skill during the beginning of the lesson. They should also have been introduced to the words compare and contrast and have some basic knowledge of their meaning. They also should have done some sort of animal studies so they are familiar with basic animal habitats. This is not necessary, but helpful.

Activity

1. Warm up: Give each student a card that says same and different on it. Explain to them that the pictures that are the same will represent something that is the same. And the card that shows two different pictures will represent something being different. Have a basket full of animals printed such as chickens or cows. Duplicate the sheet of animals printed. Tell the students that two volunteers will come up and draw an animal out of the hat. They will use their body and voice to act like the animal. It is the job of the audience to determine if they are the same animal or different. Use the cards to show your answer. Allow about 3 rounds of this activity. Let that activity lead into the goal of comparing and contrasting. Have the students flip their cards inside out and look at the words compare and contrast using the same picture clues. (Print this card front and back). Explain how comparing means showing things that are the same. Contrasting means showing things that are different.

Stellaluna (Cohn) 93

same

different
fold

compare

contrast
fold

2. Show a picture of the bird from the book (*Stellaluna*) and a bat. Ask them to tell some things that they know are the same, then some things that are different. Ask some of the following questions to drive their thinking: What does the (bat/bird) need to survive? Why? Do all animals need the same things?

3. Read the story *Stellaluna* (*Storyline Online*, www.storylineonline.net/stellaluna, has a great read aloud of this).

4. Tell the students their goal at this time is to list at least two needs of each animal. Model looking back in the book at a page and using evidence to cite a need. For example: "As I look at this page I see a soft nest made out of straw. I see three of the birds cuddled in it. I know that birds need a nest." Remind the students that they need to use evidence to explain how they know that is a need of the animal. Break the students into small groups or partners. Give them the graphic organizer and have them list at least two needs.

5. Come back together. Have the students list out their needs and record them on a chart (if you have an interactive whiteboard, record it on there. It will make it easier to use for the Venn diagram). Have the students show thumbs up or down if they agree or disagree with the statements provided.

6. Show a Venn diagram with the picture of the bat on one side and the picture of the bird on the other. Tell the students that they are going to compare and contrast the needs of the animals. Get the cards back out that were used earlier. Review the words compare and contrast. Have the Venn diagram labeled with these words. Show them where things will go if they are different in the diagram and where they will go if they are the same. (If you use the interactive whiteboard you can just drag the text you wrote into the diagram.)

7. Reflect on the Venn diagram activity with these questions: What was the same? What was different? Did they live in the same area? Why

Stellaluna (Cohn) 95

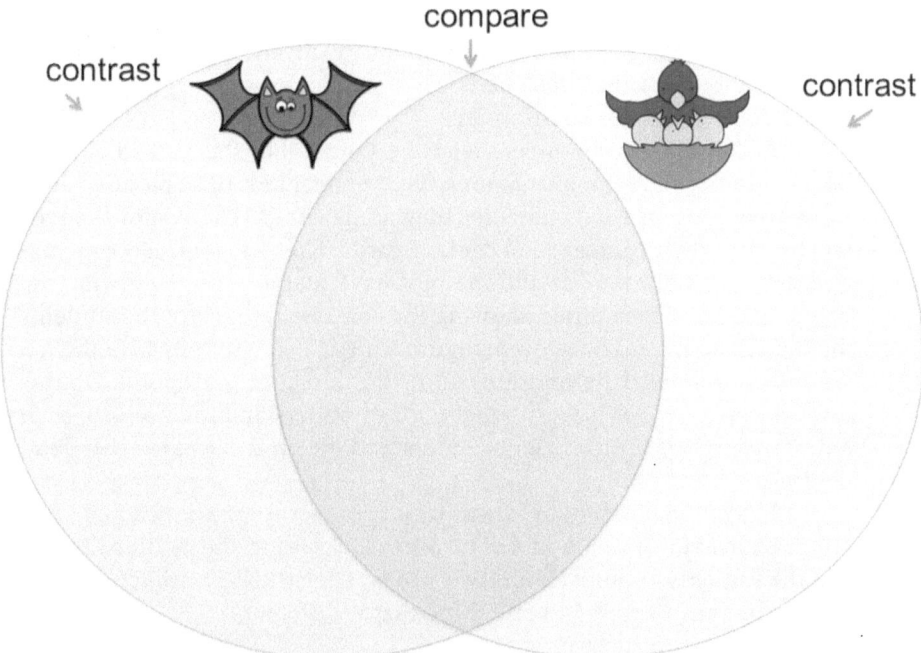

do you think they did? Can animals have different needs and live in the same area? What is an animal that would not live in that area based on its needs?

8. Tell the students they are going to be responding to the needs or non-needs using body and voice. The audience's job is to decide if their reaction should be the same or different.

9. Introduction activity: Start by just using body to respond by doing things like crossing arms, jumping up and down, crouching…. How do I feel? How do you know? What about my body told you that? Continue the same activity using voice by screaming, whimpering, growling. How do I feel? What about my voice made you think that I felt that way? How did my voice change?

10. Allow the students to practice by giving them different emotions. They are going to make an emotion gallery. You will say an emotion and give them 5 seconds to decide. They can use their body, voice, or both. As they hit their final position walk around and use evidence to talk about their emotion like, "I see Johnny with his hands pushed out and his mouth snarled up. He must not like whatever is in front of him." Do this a few times to warm the kids up for the final activity.

11. Tell the students now that they have warmed their emotions up, they will be responding to different items using mind and body. If it is

something the animal *needs* they should respond in a good way. Have the students show you how they might respond positively. Then tell them they may see something they *don't need*. They should respond negatively. Have the students show this emotion too.

12. Ask for two volunteers at a time. One will be the bat and one will be the bird from the story *Stellaluna*. (For younger kids use a picture badge to remind them of what character they are playing.) The rest of the kids will be using their compare and contrast cards. They will look at the picture and decide if both the bat and the bird have that as a need showing the compare card, if they differ, showing the contrast card. Have the students look at the board as you show a picture with a label under it. Give them 5 seconds to act out their emotion. Allow the audience to respond. Do this several times. This will assess whether they understand the needs of each animal, as well as if the students understand the meaning of compare and contrast.

13. The final assignment will be a short writing. The students will either choose to compare and contrast themselves to the bird or the bat. Tell the students to think about their needs. They will be writing one thing that is similar in needs and one thing that is different.

Writing Task

Name:_____

How are your needs the same?
_____
_____
_____

How are your needs different?
_____
_____
_____

Writing Task

Name:_____

How are your needs the same?
_____
_____
_____
_____

How are your needs different?
_____
_____
_____
_____

Assessment

I can list the needs of animals using a text. The students will be assessed in their partner groups with the pieces of information they bring back and the evidence they use to prove it.

I can compare and contrast the needs animals. Whole group assessment when categorizing the needs listed of the animals. They will also be assessed as an audience member in the theatre activity, determining if the need is something that compares that animals or something that contrasts the animals. In addition the final writing piece will reflect their knowledge on the needs of those animals along with the words compare and contrast.

I can respond as an animal to a need using body, face, gestures, and voice. This assessment takes place during the theatre activity where the students are reacting to the pictures presented. It will also be informally assessed during the warm up activity.

BIBLIOGRAPHY

- *Stellaluna* (read-aloud video). www.storylineonline.net/stellaluna
- Graphics by: aJoy2share clip art http://www.teacherspayteachers.com/Store/Betty-Jones-6757
- Graphics by: www.mycutegraphics.com
- Graphics by: Michael Rawls http://www.teacherspayteachers.com/Store/Atlteacher
- Graphics by: www.amazingclassroom.com

Graphics used by permission of Teacherspayteachers.com

"Rabbit's Tale"
A Paiute Indian Nature Myth
Lynn Rubright

CCC topics: Patterns, Cause and effect, Structure and function
POSE topics: Planning and carrying out investigations, Constructing explanations and designing solutions

The Story

"Rabbit's Tale": A Paiute Indian Nature Myth
by Lynn Rubright

> Every morning Sun comes up
> Eastern rim of the world.
> Every evening Sun goes down
> Western rim of the world.

Every morning Sun came up and Rabbit was HOT!
"Sun, why are you SO HOT?" he shouted. But Sun did not reply.
To cool himself Rabbit stretched himself in the shade of cactus. For a little while Rabbit wasn't quite so hot.
But Sun kept moving over the arc of the sky, changing shadow and shade. Once again Rabbit was HOT!
Then Rabbit saw a great rock. Rabbit hopped over and nestled himself in its shade. But that Sun kept moving over the arc of the sky, changing shadow and shade. Once again, Rabbit was HOT!
At the end of the day Sun slipped under the western rim of the world. Rabbit felt SO good resting on the cool desert floor as the moon slowly rose.

Then Rabbit remembered that in the morning Sun would come up over the Eastern rim of the world and once again he would be HOT.

Rabbit got an idea. Taking his bow and arrow he traveled all night to the Eastern rim of the world. Rabbit hid behind a rock and waited for Sun to come up.

In the morning when Sun raised its rosy head over the Eastern rim of the world, pushing back the night sky, Rabbit shot an arrow into his side.

"AAAAAAH!" cried Sun.

"Now, maybe Sun won't be SOOO HOT, " thought Rabbit. But then he saw a river of molten fire flowing from the hole his arrow had made in Sun's side. It was flowing over the desert floor, burning everything in its path. The terrified Rabbit ran. He ran to where Creosote Bush was growing.

"Help me, save me! Creosote, help!" shouted Rabbit.

But Creosote Bush, watching the fire flowing from the hole in Sun's side come closer and closer, yelled, "Soon I will be burned to ash. I can't save you! RUN, Rabbit RUN!"

Rabbit raced across the desert floor until he came to where Sagebrush was growing. "Help me! Save me! Sagebrush, HELP!"

But Sagebrush cried, "OHHH! I can't save you, Rabbit, soon I will be burned to ash. RUN, Rabbit, RUN!"

Rabbit charged in front of the river of fire to where a little bush with yellow flowers was growing. Rabbit pleaded, "Help me, save me, Yellow Bush. HELP!"

"I can't save you, Rabbit, because soon I will be burned to ash. But you can save yourself. Dig, Rabbit. DIG!"

With his front paws and hind legs, Rabbit dug, spraying the desert sand into the very face of the fire flowing from Sun's side. Rabbit dug a tunnel down to the roots of Yellow Bush. Trembling, that is where Rabbit stayed for many days and many nights.

Then one day, hungry, thirsty and lonely, Rabbit began to crawl out of his tunnel.

"Wait, Rabbit, wait," warned the roots of Yellow Bush. "It's too soon. WAIT!"

But Rabbit did not listen. He poked his ears through the crust of ash covering his rabbit hole and jumped out.

Rabbit saw that Creosote Bush, Sagebrush, and Yellow Bush had *all* been burned. Nothing but ash covered the floor of the desert.

Then the wind began to blow. And on the wind came sparks. One spark burned one of his ears. "OWWW!" cried Rabbit. Another spark burned his other ear. "Ohhhh! OWWW!"

A big spark burned his tail. "Ohhh! OWWW!" cried Rabbit, jumping down into his rabbit hole again.

"I told you it was too soon," Yellow Bush whispered to the whimpering Rabbit. She wrapped him in her roots and sang:

> Though I am burned
> I will live again.
> My roots are strong and await the rain.
> Deep in the earth
> In the cool dark earth
> Waiting and waiting for my rebirth.
> Though I am burned
> I will live again.

"Be patient," murmured Yellow Bush as she cradled the frightened Rabbit. Thirsty and hungry, Rabbit waited. And waited.

One day Yellow Bush said, "Rabbit, it's time." She nudged him with her roots.

Timidly, Rabbit crept from his burrow. He saw that new shoots of life had sprouted from the roots of Creosote Bush and Sagebrush. And tiny buds had burst open on the new branches of his Yellow Bush.

And there was cactus growing tall and straight once again. And then he saw his old friends: cactus wren, beetle, mouse, kangaroo rat, desert tortoise, and scorpion. They all sang:

> Rabbit, Rabbit where you been?
> Rabbit, Rabbit where you been?
> Rabbit, Rabbit where you been?
> When the Sun comes out
> You stay in.

Rabbit looked up. There was Sun as HOT as ever.

"What happened to your ears and tail?" asked the Creosote Bush and Sagebrush. "They're all black."

"Rabbit got a little burned when he came out too soon from the tunnel he had dug near my roots to save himself," explained Yellow Bush.

Rabbit felt the HOT Sun burning overhead. He jumped down into his cool rabbit hole. But when the Sun set over the western sky, Yellow Bush nudged him. Rabbit crept out of his tunnel and played on the cool desert floor in the moonlight among her tender branches and little flowers.

Time passed and time passed.

Today, those yellow bushes in the desert of the Great Basin in the western United States are now called rabbitbrush because they not only provide shade for rabbits during the HOT days, they also provide food and water stored in their woody stems and yellow flowers.

Those rabbits, today called jack rabbits, have ears and tails still marked with black fur as reminders of the foolish rabbit who long ago shot an arrow into Sun's side.

But old Sun still worries that someday one of those pesky jack rabbits might shoot him with an arrow again. That's why Sun comes up in a slightly different place each day. In the summer, he rises a little to the north. In the winter, he rises a little to the south … just to fool a rabbit who might be waiting to shoot him with his bow and arrow once again.

But Sun need not worry. Those jack rabbits are too happy living near the roots of the rabbitbrush shrub to ever shoot an arrow into the sun again.

> Every morning Sun comes up
> Eastern rim of the world.
> Every evening Sun goes down
> Western rim of the World.

Standards

NGSS—Earth & Space Science, Physical Science

ESS1.A: The Universe and its Stars: Patterns of the motion of the sun, moon, and stars in the sky can be observed, described, and predicted. (1-ESS1-1)

ESS1.B: Earth and the Solar System: Seasonal patterns of sunrise and sunset can be observed, described, and predicted. (1-ESS1-2)

PS4-3: Waves: Light and Sound: Plan and conduct investigations to determine the effect of placing objects made with different materials in the path of a beam of light.

CCSS-ELA—Reading Literature, Writing, Language

RL.1.1 Ask and answer questions about key details in a text.

RL.1.2 Retell stories, including key details, and demonstrate understanding of their central message or lesson.

RL.1.3 Describe characters, settings, and major events in a story, using key details.

W.1.3 Write narratives in which they recount two or more appropriately sequenced events, include some details regarding what happened, use temporal words to signal event order, and provide some sense of closure.

L.1.4 Determine or clarify the meaning of unknown and multiple-meaning words and phrases based on grade 1 reading and content, choosing flexibly from an array of strategies.

Objectives

Students grades 1 through 3 will be able to say:

102   Part One. Early Childhood (Earth and Space Science)

- I can re-tell "Rabbit's Tale" in proper sequence with understanding of setting, characters, incidents, main problem and resolution.
- I can put words from the class group Word Bank in my journal from which to write stories and poems. (*The class Word Bank is a collection of words listed by children following listening to "Rabbit's Tale" for use in children's writing to expand vocabulary, teach parts of speech [nouns, adjective, verbs] and improve grammar and spelling.*)
- I can explain that rabbit was hot because the sun burns down on the desert at about 120 degrees in summer and that he learned to stay cool by resting in the shade of rabbit brush and other shrubs during the day, coming out at night to eat and play (nocturnal).
- I can tell you that the length and angle of a shadow changes throughout the day because of the rotation of the earth.

Materials

- Crepe paper streamers of red, orange, yellow
- Tissue paper of yellow, green, and gray
- Graph paper
- Hand drum
- CD player
- Yard stick

Instructional Plan

Rationale

Cultures all over the world invented stories to explain how something came to be. These stories are called pourquoi tales, and they represent the cultures from which they come. In "Rabbit's Tale," the Paiute Indians of the Great Basin region in the western United States explained why today jackrabbits have long ears rimmed in black fur and black fur on the tops of their tails, and why they like to live near rabbitbrush (and other shrubs) to protect them from the hot sun, and provide food and water. A study of pourquoi tales helps children think about the ways nature helps creatures (both flora and fauna) evolve to cope with things in the environment that could endanger them or cause their extinction. Example: rabbits developed powerful hind legs for leaping and jumping and running to safety when chased by a predator.

Reading, studying and researching facts in print and on the internet, supplemented by creative interdisciplinary activities, help children use their imaginations and discover the connection between fact and fiction of pourquoi stories. I believe strongly in the kinesthetic connection to deep learning: it touches the brain in ways pure intellectual approach doesn't, especially for children who have trouble learning in traditional ways.

Preparation

Tell "Rabbit's Tail." Show a map of the United States and talk about North, South, East, West. Have children find states in Western United states on map or Smart Board. The Great Basin desert covers most of Nevada, and parts of Idaho, Utah, California, Wyoming, and Oregon where the Paiute Indians lived thousands of years ago and even today. The Paiute people made up this pourquoi nature myth hundreds of years ago to explain why jackrabbits who lived among them have black fur lining their long ears and the top of their tails and why they live so close to the rabbitbrush and other shrubs. Both cottontail rabbits and jackrabbits live near rabbitbrush, sagebrush and creosote bush and other shrubs that provide food, water and shelter.

Talk about the story's main idea: Sun was TOO HOT, causing the problem that Rabbit wanted to solve. Rabbit's foolish solution caused changes in his behavior forever: jackrabbits and cottontail rabbits both stay OUT of the sun during the heat of the day resting in the shade of rabbitbrush, sagebrush and creosote bushes, cacti, and other shrubs that provide shade.

The Sun and Earth

The sun is a star in the center of our solar system, at the edge of the Milky Way. It was born 4½ billion years ago and our planet, Earth, is the third planet orbiting around it, and the only planet known with water that allows animals, plants and people to live on it. Our earth is almost 92,000,000 miles from the sun. The main thing for children to know is that the sun is HOT! On its surface the sun is almost 10,000 degrees Fahrenheit. At its center it is 27 million degrees. That is why Rabbit was so HOT and tried to do something about it!

Activities

After children hear the story told (or read) twice, or listen to it on Lynn's website, www.lynnrubright.com, lead them in identifying elements of plot: setting, characters, incidents, problem and resolution. Let children take turns re-telling parts of the story from beginning to end, practicing storytelling skills.

Once thoroughly familiar with the story, begin exploring the Rabbit's experience with the Sun through some of these activities.

- Children explore qualities of Rabbit and the Sun through movement games: first sitting at desks using pantomime, then moving through space in the room, the gym or outdoors.
- Children create a class word bank of nouns, adjectives, and verbs to describe Rabbit's and Sun's experience in the story. Words should be saved so children can refer to them to expand their vocabulary and to enrich their writing short poems, expository paragraphs and short stories based on the story. (Children record the word bank in their journals.)
- Children pick a favorite scene from "Rabbit's Tale," illustrate it with torn paper mosaics, write about their scene to create a page of a class book.
- Working in pairs using yardsticks, children measure and chart the length of each other's shadows three times during a sunny day to show how the sun's movement changes the length of the shadows OR measure the changing shadow of trees or playground equipment and record those shadow changes on a sunny day.
- Children play Shadow Shapes game. Working in pairs, children hold hands and twirl each other around to the beat of the drum. When drum STOPS children let go and spin into interesting SHADOW shapes and FREEZE. REPEAT to explore high and low, wide and narrow, large and small shapes. Adding music, this exercise can be used to create a Shadow Dance.
- Children play Run Rabbit, Run! outdoors on a sunny day when there are shadows on the ground. Ten children in center of the circle play the SUN, twirling red, yellow, orange crepe paper strips in their arms. Using the space around the sun, three children arrange their bodies to become a sagebrush; three children become a rabbitbrush; three children become a creosote bush and three children become a cactus. Five children playing jackrabbits run into the space running, leaping, forwards backwards, sideways, around in circles, zig zagging to the drum beat, not too close to the sun. When the drum beat stops, rabbits must find a shady spot under a shrub or cactus and FREEZE. When drum begins, rabbits RUN again. Children playing predators (hawks, eagles, etc.) fly into the circle and try to TAG rabbits BEFORE rabbits find safety under the shade of a bush or cactus. When a predator tags a rabbit who is not safely hiding in the shade, the rabbit is OUT, and the predator becomes a rabbit.
- "Rabbit's Tale" movement games include improvisational pantomime activities: becoming like the HOT Sun; becoming Sun SHOT with Rabbit's arrow; becoming like fire flowing over the desert floor consuming shrubs: rabbitbrush, sagebrush, creosote bush, and cacti. The

"Run! Rabbit Run!" game demonstrates jackrabbits running, leaping, jumping, zigzagging to the right, left, forward, backward sideways (directionality: reinforcing understanding of left, right, up down, sideways, and north, south east and west) to escape the fire from the sun. Adding predators to the game is exciting. (*Note: during movement games, encourage children to move in SLOW MOTION to help them concentrate on the quality of their movements.*)

This story also lends itself to lessons in life science, poetry, music, and drama. For further information and loads of ideas, visit www.lynnrubright.com.

BIBLIOGRAPHY AND RESOURCES

Books

Gibbons, Gail. *The Moon Book*. New York: Scholastic, 1997.
Palmer, William R. "Why the Sun Rises Cautiously," in *Why the North Star Stands Still and other Indian Legends*. Englewood Cliffs, New Jersey: Prentice Hall, 1947, 1957. (Paiute Pourquoi Tale that inspired Rubright's *Rabbit's Tale*.)
Rubright, Lynn. *Beyond the Beanstalk: Interdisciplinary Learning through Storytelling*. Appendix B: Storytelling, Movement and Drama Exercises. Portsmouth, N.H.: Heinemann, 1995.
Tesar, Jenny. *The Sun*. Des Plaines, IL: Reed Educational and Professional Publishing, 1998.

Websites

www.desertUSA.com
www.digital-desert.com
www.firstpeople.us/FP-HTML-Legends/Rabbit Rabbit Shoots the Sun (Hopi tale). "Rabbit Shoots the Sun," a Hopi variant of the "Rabbit's Tale" story, with Cottontail as the main character. Compare with "Rabbit's Tale" for similarities and differences.
www.jayepurplewolf.com/Phoenix/Hopilore
www.wldutahedibles.com

The Big Dipper
Patterns, Inspiration and Multicultural Stories

LYNETTE J. FORD

CCC topic: Patterns
POSE topic: Asking questions and defining problems; Developing and using models; Constructing explanations and designing solutions

The Stories

Here are a few stories that focus on the Big Dipper:

"The Seven Plough Oxen" (Ancient Roman)

The Romans knew the seven stars of the Big Dipper as the "seven plough oxen," or Septentriones, but only two of the seven stars represented oxen; the other stars formed the wagon pulled by the oxen.

"Follow the Drinking Gourd" (African American)

The American folksong "Follow the Drinking Gourd" is believed to be a "map song" from the times of the Underground Railroad; African American folklore now states that the song gave people who had been enslaved a directive to use the Big Dipper asterism (or small star pattern that forms part of a constellation) to find and follow the North Star, Polaris, and make their way to freedom.

A drinking gourd is a hollowed out gourd that is used as a water dipper; in the song, that term is a code name for the Big Dipper.

"Bear and Three Hunters" (Musquakie, Iroquois Tribes, East Coast, Great Lakes)

In this story, the bowl stars of the Big Dipper form the shape of a great bear. The stars of the handle are hunters chasing the bear. Near the elbow of the handle is a tiny star, which is viewed as a small hunting dog named "Hold Tight" or "Four Eyes" (the first name is used in several Iroquois tellings; the second is Cayuga, and the little dog has two black spots over his eyes—thus, four eyes; the naming depends on the language in which the tale was originally told).

The hunters follow the little dog, who always finds the bear's trail; they chase the bear, wound him with their weapons and kill him, and eat the meat. Then the hunters look around, and realize they have chased the bear all the way into the sky. There, the bones of the bear begin to rise and become a bear again. And the hunt begins again.

The story says that, in autumn, when the Dipper is low in the sky and near the horizon, it is the great bear wounded and fallen again. The wounded bear's blood drips on the trees, turning them red and brown. But the hunt doesn't end; it continues towards spring, as the bear and hunters rise in the sky again.

"Coyote, Wolves, and Bears" (Wasco Tribe, Columbia River, Washington and Oregon)

Once, long ago, there lived five wolves who would share the meat from their hunts with Coyote. One night, as the wolves stared into the sky, Coyote asked them what they saw. "Two animals are up there," the wolves told Coyote. "It's too bad we can't get close enough to see them clearly." "I can help you get close to those creatures. That is an easy task for me," said Coyote.

Coyote used his bow to shoot an arrow into the sky. The arrow stuck there. Coyote shot another arrow; it stuck into the first one. Then Coyote shot another arrow, and another, and another, until a ladder of arrows bent from the sky and touched the ground.

Then Coyote and the five wolves and the oldest wolf's hunting dog carefully climbed the arrows into the sky. There, they could see that the two animals were grizzly bears. The bears stared; the other animals stared. The grizzly bears seemed surprised to see the wolves and the dog and Coyote in the sky.

The wolves sat looking at the bears and the bears looked back. And Coyote decided that this was a beautiful thing to see. Coyote left those animals sitting in the sky; when he climbed down to earth, he removed his ladder of arrows. Now, when we look into the sky, we see the three stars of the handle of the Big Dipper and the two stars of the bowl near the handle; they are the wolves. The two stars that make the front of the Dipper's bowl are the bears. And the tiny star by the old wolf in the middle of the handle is the hunting dog.

Big Dipper Anecdotes

- An older name for the stars of the Big Dipper comes from Scandinavian mythology. It was considered to be part of the constellation known as Odin's Wain, or Odin's Wagon, which is actually Ursa Major.
- The Big Dipper is known as the "Great Wagon" or the "Great Bear" in Germany. It is "The Great Wagon" in Romanian and many Slavic languages.
- In Hindu astronomy, the Big Dipper is referred to as Sapta Rishi, which means "the Seven (Great) Sages."
- In Malaysia, the asterism is known as Buruj Biduk (the Ladle, in direct relationship to the concept of the Drinking Gourd).

Story Notes

These stories were adapted from legends, mythologies and folktales heard at various gatherings, and from the information at several websites and in many books on constellations, including:

Branley, Franklin M. *The Big Dipper (Let's-Read-and-Find-Out Science 1)*. New York: HarperCollins, 1991.
Connelly, Bernardine. *Follow the Drinking Gourd: A Story of the Underground Railroad* (Rabbit Ears American Heroes & Legends). South Norwalk, CT: Rabbit Ears Entertainment, 2013.
Meister, Cari. *Follow the Drinking Gourd: An Underground Railroad Story* (Night Sky Stories). Mankato, MN: Picture Window Books, 2012.
Mitton, Jacqueline. *Zoo in the Sky: A Book of Animal Constellations*. Washington, D.C.: National Geographic Children's Books, 2006.
Peters, Stephanie True. *Big Dipper (Library of Constellations)*. New York: PowerKids Press, 2003.
http://www.newworldencyclopedia.org/entry/Big_Dipper
http://www.ianridpath.com/startales/startales3.htm

Standards

NGSS—Earth and Space Science

ESS1-1. Use observations of the sun, moon and stars to describe patterns that can be predicted.

CCSS-ELA—Writing, Speaking, Listening

W.1.7 Participate in shared research and writing projects.

W. 1.8 With guidance and support from adults, recall information from experiences or gather information from provided sources to answer a question.

SL.2.4 Tell a story or recount an experience with appropriate facts and relevant, descriptive details, speaking audibly in coherent sentences.

Fine Arts Anchor Standards—Create, Produce, Respond, Connect

Objectives

Second Grade Students will be able to say

- I know what an asterism is, and I know what a constellation is.
- I can find the asterism we call the Big Dipper in the night sky.
- I can tell one story about the Big Dipper, or one idea people had long ago about the Big Dipper.
- I can imagine and create my own story about how a star pattern came to be in the sky.
- I can share my story.

Materials

- Any picture books appropriate for grade levels K—2 with clear and easy to understand illustrations of the Big Dipper.
- Photographs of the Big Dipper (http://www.astropix.com/HTML/BEGINNER/DIPS.htm shares a lovely photographic image of the Big and Little Dippers in the night sky)
- Constellation patterns to print*: A simple line drawing with stars marking the pattern of the asterism, and a dot-to-dot type of image to use for creating lacing cards of the Big Dipper. Graphics are available at:
    https://docs.google.com/file/d/0B91cbdesRHx4VV85USlrZWQzVW8/edit
    https://docs.google.com/file/d/0B91cbdesRHx4RUlZcWI2REhkQjg/edit
    http://space.about.com/library/graphics/constellation_patterns.jpg
    http://kidsactivitiesblog.com/wp-content/uploads/2014/05/Constellation-Sewing-Cards2.pdf
    http://members.enchantedlearning.com/subjects/astronomy/activities/dots/bigdipper.shtml

http://belladia.typepad.com/.a/6a00d8341cc08553ef0115724c3a32970b-pi
- Dark crayons, one per child.
- One shoelace or length of string or thin yarn per child.
- Plain white copy paper or other paper suitable for illustrating and writing.
- Pencils and crayons.
- Construction paper stars, seven for each child. If you provide a pattern, children who are ready to safely use scissors may cut these out for themselves.
- Heavy black construction paper, one or two sheets per child.
- White or yellow chalk, one piece per child.

*Thank you to Stephanie at http://fullofgreatideas.blogspot.com/2012/03/diy-daytime-constellations.html for the Google documents. Some of the listed pages may be the same or similar graphic printouts; they have all been offered in the hope that web pages are still active and useful, though a search of the Internet should uncover similar material if needed. Please note that printouts can be made by members only from the Enchanted Learning website.

Instructional Plan

Rationale

As young students learn stories and facts about the Big Dipper and experience various participatory activities, they improve their ability to critically think about what they see in the night sky. Students also have opportunities to listen, respond, observe, question, imagine, and create, in processes that help them to understand both the development of star patterns and the development of stories.

Preparation

Prior to sharing the stories and activities:

- Print out a simple line drawing of the Big Dipper. Make sure the stars that create its pattern are clearly marked. Make one copy for each child.
- Create the lacing cards. Make two cards for each student. The printouts suggested under "Materials" should be enlarged if needed; the patterns should be printed on card stock. Then use a hole punch to make the pattern of the Big Dipper on each card; using a ⅛ inch circle hole punch with a 2 inch reach ensures that the punch will reach the center of the star images.

- Share picture books and reference books about various constellations. Show website images of various constellations and asterisms, including the Big Dipper.
- Explain what "asterisms" are: smaller formations of stars within the larger patterns of constellations. The word "constellation" comes from the Latin words *com* and *stella*, meaning "stars together." The word "asterism" comes from the Greek word *asterismos*, meaning "a marking with stars." For example: the Big Dipper is a pattern of stars, but it is part of the constellation Ursa Major.
- Introduce the following vocabulary:

  Star—a big ball of gas that gives off heat and light. The sun is the star nearest to Earth; it is 93 million miles away. After the sun, the next nearest star is 4.3 light years away.

  > "If you were riding in a car going 65 miles per hour, you would have to travel nonstop 24 hours a day for almost 200 years to reach the sun. (And that's only one way.)"
  > "The next-closest star to our sun is called Proxima Centauri. It is about 25.2 trillion (a 25 with 12 zeroes after it) miles away."—Information quoted from myspace.com/truemonge

  Constellation—a pattern of stars visible in the night sky.

  Asterism—a smaller formation of stars within the larger pattern of a constellation.

  The North Star—a star that always in the direction of north; as we observe the northern night sky throughout the seasons, the other stars in the sky seem to circle around the North Star, which is also known as Polaris (short for *stella polaris*, Latin for "polar star").

  The Big Dipper—an asterism of seven stars within the constellation known as Ursa Major, or the Great Bear.

  The Little Dipper—an asterism in the constellation of Ursa Minor, the Little Bear. The most famous star in the Little Dipper is Polaris, which is also known as the North Star or Pole Star. This was the guide star for those escaping slavery and heading North in the times of the Underground Railroad.

  Nebula—a cloud of dust, hydrogen, helium, and other ionized gases in which stars are often formed. Gas, dust, and other materials "clump" or bunch together to form larger masses; these masses attract more materials, and eventually become big enough to form stars.

- Discuss the patterns of several constellations. Ask students why people might have wanted to name these star patterns and tell stories about

them. Ask students how we know that these stories are fiction and never happened.
- Tell students that the Big Dipper is the most visible part of the constellation Ursa Major (the Great Bear), which is the third largest of all the 88 constellations. The Big Dipper is seen in many places around the world, and many different stories have been told to explain what it is, or how it came to be in the sky; it has even become a symbol of freedom. Let students know they will hear a few stories about the Big Dipper.

Activities

- Share at least three different stories about the Big Dipper from various places in the world. On a map, show the places where these stories originated.

  After each story is told or read, discuss the way the story begins, its characters and its setting. At the end of each story, have the characters changed in any way? If so, how have they changed? At the end of the story, where are they? How did they get there? How is this place different from the setting at the beginning of the story? What do you think you know about the details of the story?
- Reintroduce pictures of the Big Dipper in photographs, reference books, or on the Internet. Then share a simple line drawing of the Big Dipper, pointing to each star in its pattern.

  Pass out copies of this line drawing. Students will follow the line drawing with their pointer fingers, then draw over the line with crayons.

  Pass out one card with the simpler dot-to-dot, hole-punched image you've created. Give each child a shoestring or piece of yarn. Students lace the shoestring or yarn through the holes, so that the shape of the Big Dipper is evident.
- After the visual-art activities have been completed, ask students to tell their favorite of the three Big Dipper stories they heard. Ask students to tell why their particular stories were chosen, using a simple narrative-essay format: "My favorite Big Dipper story was ... because...." Tell students to illustrate and/or write their favorite Big Dipper story, depending on their skill levels. Display and share these stories.
- Give each student seven construction paper stars. In a large room or gymnasium, students stand and drop their stars on the floor, then arrange them to create a constellation, noting that these are not

asterisms, since there are no smaller star patterns within the larger collection image of stars.

Students draw their constellations on large pieces of paper. Then they create their own stories of how these new constellations came to be in the sky. Students then give their constellations names based on the stories. These stories are then written by scribes (older students; parents; volunteers) or the students themselves, depending on their skill levels.

- In addition to or instead of the aforementioned activity, students can create their own constellations using chalk dots drawn on black paper. If a student doesn't like the position of one of the dots, he or she simply rubs it out with thumb or finger; this smudge becomes a gaseous cloud or nebula, in which stars are formed.

  First, students draw their dots (more than four but no more than nine is a suggested number). Then they connect the dots to create a shape. The paper is turned in different directions until the student decides he or she sees an image that could become a story. That image is given a name: the Chocolate Chip Cookie constellation; the Pizza; the Kite, etc.

  Students create stories explaining how these named objects came to be in the sky. Display the illustrations and share these stories.

  Remind students that this is the way the asterisms and constellations got their names and their stories among people around the world centuries ago.

- In a cross-curricular study that emphasizes the topic of the Underground Railroad, these Big Dipper activities can lead to the utilization of the song, "Follow the Drinking Gourd," and the introduction of books on this subject.

  The song was first published in 1928 by H.P. Parks. "Follow the Drinking Gourd" became an important song of freedom, hope, and strength in the 1950s and 1960s, during the Civil Rights and folk revival movements. It is considered a unique composition, although its origins and history are still debated by historians, for no other such map songs are known.

  The following explanation of the lyrics of "Follow the Drinking Gourd" are derived from information at the website of the National Aeronautic and Space Administration: http://quest.arc.nasa.gov/ltc/special/mlk/gourd2.html

"Follow the Drinking Gourd"

When the sun comes back and the first quail calls,
Follow the Drinking Gourd.

For the old man is waiting for to carry you to freedom,
If you follow the Drinking Gourd.[1]

The river bank makes a very good road,
The dead trees show you the way,
Left foot, peg foot, traveling on
Follow the Drinking Gourd.[2]

The river ends between two hills,
Follow the Drinking Gourd.
There's another river on the other side,
Follow the Drinking Gourd.[3]

Where the great big river meets the little river,
Follow the Drinking Gourd.
For the old man is awaiting to carry you to freedom if you
follow the Drinking Gourd.[4]

Assessment

Acquired knowledge can be assessed through the illustrations and storytelling the students share. Note vocabulary used, details of narrative process (beginning, middle, and end, characters, settings, action, spoken-word and visual imagery), critical thinking that orders ideas to create a new story, distinction between fact and fiction, and reference to other stories.

Notes

1. "When the sun comes back" may mean the seasonal time of late winter and spring, when the sun at noon gets higher each day. Quail are migratory birds who winter in the South, and whose calls can often be heard in April. The Drinking Gourd is the Big Dipper. The old man is Peg Leg Joe, who, despite having lost a leg and replaced it with a wooden peg, worked as a guide, conductor, or leader, on the Underground Railroad.

The verse tells escaping African captives to leave in the winter and walk towards the Drinking Gourd; the two stars that make up the outermost side of the dipper's bowl point to Polaris. If those escaping walk in that direction, they will eventually meet the man who will guide them for the remainder of the trip. Most escapees had to cross the Ohio River which is too wide and too swift to swim (although, in the 1800s, some parts of the river were low enough for escaping, to "wade in the water"). Conductors for the Underground Railroad believed that winter, when the river was frozen, was probably the best time to cross. The journey from the Deep South to the Ohio River took most escapees a year, so it became urgent for escapees to begin their trip in winter, in order to be at the Ohio River by the next winter.

2. Dead trees along the bank of the Tombigbee River north were marked with drawings of a left foot and a peg foot, the symbols of Peg Leg Joe. These markings distinguished the Tombigbee from other north-south rivers.

3. When those escaping reached the headwaters of the Tombigbee, they were to

continue going north over the hills until the Tombigbee River met the Tennessee River. Then they were to travel north along the Tennessee River.

 4. This verse told the slaves that the Tennessee joined another river, the Ohio River. They were to cross the Ohio River, and on the north bank, they would meet another guide from the Underground Railroad.

"Un Lazo a La Luna" and Other Tales
Observing the Moon

JANE STENSON

CCC topics: Patterns, Cause and effect, Structure and function, Stability and change
POSE topics: Asking questions and defining problems, Developing and using models, Planning and carrying out investigations, Analyzing and interpreting data, Obtaining, evaluating, and communication information

The Stories

Un Lazo a la Luna *by Lois Ehlert*

A beautiful picture book with a shining silver moon throughout, the Peruvian folktale "The Fox and the Moon" recounts Fox's desire to get to the moon.

Moon Bear series *by Frank Asch*

So many fun books about a bear that loved the moon, and they are jam packed with important and fun science. Children particularly enjoy "Happy Birthday, Moon!"

The Man in the Moon in Love *by Jeffrey Brumbeau*

A woman living alone in her house in the woods crawls up on her roof one night and falls in love with the Man in the Moon … and he with her.

Moonman *by Tomi Ungerer*

The Man in the Moon comes to Earth because he is bored living on the moon. He gets into all kinds of interesting situations, is thrown in jail and simply phases out!

Standards

NGSS

ESS1.A—The Universe and its Stars: Patterns of the motion of the sun, moon, and stars in the sky can be observed, described and predicted. Scientific knowledge assumes an order and consistency in natural systems ... science assumes natural events happen today as they happened in the past.

ESS1.B—Earth and the Solar System: Seasonal patterns of the sunrise and sunset can be observed, described, and predicted.

CCSS/ELA

W.1.7—Participate in shared research and writing projects

W.1.8—With guidance and support from adults, recall information from experiences or gather information from provided sources to answer a question.

Instructional Plan

Rationale

Many folktales and stories about the moon and the phases of the moon are structured around a pair, the Man-Lady, Fox-Rabbit, etc. We are fascinated by the moon. Has the moon ever followed you as you drive in a car? Has it made a shimmering path across the sea waters? Has it peeked in your window late at night and beckoned you outside? Was it still up in the morning as you drove to work? The moon is always there and yet we cannot always see it. The mystery! The science! Do you understand the physical relationship between the sun or light source, the moon—shining reflected light, and the earth—the recipient of the light of the sun and the moon? So, let's begin by observing and recording the observation and responding artistically to what we see and containing all in a Moon Journal.

"Presented with the challenge of discovering something new, unique, and compelling in the moon every night, they (students) become active learners, questioning scientists, patient researchers, expressive artists, and detailed writers."[1]

Preparation

The driest and clearest skies in our part of the world happens in late September and early October, so that is when we determine to send the children outside at night for an entire month to make scientific observations and artistic responses. Parents are included in these observations, of course, and often have as much delight and wonder as their children. While in the classroom we discuss our observations and create visual and poetic responses to the nightly activity.

Assemble books, maps, charts, newspapers, internet resources so that when the scientific study begins—when students have questions ... after and during this artistic experiences ... you have appropriate materials. The observations generate many student questions which may or may not be answered as you proceed. About half way through the month these questions can form the basis for research and inquiry with the assembled materials.

Google "Photos of the moon and the earth" and find some glorious, meaningful photos that will cause wonder. Choose one or two to share in class.

Activities

Beginning with the new moon, each student will go outside to a place where the sky is open enough to view/observe the moon at approximately the same time each night, and 1. Draw what you see; 2. Include the date, time, condition of night sky, and weather in text and drawing; 3. What else do you see at night—airplanes, satellites, planets, any stars, how much do city lights distract from your observation? 4. And what is happening on the Earth as you observe? birds? children? voices of people you can't see? silhouettes of houses? signs of the season, and...

As the month proceeds, discuss some wonderings: the lunar versus the gregorian calendar (This September–October timeline offers a chance to discuss the Jewish high holidays which are based on the lunar calendar), navigating ships on the ocean, the lure of wonderful legends and folktales—what other people wondered about. and searching for "linguistic spillovers" from the stories to the visual and poetic activities.

Associated activities may involve exploration of sunsets, clouds, as well as the moon:

- Writing—similes, "metaphor moon" writings, students consider/write about their own "phases";
- Reading—legends and folktales about the moon; expository text about the Apollo missions;
- Visual Art: water color wash (for sunsets), chalk and oil pastels, the

"community papers" of Eric Carle to use in collage, silhouettes, watercolor weavings, colored pencils.

Activity from ETSU student Kate Nuttall Young at the Weber State Story Symposium 2014 on Exploring the Science in Stories: Aligning Folktales with the Next Generation Science Standards to Keep Knowledge Whole with instructor Jane Stenson

1. Google "moon" and look for photos. Arrange to project the chosen photo(s).

2. Present image to students on projector screen so everyone can see it clearly and in as much detail as possible. Allow 2 to 3 minutes of silent observation time.

3. Use Thinking Routine: See-Think-Wonder from *Making Thinking Visible* by Rictchhart, Church, and Morrison. Looking at the image(s) you will ask students

4. What do you see? *See:* Ask student to state what they notice. This is not a time for interpretations. This is just simply what they see. The students say "I see...."

5. What do you think is going on? *Think:* Ask students what they think is going on. The goal is to build a layer of interpretation. Follow up with "What else is going on here?" or "What do you see that makes you say that?" This will encourage students to use supporting evidence.

6. What does it make you wonder? *Wonder:* Ask the students what they are now wondering about based on what they have seen and think.

7. *Assessment*: During "see" look for improvements in students' ability to notice details and go deeper in the image. During "think" see if students can support their interpretation or are basing it on opinion. In "wonder" look for questions that are bold and adventurous (this may take time if this is the first time you are using this routine). The depth of questions posed will give you an idea of students' understanding.[2]

Assessment

Recording reflections and impressions is a never-ending inquiry project, which once established, never ends.

NOTES

1. Joni Chacer and Gina Resster-Zodrow, *Moon Journals: Writing, Art, and Inquiry through Focused Nature Study* (Portsmouth, NH: Heinemann, 1997), p xi.
2. Ron Ritchhart and Mark Church and Karin Morrison, *Making Thinking Visible: How to Promote Engagement, Understanding and Independence for All Learners* (Los Angeles, CA: Jossey-Bass, 2011).

"Old Man Coyote and the Rock"
The Rock Cycle

JANE STENSON

CCC topics: Patterns, Cause and effect, Stability and change
POSE topics: Developing and using models, Analyzing and interpreting data, Obtaining, evaluating and communicating information

The Story

"Old Man Coyote and the Rock"
Pawnee Great Plains
source: Joseph Bruchac's *Native American Stories*,
retold by Jane Stenson

Old Man Coyote was going along. It had been quite a while since he had eaten and he was feeling cut in half by hunger. Even the grey hair on his sides and skull couldn't hide the fact that his bones stuck out. He sniffed and sniffed again and all that came back was the desert sand and hot sun. He came to a very large dessert rock and caught a glint from the sun.

"Grandfather," Old Man Coyote said to the rock ... pulling up something from the side of his leg, "I give you this fine—very fine—knife. Now help me in some way, because I am very, very hungry."

Then Old Man Coyote went along further.

He went over the top of the hill and, looking down, there at the bottom of the hill was a buffalo that had just been killed.

"How lucky I am," Old Man Coyote said. "But how can I butcher this buffalo without a knife? Hmm, where did I leave my knife?"

Then Old Man Coyote walked along, back up the hill until he saw the big rock. "You don't need this knife," he said to the big rock. He picked it up and ran back to the place where he had left the buffalo. Now, though, where there had been a freshly killed buffalo, there were only buffalo bones and the bones were old and grey. And, behind him, he heard a rumbling noise. Turning around and looking up, he saw Grandfather Rock rolling down the hill straight for him. GA-DA-RUM, GA-DA-RUM, GA-DA-RUM, GA-DA-RUM.

Old Man Coyote began to run. He ran and he ran, this way and then that, but the stone still rumbled after him. GA-DA-RUM, GA-DA-RUM, GA-DA-RUM, Ga-DA-RUM Old Man Coyote ran until he came to a bear's den. "HELP ME!" he called in to the bears.

The bears looked out and saw what was chasing Old Man Coyote. "We can't help you against Grandfather Rock," they said. GA-DA-RUM, GA-DA-RUM, GA-DA-RUM, GA-DA-RUM.

The Big Rock kept coming and Old Man Coyote kept running. Now he came to a cave where mountain lions lived and he called out again. "HELP ME. I am about to be killed!"

The mountain lions looked out and saw what was after Old Man Coyote. "No," they said. "We can't help you if you have angered Grandfather Rock. Grrr." GA-DA-RUM, GA-DA-RUM, GA-DA-RUM, GA-DA-RUM.

The Big Rock kept rumbling after Old Man Coyote and he kept running. Now he came to the plain—the flat place—where the bull buffalo was grazing. "HELP ME! That big rock said it was going to kill all the buffalo. When I tried to stop it, it started to chase *me*."

The bull buffalo braced his legs and thrust his head out to stop the rock. But the rock just brushed the bull buffalo aside and left him standing there dazed, with his horns bent and his head pushed back into his shoulders. To this day buffalo still look like that. GA-DA-RUM, GA-DA-RUM, GA-DA-RUM, GA-DA-RUM. The big rock kept rolling after Old Man Coyote. And Old Man Coyote kept on running.

But Old Man Coyote was getting tired and the big rock was getting closer.

"My friend," Coyote yelled up to the nighthawk, "My friend that big rock is chasing me and it said you have a wide mouth and your eyes are too big and your beak is all pinched up. I told it not to say that and then the rock started to chase *me*."

Now the nighthawk heard what Old Man Coyote said and grew very angry. He called all the other nighthawks. They began to swoop down and strike at the big rock with their beaks. Each time they struck the big rock a piece broke off and stopped rolling. GA-DA-RUM, GA-DA-RUM, GA-DA-RUM, GA-DA-RUM. The rock kept rolling and Old Man Coyote kept running, but now the rock was much smaller. The nighthawks kept swooping down and breaking off pieces. Finally, the rock was nothing but small pebbles … and couldn't chase Coyote anymore.

Old Man Coyote stopped running, and looked at the small stones. "My, my, WHY did you wide-mouthed, big-eyed, pinched beak bird do that to my old friend, Grandfather Rock?" And Old Man Coyote laughed and laughed and started on his way again.

Now the nighthawks were very angry at Old Man Coyote. They gathered together all the pieces of the big rock and framed them with their broad wings. And the next thing Old Man Coyote knew, he heard a familiar sound behind him. GA-DA-RUM, GA-DA-RUM. GA-DA-RUM, GA-DA-RUM. He tried to run but he was so tired now that he could not get away. and that big rock? Well, it rolled right over him and flattened him out! SPLAT, and kept on rolling. GA-DA-RUM.

Standards

NGSS—Earth and Space Science

2-PS1-1. Plan and conduct an investigation to describe and classify different kinds of materials by their observable properties.

2-PS1-2. Analyze data obtained from testing different materials to determine which materials have the properties that are best suited for an intended purpose.

CROSSCUTTING CONCEPTS
- Patterns in the natural and human designed world can be observed.
- Events have causes that generate observable patterns.
- Simple tests can be designed to gather evidence to support or refute student ideas about causes.
- Objects may break into smaller pieces and be put together into larger pieces, or changed shapes.
- Every human-made product is designed by applying some knowledge of the natural world and is built using materials derived from the natural world.

CCSS for ELA

CCSS.ELA-LITERACY.W.2.2—Write informative/explanatory texts in which they introduce a topic, use facts and definitions to develop points, and provide a concluding statement or section.

CCSS.ELA-LITERACY.W.2.7—Participate in shared research and writing projects (e.g., read a number of books on a single topic to produce a report; record science observations).

CCSS.ELA-LITERACY.W.2.8—Recall information from experiences or gather information from provided sources to answer a question.

Objectives

Second Grade students will be able to say

- I can explain the rock cycle in terms of erosion and gravity.
- I can sequence the density/weight of rocks using a balance scale—the Mohs Scale of Hardness
- I can identify some rocks by sight and weight.
- I can explain the difference between rocks and minerals

Materials

- balance scale
- large box of rocks for classroom use—such as those offered by rocksandminerals.com or americaneducationalsupply.com or geology.com
- Murphy, Stuart. *Dave's Down-to-Earth Rock Shop (Math Start 3)*. New York: HarperCollins, 2000.

Instructional Plan

Rationale

Children love rocks and making rock collections. Classifying rocks in order to show their collections is a never-ending engaging part of childhood! Thinking about the earth's time-table of pressure down on our rock foundation, erosion, and the various ways hills and mountains are created and established is endlessly fascinating.

Preparation

Rock collections are easily available for purchase and should be varied enough to spark a study of their attributes. Children will want to share their collections; provide space, as well as some help in organizing and labeling. Determine a rock trail where children can view the ways rocks are used in buildings and construction.

Activity

Begin the study with the story about the rock cycle "Old Man Coyote and the Rock." It's fun and it is not the only folktale about rocks ... and minerals. Ask students what questions they have about rocks and minerals, and continue generating questions, the more you know, the more questions you will ask!... These questions will form the basis of their research. Eventually volcanoes, plate tectonics, gemstones, landslides, fossils, et al, will provide questions as student awareness of the topic emerges.

Activity one: The book *Dave's Down-to-Earth Rock Shop* by Stuart Murphy offers strong skills about establishing collections and categorizing rocks, and provides a great opportunity to bring in some math. Invite a local rock hound to speak about collecting in the area.

Activity two: Weighing Rocks with a Balance Scale. This is a skill-oriented activity and can be easily worked by partners and written up as a "lab report." Using about 12 different rocks, place one rock in one basket of the balance scale and one in the other basket. Record the heavier and lighter rock. Continue with all rocks until you determine the weight sequence of the 12 rocks. It is hoped (or as teacher you can request) that there will be documentation of visible attributes of each rock.

Activity three: Identifying rocks. Using the classroom box of rocks note defining characteristics of the three major categories—sedimentary, igneous, and metamorphic. Determine which rocks fit in these categories and determine possible use(s) of the rocks. Students will enjoy going on rock hunts to find examples—what they "must" find depends on your location. Remind students to always note the location of the rock sample they collect.

Activity four: Take a walk to find building materials made of rock. Identify and draw what you can, and draw the materials you can't identify, noting their locations. Ask students to determine how they can identify unknown materials.

Assessment

- Students shall provide oral, written, or artistic renderings of the rock cycle including some examples of real events from current events or history.
- Students shall be provided a form to state results of their activity with the balance scale to sequence the rocks.
- Student collections of rocks shall demonstrate sedimentary, igneous and metamorphic rocks.

BIBLIOGRAPHY

Bruchac, Joseph, and Michael Caduto. *Native American Stories: From Keepers of the Earth*. Golden, CO: Fulcrum Publishing, 1991.

PART TWO

Upper Elementary
Grades Three through Six

"*There are only two lasting bequests we can hope to give our children. One of these is roots; the other, wings.*"—William Hodding Carter, Jr.

Introduction

SHERRY NORFOLK

"I have no special talents. I am only passionately curious."—
Albert Einstein[1]

Once there was, and is, and always will be ... a gigantic ash tree called Yggdrasil. Yggdrasil is the World Tree that links, nurtures and shelters all the worlds. It connects heaven to hell, humans to animals to plants, and wisdom to fate. In Norse mythology, the tree Yggdrasil is a symbol for the interdependence of all forms of life.

Yggdrasil seemed a fitting place to start this chapter, as we explore the ways storytelling can plant seeds—of understanding, of passion, of curiosity, of delight—in upper elementary students. Like Yggdrasil, stories connect and nurture us. They provide metaphors to help us understand our place in this world and our responsibilities to it. They ignite interest, which leads to discovery and insight.

In Ted Perry's 1972 movie *Home*, Chief Seattle is (wrongfully) credited with saying, "All things are connected. Whatever befalls the earth befalls the sons of the earth. Man does not weave the web of life; he is merely a strand of it. Whatever he does to the web, he does to himself."

While those are beautiful words and a concept we *want* children to understand and embrace, they are not necessarily words that children *can* understand and embrace. But in Zaire, they tell the story "All Things Are Connected," a story and lesson plan found in this section.

For many children, this story creates an "a ha!" moment—a sudden and almost intuitive leap from "huh?" to "I get it!" The next leap is to curiosity: "Is it true?" and from there to, "What can I do?" And from there, the possibilities are endless!

What makes storytelling work?

According to research, in order for us to learn, the information we are learning *must make sense, and it must having meaning.* "Sense" means that the learner can fit the information into existing understanding. "Meaning" means that the information is regarded as relevant to the learner.

Story helps children make sense of new information because it puts information into a *meaningful* context, to which other information can be "attached." Story also puts information into an *emotional* context, and research indicates that emotions play an essential role in both memory and motivation. When emotions are present, hormones released to the brain act as a memory fixative. Story is engaging—it evokes emotion and curiosity, which provokes learning!

News flash: in almost every classroom, there are some students who are not excited about science. In fact, by the time they reach third grade, there are students who have already disengaged from the entire learning process. Maybe they are struggling so much with the fundamental skills of reading that they have already given up. Or they simply do not see any relevance to their own lives. They have lost interest.

Why does this matter?

Pioneering research reveals a secret ingredient for fostering real learning: interest, as demonstrated by the work of Paul Silvia (UNC), Judith Harackiewicz (Wisconsin) and Suzanne Hidi (Toronto) (Annie Murphy Paul, "The Science of Interest," *School Library Journal*, November 2013 p. 24–27). According to Paul, "Silvia speculates that interest acts as an 'approach urge' that pushes back against the 'avoid urges' that would keep us in the realm of the safe and familiar. Interest pulls us toward the new, the edgy, the exotic."

How do we create interest and curiosity?

Brain research has found that *the brain pays closer attention to things that are new and different.* In *The Way of Kings*,[2] Brandon Sanderson hit the nail on the head: "The purpose of a storyteller is not to tell you how to think, but to give you questions to think upon."

Catching student interest is about seizing attention and providing stimulation. Holding it is about finding deeper meaning and purpose. That's why stories and science, paired together, are a winning combination for sparking interest, gaining knowledge, and fostering real learning. Through stories, science facts take on a relevance and immediacy that help students remember them and apply them in their own lives. Storytelling also inspires children to research science topics in greater depth, according to Kathleen Allen[3] writing about the way stories are used in Montessori classrooms.

There are a plethora of professional books that explore the relationship between literature and science—so why *tell* the story rather than read it aloud or requiring the students to read it for themselves? A story is a story, right? A story is a story—but the mode of delivery can make all the difference! The oral story provides an opportunity for students from all reading levels to understand. It introduces vocabulary and concepts through a combination of vocal inflection, body language, and facial expression. It enhances development of higher thinking and analytical skills. It strengthens the ability for recognition and memory of details.

That's why a "focus on oral language is of greatest importance for the children most at risk—children for whom English is a second language and children who have not been exposed at home to the kind of language found in written texts.[4] Ensuring that all children have access to an excellent education requires that issues of oral language come to the fore in elementary classrooms. "By reading a story or nonfiction selection aloud, teachers allow children to experience written language without the burden of decoding, granting them access to content that they may not be able to read and understand by themselves. Children are then free to focus their mental energy on the words and ideas presented in the text, and they will eventually be better prepared to tackle rich written content on their own."[5]

Beyond all of that, when the teacher puts down the book, looks straight into the students' eyes, and tells them a story, she communicates her enthusiasm and passion for learning—and that's contagious! In her research, Margaret Meyers found a "significant increase in positive attitude toward science after the [storytelling] presentations."[6]

Storytelling is a natural, fun and easy way to get kids involved in exploring the world around them. Stories plant seeds of curiosity, excitement, and delight. They nurture understanding and invite reflection. They create the a ha! moments that lead to discovery.

Rudolph Steiner, founder of the Waldorf School System, stated, "In the years of kindergarten through eighth grade, maintaining a strong sense of wonder is far more important than dissemination of information. The scientist's gift is question. With each question, an adventure begins to unfold—the doors to the secret halls of mystery are opened and we are beckoned to enter."[7] In this part of the book, we beckon third, fourth and fifth graders into the secret halls of Physical Science, Earth & Space Science, and Life Science!

NOTES

1. Albert Einstein to Carl Seelig, March 11, 1952. AEA 39–013.
2. Brandon Sanderson, *The Way of Kings* (New York: Tor Books, 2010). Retrieved on March 8, 2014, from http://www.goodreads.com/quotes/tag/storytelling?page=1
3. Margaret B. Meyers, "Telling the Stars: A Quantitative Approach to Assessing the Use of Folk Tales in Science Education." A thesis presented to the faculty of the Department of Curriculum and Instruction East Tennessee State University, 2005.
    This research examines the impact of folk tales and science explanations on students in third through sixth grades who viewed program modules from the SkyTeller Project of Lynn Moroney and the Lunar and Planetary Institute of Houston, Texas.
4. D. K. Dickinson and M.W. Smith. (1994). "Long-term effects of preschool

teachers' book readings on low-income children's vocabulary and story comprehension." *Reading Research Quarterly*, vol. 29 (1994), 104–123.

 5. Appendix A of the Common Core State Standards for English Language Arts, p. 27.

 6. Kathleen Allen, "Story Upon Story," *North American Montessori Teachers' Association Journal*, vol. 24 no. 1 (winter 1999), 225–43.

This article discusses how stories can be used to "teach" history and science. It provides many examples of how this is done in the author's Montessori classroom. Explains the ramifications of using stories in classrooms and how it inspires children to research a topic in greater depth.

 7. Quoted from Susan Strauss, *The Passionate Fact: Storytelling in Natural History and Cultural Interpretation* (Golden, CO: North American Press, 1996), p. 88.

Physical Science

"Turtle Wants to Fly"
Gravity, Force, Thrust and Failure

Lynette J. Ford

CCC topics: Cause and effect, Scale, proportion and quantity, Structure and function

POSE topics: Developing and using models, Constructing explanations and designing solutions, Obtaining, evaluating, and communicating information

The Story

Turtle Wants to Fly

From an African American variant, retold by the author

Turtle isn't happy being who he is; although he can carry his home on his back, and is never lost or far from home, Turtle wants to fly like the birds. Turtle disturbs the forest's critters with his whining and crying. Finally, two crows offer to help Turtle fly by carrying him into the sky; in return Turtle must stop all his fussing and keep his big mouth shut. The crows hold a stick in their talons and tell Turtle to close his mouth on it. He does, but, as he is carried into the air, Turtle wants to brag and get the attention of his fellow turtles and the birds who told him he would never be able to fly. He loudly mumbles, but he keeps his mouth closed on the stick, until he realizes no one on the ground seems to be paying attention. Turtle opens his mouth and yells, "Hey, look at me! I can fly!" He falls, landing on his back, and cracking his shell into the shell all turtles wear to this day. That shell reminds them of two things we all need to remember: we should be happy being who we are, and, sometimes, we all need to refrain from boasting and keep our mouths shut.

- Public Domain Sources:

Emma M. Backus, "Animal Tales from North Carolina," *The Journal of American Folklore*, vol. 11, no. 43 (Oct.–Dec. 1898), pp. 285–86.

Sir Roger L'Estrange, *Fables of Æsop and Other Eminent Mythologists: With Morals and Reflexions* (London, 1692), no. 220, pp. 192–93.

- Contemporary Sources:

http://www.mikelockett.com/stories.php?action=View&id=199

http://www.worldstories.org.uk/stories/story/133-the-boastful-turtle

The Flying Tortoise: An Igbo Tale retold by Tololwa M. Mollel. Stoddart Kids, 1994.

Standards

NGSS—Physical Science—force and motion, Earth and Space Science

5-PS2-1 Motion and Stability: Forces and Interaction: Support an argument that the gravitational force exerted by Earth on objects is directed down. [Clarification Statement: "Down" is a local description of the direction that points toward the center of the spherical Earth.]

3–5 Engineering Design

3–5-ETS1-1 Define a simple design problem reflecting a need or want that includes specific criteria for success and constraints on materials, time, or cost.

3–5-ETS1-2 Generate and compare multiple possible solutions to a problem based on how well each is likely to meet the criteria and constraints of the problem.

CCSS—writing, Speaking, Listening and mathematics

ELA/Literacy

W.3.8 Recall information from experiences or gather information from print and digital sources; take brief notes on sources and sort evidence into provided categories.

SL.3.2 Determine the main ideas and supporting details of a text read aloud or information presented in diverse media and formats, including visually, quantitatively, and orally.

SL.3.3 Ask and answer questions about information from a speaker, offering appropriate elaboration and detail.

SL.3.4 Report on a topic or text, tell a story, or recount an experience with appropriate facts and relevant, descriptive details, speaking clearly at an understandable pace.

Mathematics MP.2 Reason abstractly and quantitatively.

Objectives

Grades 3–5 students will be able to say

- I can apply scientific thinking to a nonscientific narrative experience.
- I can recall and relate evidence of the force of gravity in this narrative
- I can determine and list or state the design problems that prevent Turtle's flight.
- I can generate possible solutions for Turtle's design flaws, and research materials needed to create these solutions, as well as the cost of materials.

Materials

For science:
- access to computers for research on turtles, crows, and the flight of birds
- access to books about same
- small scale
- 3–5 small rocks, or small objects of varying weights
- small weights (weighing less than 1 pound–3 pounds)
- 1-quart or sandwich-sized plastic bags, one for each rock or object
- yardstick and 3 sturdy clamps
- five soft, sponge balls of various sizes (balls for playing jacks to basketball is a good variety)
- drawing paper and pencils
- writing paper
- blueprints for planes, houses, any constructed concept, if possible.

For storytelling:
- access to computers for story research
- several versions of the story in picture book format (see "Contemporary Resources")
- writing paper and pencils

Instructional Plan

Rationale

This story is an ancient attempt at an explanation (pourquoi or how-and-why tale) of why the turtle or tortoise's shell is cracked. It is proof that, throughout history, people have wanted to *know*. The word "science" comes from this curiosity; its Latin root word, *scientia*, means "knowledge." Story helps students creatively approach their own revelations through critical thinking.

Preparation

Collect items that will fit into 1 quart or sandwich-sized plastic bags.

Attach paper clamps to the yardstick; one clamp on either end of the stick represents a crow's talons, and the clamp in the middle represents Turtle's mouth. Bags holding items will be clamped to the yardstick, one at a time.

Determine how the story will be shared: oral format, literary reading, or copies of the story for each student to read (*telling* the story is recommended, both as a community-building experience for the experiments to follow, and as a shared experience for all types of learners).

Activities

1. Tell the story. Reflect on its lesson, and why a turtle and crows might have been chosen as the important characters in the story.

2. Facilitate students' research regarding the facts about the "design," average weight, and movement of turtles and crows. List their findings about each animal, for comparison, under the titles "The Fictional Turtle" and "The Factual Turtle," and "The Fictional Crow" and "The Factual Crow."

3. Facilitate students' research about the flight of birds, with an emphasis on: the design and wingspan of a crow's (or any other bird's) wings; the movement required for birds to take flight, and the movement that allows a bird to resist gravity and remain in the sky.

4. Play with gravitational force by: tossing the sponge balls up and letting them bounce; tossing the balls to one another in a circle, discussing what happens when someone drops or misses the ball; deliberately bouncing the balls as high as possible (or as high as your classroom or play space ceiling permits), and letting them continue to bounce until they eventually stop. Ask students to consider why the balls didn't float off into space. Relate this to Turtle, comparing the weight of the heaviest ball to the weight of the average turtle; reflect on Turtle's body substance (he was not made of spongy material), why Turtle couldn't fly, and why he didn't bounce.

5. Introduce the students to the scale and the items to be weighed on it. Students will record the weight of each item.

6. Select an item to be "Turtle." In this experiment, how much does Turtle weigh? Put the item in a plastic bag, and clip the bag to the middle

of the yardstick. Have two students pretend to be the crows, remove their shoes and socks, and try to pick up the ruler with their toes. Take turns trying this. Can any pair of students lift Turtle?

7. Reflections to be shared orally and in writing: How do the crow's talons differ from people toes? How much might each crow weigh? How would they build resistance to gravitational force in order to take off from the ground, and in order to fly while carrying Turtle? (*Note:* For #6 and #7, if at all possible, permit students to work in pairs, with each pair having its own yardstick, clamps, and items to weigh.)

8. Repeat the activity with different items of different weights. After students have orally presented reflections, permit them to write both these reflections and their own questions and thoughts about the experience. Discuss possible ways to find the answers to their questions, and permit students to do their own research.

9. Encourage students to: invent and design their own methods and modes of flight for Turtle, and write about and draw these designs; imagine and research the materials needed for their designs, and the cost of materials. This is a rough-draft project.

10. If you have blueprints available, share them and discuss their clear and useful language and imagery. Encourage students to redo their work, making their own writing and illustrations clearer.

11. Facilitate students' search for other versions of the story, or share books or printouts of the story. Compare these variants with the story you shared.

12. Instruct students to write their own version of the story, using their inventions as the means of Turtle's flight, and relating the changed outcome as the end of the story.

Assessments

5-PS2-1 Students will individually use balls to show that the gravitational force exerted by the earth is directed "down," or toward the center of the spherical Earth; each student will recount a statement or statements similar to the following: On earth, a ball thrown or bounced in any direction will always come down to earth, because of Earth's gravitational force (or gravity, or gravitational pull). It may bounce "up," but it will come back "down." Alternatively, try this with items that have differing attributes—feathers, matchbox cars, paper, tires, etc. It can't fly off into space because…

3–5 Engineering Design Students will individually tell and write their evaluation of the predicament that prevents Turtle's flight: size, weight, shell, physical design, etc. Students will present a list of materials that might be used to enable Turtle to fly, as well as the costs of these materials. Students will design and illustrate their solution to Turtle's flight problems. Additional assessment (or simply a fun project): As a group, or in small groups, students will design and, if time, materials, and supervision permit, create a "flying-enabled turtle."

"Paddy the Bricklayer"
Working and Playing with Pulleys

Jane Stenson

CCC topic: Patterns, Cause and effect, Energy and matter, Stability and change

POSE topic: Asking questions and defining problems, Developing and using models, Planning and carrying out investigations, Using mathematical and computational thinking

The Story

"Paddy the Bricklayer" can be found in the Clancy Brothers and Dubliners repertoires.

> Dear Boss, I write this note today to tell you of me plight.
> And at the time of writing, I am not a pretty sight.
> Me body is all black and blue, me face an ashen gray,
> And I hope you'll understand why Paddy is not at work today.
> While working on the fourteenth floor some bricks I had to clear.
> And throwin' 'em down from such a height was not a good idea.
> The foreman he was none too pleased, him being such a sod,
> He said I had to carry them down the ladder in my hod.
> But carrying all them bricks by hand, it seemed so awful slow.
> So I hoisted up a barrel and secured the rope below.
> But in me haste to do the job I was too blind to see
> That a barrel full of building blocks was heavier than me!
> So I went down and cut the rope, and the barrel fell like lead.
> And clinging tightly to the rope I started up instead.
> I shot up like a rocket, and to my surprise I found
> That halfway up I met the bloody barrel coming down.
> The barrel struck me shoulder hard as to the ground it sped.

And when I reached the top I hit the pulley with me head.
I still hung on though numbed and shocked from the almighty blow
When the barrel dumped out half its bricks some fourteen floors below.
When the bricks had fallen from the barrel to the floor,
I then outweighed the barrel and started down once more.
Still clinging tightly to the rope, I headed for the ground,
And fell upon the building blocks that were scattered all around.
I lay there moaning on the floor. I thought I'd seen the worst,
When the barrel hit the pulley and then the bottom burst.
A rain of bricks fell down on me, I hadn't got a hope,
And as I became unconscious I let go the bloody rope.
The barrel now the heavier, it started down once more
And landed right across me as I lay there on the floor.
It broke some ribs and my left arm, and I can only say
That I hope you'll understand why Paddy's not at work today.

Standards

NGSS—Physical Science—pulleys

PS2.A.1. Each force acts on one particular object and has both strength and a direction. An object at rest typically has multiple forces acting on it, but they add to give zero net force on the object. Forces that do not sum to zero can cause changes in the objects speed or direction of motion.

PS2.A.2. The patterns of an object's motion in various situations can be observed and measured; when that past motion exhibits a regular pattern, future motion can be predicted from it.

PS2.B.1. Types of Interactions—Objects in contact exert force on each other.

CCSS—Speaking, Listening, Reading, Writing

SL.K.4 Describe familiar people, places, things, and events and, with prompting and support, provide additional detail.

SL.K.5 Add drawings or other visual displays to descriptions as desired to provide additional detail.

SL.K.6 Speak audibly and express thoughts, feelings, and ideas clearly.

RL3.1 Ask and answer questions to demonstrate understanding of a text, referring explicitly to the text for answers.

RL3.3 Describe the relationship between a series of historical events, scientific ideas, or concepts, or steps in technical procedures in a text, using language that pertains to time, sequence, and cause/effect.

RL2. Recount stories, including fables, folktales, and myths from diverse cultures; determine the central message, lesson, or moral and explain how it is conveyed through key details in the text.

W.2 Write informative, explanatory texts to examine a topic and convey ideas and information clearly.

W.3 Conduct short research projects that build knowledge about a topic.

Objectives

Third Grade students will be able to say:

- I can picture/visualize and determine how a pulley is used to vertically or horizontally transfer items from one place to another.
- I can in my environment find and explain examples of pulleys, such as a flagpole pulley, winch, block and tackle, steam shovel, and window blinds.
- I can demonstrate that science questions can be answered with a narrative.
- I can cartoon (graphic short) a story that contains information about a pulley embedded in the narrative.

Materials

For science:

- many sizes and varieties of pulleys,
- ropes
- empty milk jugs
- items to transfer
- a bicycle

For storytelling and writing:

- paper
- colored pencils

Instructional Plan

Rationale

Raising student awareness of the technologies that support out lives can be as simple as walking around and pointing out examples of tools people invented to make our lives simpler. Pulleys aid in the transfer of (heavy) items and, used in conjunction with other technologies such as a gears, allow people to accomplish more.

Preparation

Gather several sizes of pulleys, including double pulleys, and hopefully a block and tackle (can it lift a student?). Gather ropes which fit into the pulleys and milk jugs with water and heavy items. Determine ways to hang the pulleys and know where pulleys exist and work in nearby buildings. You may need to speak with a garage mechanic or a man who works on an oil derrick and ask him to speak your class.

Activity

Play Tell/Re-Tell. Place students in triads knee to knee. Tell the story "Paddy the Bricklayer." Number off 1, 2, 3 and Number I begins to retell the story—in her own words—as 2 and 3 listen. Say to students, "You will and can tell it ugly, because the words haven't had time to form in your mouths. But as you proceed you will find yourselves becoming more fluent; you don't have to have the words exactly like the told story, although the rhymes are fun! Put it in your own words. Each Number continues the tale where the prior person left off. Have the story run about three times in total. You will each listen twice and tell once—a good rule for storytellers (two ears and one mouth)!"

Have each person tell for a minute and a half or so, increasing the telling time throughout. Keep going, over and over until each group has gone through the story about three times. Then as a large group, reflect on the experience.

Because the story is rhymed and a "foreign" culture to many, have students use rhymes they remember, but simply tell what happened (plot). Have them visualize the relationship between Paddy and the bricks—what goes up and what goes down and why.

In their small groups, draw the pictures that track the pulley's movement and Paddy's movement. It is tremendous fun for students to act out this story, but impulse control is paramount.

Looking at the assembled pulleys, ask students "Tell me what you know about these things."

Next ask students to create an hypothesis and determine ways to experiment so they can collect data of the pulley activity. What associated math ideas or questions does the pulley create? Have students analyze the data they collected and form a conclusion about the pulley.

DRAW a comic strip depicting why Paddy is not at work today. And share the strips and the story.

Assessment

Plan and conduct an investigation to provide evidence of the effects of balanced and unbalanced forces on the motion of an object. Examples might include an unbalanced force on one side of the pulley as heavy items are transferred, being certain students use one variable (number, size, or direction of forces) at a time. Make observations and/or measurements of an object's motion to provide evidence that a pattern can be used to predict future motion. The documentation of these experiments—predictions, text and pictures—can be used to assess student understanding.

The comic strip or graphic response to the story poem Paddy the Bricklayer can be used to assess student understanding.

Author's note: I would like to acknowledge Kate Young, Gena Lotta, Lena Foster, and Melissa Dorronsorro, students in the 2014 Weber State Story Symposium "Story and Science," for their work with this science story.

"The Lady Who Put Salt in Her Coffee"
Life Science, Chemistry and Problem-Solving Strategies

VITO M. DIPINTO

CCC topics: Cause & Effect, and Structure & Function
POSE topics: Explanations and designing solutions; Engaging in argument from evidence; obtaining, evaluating and communicating information.

The Story (reprise)

"The Lady Who Put Salt in Her Coffee"
retold by Vito M. Dipinto
The video https://www.youtube.com/watch?v=Y8Y8CfoHvQc

Mrs. Peterson got up in the morning and needed a cup of coffee to begin her day. She made a fresh pot of coffee, poured a cup, and put what she thought is sugar into it. She took a sip. YUCK!! There was salt instead of sugar in her coffee. What was she to do? Having no solution, she sat down to ponder her situation.

Soon Mr. Peterson came downstairs for breakfast. Seeing his wife obviously distressed, he asked, "What is the problem?"

Mrs. Peterson explained about *how she got up in the morning and needed a cup of coffee to begin her day, made a fresh pot of coffee, poured a cup, and put what she thought was sugar into it, took a sip, and YUCK!! There was salt instead of sugar in her coffee*, and perhaps he had a solution.

Mr. Peterson had no solution. Fairly soon, all the Peterson children came into the kitchen and saw their mother and father obviously distressed. They asked, "What is the problem?"

Mr. Peterson explained about how *Mrs. Peterson got up in the morning and needed a cup of coffee to begin her day, made a fresh pot of coffee, poured a cup, and put what she thought was sugar into it, took a sip, and YUCK!! There was salt instead of sugar in her coffee.*

And perhaps they had a solution.

The children had no solution so it became a family crisis. They adjourned to their family crisis room: the dining room. They thought and thought and finally Agamemnon, who had gone to college, remembered that there was a chemist who lived down the street. Perhaps he could help. Mr. Peterson said, "Oh, well" and Mrs. Person said, "Oh, my." All the Peterson children jumped for joy, put on their red India rubber boots, and went over to the chemist's house. The chemist was definitely weird. He had this idea: he thought he could turn ordinary things into precious metals. Unfortunately, he had used all the precious metals in house except his wife's wedding ring. He had been on his knees for hours begging, pleading, and cajoling his wife to donate the ring to the cause of science. This time the experiment was sure to be a successful and they would be rich beyond imagining. She was just about to acquiesce when in tromped the Peterson children. The chemist's wife left. The chemist was mightily miffed. However, he put on his best professional face and asked, "May I help you?" Agamemnon explained about how

refrain

the chemist was about to kick them out on their proverbials when Agamemnon said they could pay in gold. He gathered all sort of chemicals and chemical paraphernalia. He went over to the Peterson's house. He picked up the cup of coffee, looked at it, smelled it, and tasted it, and YUCK!! It had salt instead of sugar in it. He began to work a bit of chemical magic. But everything he added, although it made the salted coffee taste interesting, did not make it taste precisely like coffee. He threw up his hands in despair saying, "The theory was correct but the experiment was a failure. Pay up!"

They returned to the dining room where they all pondered the situation more. Finally Solomon John remembered there was an herb lady who lived at the other end of the street. Mr. Peterson said, "Oh, well" and Mrs. Person said, "Oh, my." All the Peterson children jumped for joy, put on their red India rubber boots, and headed over to the herb lady's house. Now the herb lady's house was a wondrous place filled with plants and plant stuff. Solomon John explained about how

refrain

and that the chemist had made it quite worse, and could she help? She agreed and gathered all sort of plants and plant stuff. She went to the Peterson household, picked up the cup of coffee, looked at it, smelled, tasted it and YUCK!! It had salt instead sugar in it. She began to work a bit of botanical magic. Everything she added made the cup of coffee taste worse and worse. Finally she held up her hands in despair saying that the coffee was bewitched. After Solomon John paid an honorarium for her troubles, she left.

It was getting dark and Mrs. Peterson still had not begun her day. Finally Elizabeth Eliza remembered that the lady from Philadelphia was in town and she had a reputation for wisdom. Perhaps she could help. Mr. Peterson said, "Oh, well" and Mrs. Person said, "Oh, my." Elizabeth Eliza jumped for joy, put on her red India rubber boots, and headed over to the lady from Philadelphia's house. Now the lady from Philadelphia got her reputation for wisdom for two reasons. One, like all of you, she was a good listener and two, she could ask good questions. So when Elizabeth Eliza explained about how

refrain

and the chemist and the herb lady had made it quite worse, could she help? The lady from Philadelphia listened carefully to Elizabeth's words, asked her a few questions, and pondered the responses. Then she said, "Elizabeth, go home. Tell your mother to throw out that cup of coffee. Make a new pot. Pour a fresh cup and taste the sugar before putting it in." Elizabeth Eliza went home and told her mother the advice from the lady from Philadelphia. Mrs. Peterson made herself a fresh pot of coffee, poured herself a steaming hot cup, and put sugar (for sure) into her cup. She drank the cup and she and the family immediately went to bed.

Based on *The Peterkin Papers* by Lucretia P. Hale (1820–1900). Boston and New York: Houghton Mifflin, 1886, 1914; A. Schwartz, (1989). The lady who put salt in her coffee. New York: Harcourt Brace Jovanovich.

Author's note: I have used this same story for 2nd, 5th, and 8th grades. The science that is pursued is grade appropriate, yet the story works at all levels. The 5th grade activity is here and the 2nd grade activity is in Part One.

Objectives

Fifth Grade students will be able to say:

- I can identify chlorophyll as the green pigment in plant leaves.
- I can write an argument based on evidence that supports my identification of chlorophyll being the green pigment in plant leaves.

- I can determine the spices as "beginning" chemistry
- I can retell the story The Lady Who Put Salt in her Coffee

Materials

- The video https://www.youtube.com/watch?v=Y8Y8CfoHvQc
- simple protocol for extracting chlorophyll
    http://www.scienceprojectlab.com/easy-science-project-chlorophyll.html
- Dark green leaves of any plant.
- Cup
- Scissors
- Water
- Paper towel
- Foil
- Oven
- Mortar and pestle
- Glass test tubes with lids or small glass jars with tight lids
- coffee (optional)

You may try one of the following solvents:

- Rubbing alcohol/ethanol
- Rubbing alcohol/91percent isopropanol

All these solvents can be used for chlorophyll extraction. However they have different property called *polarity*. This property affects the efficiency as a chlorophyll solvent.

Note: solvent mixtures can give better results in extraction of the full complex of plant pigment then individual solvent. You could study how good are the different solvents and their mixtures for chlorophyll extraction.

Instructional Plan

Rationale

General Science: Usually around fifth grade, students are being asked to describe their problem solving strategies in science, math and social studies. One of the best problem solving strategies is this: When the investigation doesn't work, start all over (just like in the story). Give the students sets of data that have obvious errors and some that are not so obvious. Measurement data works best, i.e., a set of data of masses of individual and sets of the same size metal washers or volume measurements of water from different containers. Students have to identify the suspect data; speculate on the experimental procedure used to collect the data; and test that speculation. Finally, the students use the tested experimental procedure to collect a new set of data. Students look for experimental, instrumental and human errors. All this comes as a result of the advice from the Lady from Philadelphia.

Chemistry: The other kind of chemicals that are derived from plants is medicinal compounds. People have been "doctoring" with plants as long as there have been people. Major pharmaceutical houses have ethnobotanists on staff that visit traditional cultures around the world. They speak with the person in charge of "doctoring"—the shaman, the crone or the medicine man or woman. One of the most famous ethnobotanist is Mark Plotkin. His book *Tales of a Shaman's Apprentice* is an excellent read for middle school students. He also co-authored a children's picture storybook with Lynn Cherry with the same title. He tells the story of visiting a shaman in the Amazon rainforest. The procedure was that they would gather plants together. The shaman and Mark would then sit down; Mark would point to a plant and the shaman would tell how it is used. When Mark pointed to the rosy periwinkle, the shaman said it was used to treat blood problems with children. This was a promising sign. After taking the plant back to the States, the first step is to remove the chlorophyll, do a crude extraction of all the chemicals in the plant usually only the stem, leaves, roots or flower. This crude extract is tested for activity in tissue culture samples of various diseased cells. If there is any activity, the crude extract is separated into the individual chemical components. Each chemical is manipulated until it is at least 98 percent pure. These are tested individually in the diseased cells where the crude extract had activity. The specific chemical or chemicals that now affect the tissue culture samples are identified. The structure of the compounds is determined and chemical modifications are made to enhance the effect of the drug. Starting with the shaman to the final work in the lab, we now have a treatment for a common type of juvenile leukemia. (This is a very interpretative retelling of the story. It is best to read the book yourself.) The fifth grade students begin to explore the literature on plants that have been used to "doctor" people and what kind of chemicals are in them. For instance, in the northern Illinois area if you came to the medicine man with a headache, he would prescribe a tea made out of willow bark. Aspirin is in willow bark. This is a good time to either show or have the students do the standard extraction of chlorophyll from geranium leaves. Another easy extraction is eugenol—the main chemical in cloves. We now have bridged the world of the herb lady to the world of the chemist.

Preparation

Watch video for protocols for extraction. Gather the materials.

Activity

- The fifth grade students begin to explore the literature on plants that have been used to "doctor" people and what kind of chemicals are in them. For instance, in the northern Illinois area if you came to the medicine man with a headache, he would prescribe a tea made out of willow bark. Aspirin is in willow bark.
- This is a good time to either show or have the students do the standard extraction of chlorophyll from geranium leaves.
- Another easy extraction is eugenol—the main chemical in cloves. We now have bridged the world of the herb lady to the world of the chemist.

Chlorophyll extraction procedure.

A. For a simpler yet effective extraction following the steps in the video listed in the Materials section.

B. What follows is a more detailed scientific procedure to effectively extract the chlorophyll in a very pure form that can be used in other scientific investigations.

1. Put leaves in the cup, pour in boiling water until it covers the sample. Leave for ~30 sec—1 min. Remove leaves from water and dry them with paper towel.

2. Boiling water kills the cells and destroys enzymes which can promote chlorophyll degradation. It also breaks chloroplasts which makes chlorophyll extraction easier.

3. Take the leaves and remove petioles and central veins—these parts of leaf do not contain a lot of pigments. Throw them away. Cut the rest of the leaf material into the small 1–2 mm pieces. Spread them evenly on the foil and put it in the oven for 20 minutes at temperature 104F (40C). Have a cup of tea.

4. Put dry leaf pieces in the mortar (make sure mortar and pestle are perfectly dry!) and grind them. Continue until they turn into uniform yellow-green powder. Grinding breaks cell walls and at the same time increases area of the surface. Leaf grinds will release more pigment.

5. Put powder in a test tube with tight lid. Add few ml of solvent, close the lid and shake.

Note: try to use reasonably small amount of solvent. Five to ten ml is a good volume. Solvents are toxic and the less you deal with them the better. Make sure that your working place is well ventilated!

6. Have a cup of coffee, hold the salt. After the coffee break, check your chlorophyll. There should be emerald-green slightly opalescent liquid on top of dark green powder (which will sink to the bottom of the test tube). This is it. Chlorophyll is extracted. At the moment it's pretty diluted and solution contaminated with fine debris from the broken cells. Remains of chloroplasts and other cell components are floating in liquid making it slightly foggy. To wrap this experiment nicely we would recommend clean and concentrate extracted pigments.

Since we don't have a centrifuge let's make time and gravity work. In other, more scientific words we'll do *sedimentation of the leaf cells debris* (two more jars/test tubes needed).

Here is how:

1. Wait for another 10–15 minutes for the leaf powder to settle on the bottom of the test tube.

2. Extremely carefully pour 90 percent of emerald-green liquid into second test tube. Close with tight lid. Put it in a cool dark place for few hours (24 is a good number).

3. Very carefully pour 90 percent of the liquid from the second test tube to the third test tube. This time leave it open and place it in well ventilated place. Check it from time to time. All used solvents are pretty volatile. After a while most of solvent is gone and what's left is a pretty clean and concentrated plant pigments extract.

If students are ready/interested: Eugenol extraction procedure: Eugenol from cloves. It is difficult to extract eugenol from cloves without doing a steam distillation; however this is a good way to extract the eugenol into olive oil in order to create clove oil. Follow procedures outlined in the video http://www.wikihow.com/Make-Clove-Oil.

Assessment

Students will write up the lab activity following established guidelines, including materials, step-by-step activity, results. Students will include their understanding of the story and their research on medicinal properties of plants.

A Folktale Puppet Opportunity
Lights and Shadows
Jane Stenson *with* Julie Tubbs

CCC topics: Cause and effect, Scale, proportion and quantity, Structure and function, Stability and change

POSE topics: Asking questions and defining problems, Developing and using models, Construction explanations and designing solutions, Obtaining, evaluating and communicating information

A Possible Story Script

"Rumplestiltskin"

MILLER: "My daughter can spin straw into gold, your Royal Highness."
KING: "Send her to me at once."
(*Miller's Daughter enters.*) "Spin this straw into goodly by morning or you shall die."
(*King and Miller exit.*)
MILLER'S DAUGHTER: "Oh, what is to become of me?" (*Manikin enters.*)
MANIKIN: "Why are you crying?"
M.D.: "My father has told the king a falsehood. I cannot spin straw into gold and now I must die."
MANIKIN: I will do it for you. What will you give me?"
M.D.: "Take my necklace." (*Manikin spins the straw into gold and exits.*)
--------Next Morning--------
KING: "Ah! What beautiful gold!"
(*King brings in even more straw.*) "Spin this straw into gold or you shall die."
(*exit King.*)
M.D.: "Oh! Woe is me!"
MANIKIN: Why do you still cry, fair child?"
M.D.: "The king would have me spin this straw into gold or lose my life if I cannot."

MANIKIN: "I will do it. What will you give me?"
M.D.: "Take my ring." (*Manikin spins the straw into gold and exits.*)

--------Next Morning--------

KING: "Wondrous gold!" (*King brings in yet more straw.*)
"Spin this straw into gold by morning and I shall take you for my wife!" (*King exits.*)
M.D.: "My life is surely at an end."
MANIKIN: "Why do you still cry?"
M.D.: I must spin this straw into gold."
MANIKIN: "I will do it for you. What will you give me?"
M.D.: "I have nothing left to give you."
MANIKIN: "Then give me your firstborn child when you have married the king."
M.D.: "That will do." (*Manikin spins the straw into gold and exits.*)

--------Next Morning--------

KING: "You have done well and now you shall become my bride." (*King and Queen dance together.*)

--------A Year Later--------

QUEEN: (*surprised*) "Why have you come?"
MANIKIN: "I have come for your newborn child."
QUEEN: "Have mercy on me! I will give you anything, but spare my child."
MANIKIN: "I will spare your child if you can tell me my name within three days." (*exit Manikin.*)
QUEEN (*to Messenger*): "Search the kingdom for the most unusual names you can think of."

--------The Next Day--------

QUEEN: "Is your name Casper, Melchior or Balthazar?"
MANIKIN: "That is not my name."
QUEEN: "Perhaps your name is Shortshanks, Sheepshanks, or Laceless?"
MANIKIN: "That is not my name."

--------The Third Day--------

MESSENGER: "I have found no new names but I did find a little house with a little man jumping around a fire, singing 'Rumpelstiltskin is my name. The Queen's child will be my fame.'"
QUEEN: "Thank you, you have done well!" (*Messenger exits and Manikin enters.*)
MANIKIN: "Now Mistress Queen, what is my name?"
QUEEN: "Is your name Conrad? Harry?"
MANIKIN: "No."
QUEEN: Is your name Rumpelstiltskin?"
MANIKIN: "The devil has told you that! The devil has told you that!" (*Manikin stomps his feet so hard that he disappears into the earth.*)
(*End*)

Standards

NGSS—Physical Science—light and shadows

1-PS4-2. Make observations to construct an evidence-based account that objects in darkness can be seen only when illuminated.

1-PS4-3. Plan and conduct investigations to determine the effect of placing objects made with different materials in the path of a beam of light. Examples of materials could include those that are transparent (such as clear plastic), translucent (such as waxed paper), opaque (such as cardboard), and reflective (such as a mirror).

1-PS-4-4. Use tools and materials to design and build a device that uses light or sound to solve the problem of communicating over a distance.

4-PSS-2. Develop a model to describe that light reflecting from objects and entering the eye allows objects to be seen.

4-PS-4. An object broken into pieces can reform into another object

CCSS—Reading, Writing, Speaking, Listening

RL.4.2. Determine a theme of a story, drama, or poem from details in the text; summarize the text.

RL.4.3. Describe in depth a character, setting, or event in a story or drama, drawing on specific details in the text (e.g., a character's thoughts, words, or actions).

W.4. Produce clear and coherent writing in which the development, organization, and style are appropriate to task, purpose, and audience.

W.5. Develop and strengthen writing as needed by planning, revising, editing, rewriting, or trying a new approach.

W.6. Use technology, including the Internet, to produce and publish writing and to interact and collaborate with others.

SL1. Prepare for and participate effectively in a range of conversations and collaborations with diverse partners, building on others' ideas and expressing their own clearly and persuasively.

Objectives

Grade Four students will be able to say:

- I can demonstrate that an object moving closer to and away from a light source will change its image in size and clarity.
- I can explain a silhouette in terms of positive and negative space and determine the face versus side view of the silhouette to the light source/audience.

- I can work collaboratively to create a good shadow puppet story from a well known folktale that shows I understand the science.

Materials

for science study:
- various prisms
- light sources such as flashlights
- overhead projector or LED projector

for puppets:
- black tagboard or construction paper
- scissors
- straws
- masking tape
- brass fasteners
- tabletop model (small) of shadow theaters
- a large projection site: a sheet and frame at least child-high
- light projecting ability
- silhouettes provided at conclusion of article, if desired

for writing:
- papers—transparent, translucent, opaque, reflective
- pencils
- drawing paper
- erasers

Instructional Plan

Rationale

Student will apply the study of lights and shadows to create a visually appealing rendition of the folktale that demonstrates their learned understandings. This is a STEAM activity where the physical science and the storytelling support and enhance each other.

Preparation

Copies of old folktales will need to be gathered in the classroom for student use. The study of light sources and shadow opportunities will be taught before this culminating activity is begun. Plan for collaboration time for students.

Activity

1. Initial puppet show activity: Students will create silhouette shadow puppets or use premade shadow puppets for common folktales, perhaps "Little Red Riding Hood," "The Three Billy Goats Gruff," and "Rumpelstiltskin." Students will experiment with the light source, puppets, and stories. Students should experiment—create different images—with the light and the screen. They may wish to construct a tabletop theater.
2. Reflect on the initial experience.
3. Work collaboratively to write and present a story for shadow puppets while including the following in the theatre piece:
    a. use a variety of materials that demonstrate your understanding of how light images are formed;
    b. during the story move your puppets to show changes in their image (s);
    c. have at least one puppet with movable parts.
    d. use a mirror or prism to move/channel the light in a new direction ... and change the image(s) portrayed;
    e. include an object that will be broken into pieces and reformed (into the same or a different shape) on the shadow theatre;

Assessment

As this is a science application to storytelling, the demonstration of science understanding is paramount. In developing the folktale script, opportunities for students to employ various types of surfaces and papers and angles and distances allow them to demonstrate their knowledge of lights and shadows within a familiar tale

* * * * *

Here is a wonderful activity which students may wish to incorporate into their puppet shows. If not, at the very least, this should be demonstrated and available for student use. It is by Julie Tubbs, and the activity is called "Colorful Shadows: Not all shadows are black."

Materials

- power strip
- 3 plug-in light sockets
- red, green and blue light bulbs

A Folktale Puppet Opportunity (J. Stenson & Tubbs) 153

Silhouettes for use in "Rumpelstiltskin."

Procedure

- Screw the colored bulbs into the light sockets.
- Plug each socket into the power strip. For best results, put the green bulb between the red and blue bulbs.
- Darken the room as much as possible and then turn on the colored lights.
- Experiment by making color shadow with your hand.

What's Happening?

The retina of the human eye has three receptors for colored light. One type of receptor is most sensitive to red light, one to green light, and one to blue light. With these three color receptors, we are able to perceive more than a million different shades of color.

When a red, blue and a green light all shine on the screen, the screen looks white because these three colored lights stimulate all three color receptors on your retina almost equally, giving the sensation of white. Red, green and blue are called *additive primaries of light.*

With these three lights you can make shadows of seven different colors: blue, red, green, black, cyan (blue-green), magenta (a mixture of red and blue), and yellow (a mixture of red and green). If you block two of the three lights, you get a shadow of the third color—for example, block the red and green lights, and you get a blue shadow. If you block all three lights, you get a black shadow. And if you block one of the three lights, you get a shadow whose color is a mixture of the two other colors. If the blue and green mix, they make cyan; red and blue make magenta; red and green make yellow.

RESOURCES

- Use the web to provide a variety of traditional folktales from many cultures. Asian cultures in particular have worked extensively with shadow puppets.
- http://www.exploratorium.edu/snacks/colored_shadows/ (more things to do with colored shadows!)

Life Science

"All Things Are Connected"
Interdependence

Sherry Norfolk

POSE topics: constructing explanations and designing solutions; Engaging in argument from evidence; Developing and using models.

The Story

"All Things Are Connected"
Adapted by Sherry Norfolk

There was once a small village in central Africa where the people were happy and prosperous, and their chieftain was usually wise. The village was surrounded by flowering trees and bushes, where colorful parrots and playful monkeys lived, and nearby flowed a river with cool, clean water.

Frogs of all sizes lived near the river, and every night, they sang the people to sleep.

Bellydeep, bellydeep, bellydeep*, kneedeep, kneedeep, kneedeep, ankledeep, ankledeep, ankledeep.*

Now, I told you that the chieftain was usually wise—but no one can be wise all the time. One night, he was sung to sleep as usual but the frog choir. But in the middle of the night, the chieftain woke up with a headache. As he tossed and he turned, the sound of the frogs seemed to be invading his head.

Bellydeep, bellydeep, bellydeep*, kneedeep, kneedeep, KNEEDEEP, ankledeep, ankledeep, ankledeep.*

"Those frogs aren't singing!" cried the chief. "They're yelling! They're keeping me awake and giving me a headache!"

Bellydeep, bellydeep, bellydeep, *kneedeep, kneedeep, kneedeep, ankledeep, ankledeep, ankledeep.*

He went outside and yelled, "QUIET! Stop that croaking!"

But of course, the frogs kept on singing.

Bellydeep, bellydeep, bellydeep, *kneedeep, kneedeep, kneedeep, ankledeep, ankledeep, ankledeep.*

The frogs kept him awake for the rest of the night, and for the rest of the night, the chief's headache grew worse and worse. He couldn't think straight—his wisdom was drowned in pain.

The next morning, all he could think of was getting rid of those noisy frogs. He called the people together and ordered, "Go to the river and kill those frogs! If I hear a single croak of a single frog tonight, I will punish YOU."

The people started to protest, but the Chief was adamant. "Kill the frogs!"

So with great reluctance, the villagers grabbed their sticks and obeyed—all but one of the villagers, that is. A very old woman stood firm, shaking her head from side to side.

"Since you are so old and weak, I will allow you to stay in the village," said the chief. "But stop shaking your head like that!"

"And since you are so young and foolish, I will tell you why I shake my head at you," said the old woman. "All things are connected."

"What do you mean by that?" demanded the chief.

"You will soon see," she answered. "You will soon see."

The villagers returned from their sad task, and after a long and tiring day, they went to their beds. But without the chorus of frogs they had heard every night of their lives, they couldn't sleep. The chief, however, after being up all night before, was able to sleep soundly. Just before he nodded off, he remembered the old woman. "Foolish old thing!" he thought, and he went to sleep.

Several days and nights went by like this: the chief slept, the people tossed and turned. Then one night a different sound disturbed his sleep. *Bzzzz, bzzzz, bzzzz.*

Mosquitoes!

Mosquitoes came swarming into the chief's home and bit him all over! *Bzzzz, bzzzz, bzzzz.*

The chief woke up, slapping a thousand mosquitoes away from his head and ears and neck and arms. "Go away! Leave me alone!" he thundered. "Get out of here or I'll have you killed, too!"

In reply, the mosquitoes buzzed more loudly. *Bzzzz, bzzzz, bzzzz.* Slap! Slap! Slap!

By morning, the chief and all of the people were covered in itchy red bumps. This time, when the chief gave his orders, "Kill the mosquitoes!" the people were eager to obey. They rushed down to the river—all but the old woman.

She stood shaking her head. "Um, um, um."

"What are you shaking your head about now, old woman?" demanded the chief.

She just shook her head. "Um, um, um."

The people came back, but they had not been successful. As hard as they tried—and they really tried!—they couldn't kill all of the mosquitoes. And without frogs to eat the larvae, the mosquito population grew quickly.

Itching and slapping and thoroughly miserable, the chief finally realized that the village would have to be moved away from the mosquitoes and the beautiful river. And he finally understood what the old woman meant when she said, "All things are connected."

Standards

NGSS—Life Science

5LS2.A: Interdependent Relationships in Ecosystems
5LS2.B: Cycles of Matter and Energy Transfer in Ecosystems

CCSS for ELA—Reading, Writing, Speaking, Listening

RI.5.7. Draw on information from multiple print or digital sources, demonstrating the ability to locate an answer, to a question quickly or to solve a problem efficiently.

W.5.3. Write narratives to develop real or imagined experiences or events using effective technique, descriptive details, and clear event sequences.

W.5.4. Produce clear and coherent writing in which the development and organization are appropriate to task, purpose, and audience.

W.5.7. Conduct short research projects that use several sources to build knowledge through investigation of different aspects of a topic.

W.5.9. Draw evidence from literary or informational texts to support analysis, reflection, and research.

SL.5.4. Report on a topic or text or present an opinion, sequencing ideas logically and using appropriate facts and relevant, descriptive details to support main ideas or themes; speak clearly at an understandable pace.

NCAS

Create, Present, Respond, Connect

Objectives

Fifth Grade Students will be able to say:

- I can research interdependent flora and/or fauna within specific ecosystems,
- I can write, revise, edit and publish a fictional narrative which includes scientifically accurate information that describes the movement of matter among plants, animals, decomposers, and the environment.
- I can perform stories for class, and
- I can provide positive peer feedback.

Materials

- "All Things Are Connected," in de Spain, Pleasant. *Eleven Nature Tales: a Multicultural Journey.* Little Rock, AR: August House, 1996.
- student access to print or non-print research materials

Instructional Plan

Rationale

The authors of the Next Generation Science Standards indicate that understanding of interdependent relationships within ecosystems can be demonstrated by developing a model to describe the movement of matter among plants, animals, decomposers, and the environment. But that model does not have to be a physical model—it can be in the form of a story!

The short, poignant Zairian folktale underscores the interdependence of living things: don't mess with Mother Nature! The simple structure of this tale provides a sturdy scaffold for student research and story (model) development.

Preparation

Tell the story!

Instructional Plan

After telling the story, ask students to explain why the old woman told the chieftain that all things are connected. What was meant by that? Why do they draw that inference? Does it only apply to frogs and mosquitoes, or to ALL things?

Following the discussion, analyze the story: Who are the characters? Where does it take place (what kind of habitat)? What animals are involved in the story? When does the story take place? What is the problem? How/why is the problem created? What is the resolution?

Can we move this story to a different habitat/locale? If so, what would the interdependencies be and what would happen in the story? Generate a story together as a group, brainstorming ideas and consulting resources to answer these questions:

- Where will the story take place?
- Who are the human characters?
- What kinds of plants and animals live in that ecosystem? (How can we find out?)
- What interdependencies would be upset if one of these living things was either removed or greatly multiplied? (How can we find out?)
- What causes the imbalance and why?
- What is the result of the imbalance?
- How does the story end?

When the outline is complete, tell the resulting story to the class, then ask students to work in pairs to develop their own outlines by using print and/or non-print resources to choose a locale/ecosystem and answer the remaining questions.

After the research has been completed, students will work independently, each drafting their own version of the story they have outlined. Then revise and edit using storyteller's tools such as body language, facial expression, movement, and character voices, and translating that paralinguistic information into descriptive words and phrases. Students work in pairs or groups of three to listen to each other's stories and ask questions and/or suggest changes.

Final drafts can be produced on the computer, adding appropriate images and graphics. Once these are complete, students rehearse and then tell their stories to the class.

Assessment

Stories can be assessed for effective technique, descriptive details, clear event sequences, choice of relevant graphics, and inclusion of accurate ecological details using a rubric. Performances can be assessed for clear speaking voice, eye contact, appropriate use of gesture, and fluency.

Insects and Plants
Finding the Food Connection
MARY HAMILTON *and* CHARLES WRIGHT

CCC topics: Patterns, Cause and effect, Structure and function
POSE topics: Asking questions and defining problems, Planning and carrying out investigations, Analyzing and interpreting data, Obtaining, evaluating, and communicating information

Short Text—Reprise from "Thinking Like a Scientist"

This first-person anecdote is a true story retelling an incident experienced by Mary followed by a conversation with her husband Charles.

One day I was carrying bags of groceries into my house, and I saw a blue-black wasp caught in a spider's web near the front door. "Uh oh," I thought, "that wasp is going to be a spider's dinner." But then I noticed that only two of the wasp's six legs were touching the web. "Wait just a minute," I said to myself, "I've seen moths with more legs caught escape from spider webs. Something's up. I wonder what?" So, I set my groceries down, and I watched.

The wasp shook the web and shook the web, as if struggling to escape. The spider ran toward the wasp, then stopped, and ran away. Again, the wasp shook the web, as if to say, "Help! Help! I'm caught!" Again the spider ran toward it, but once again it stopped and ran away. The wasp shook the web even more. This time, when the spider ran toward the wasp, it did not stop.

I expected the spider to grab the wasp. Instead, the wasp grabbed the spider. Then the wasp flew over to a window shutter and crawled behind it while still holding the spider. From behind the shutter I heard a high pitched whine. After that, I picked up my grocery bags and carried them inside.

Later my husband Charles came home. I said, "Charles, today I saw a blue-black wasp catch a spider! It took it back behind the shutter, and I heard it eat it!"

Charles is an entomologist so he's been learning about insects for years. He said, "I don't believe you heard the wasp eat the spider. I think you saw a kind of wasp called a mud dauber. Some mud daubers are blue-black and they build their nests in sheltered places, like behind our shutter.

"When a mud dauber catches a spider it doesn't eat it. Instead, it stings the spider to paralyze it, not kill it. Then, the mud dauber carries the spider to its nest, stuffs it in and lays an egg on it. When the mud dauber egg hatches, the larva eats the spider."

"Oh my," I gasped, "that's amazing!"

"But that's not all. If a small bright blue cuckoo wasp happened to be nearby, it would wait for the mud dauber to leave the newly made nest. Then the cuckoo wasp would fly in, and lay its egg on the spider. Because its egg would hatch first, the cuckoo wasp larva would have both mud dauber egg and spider to eat."

Wow! I thought spiders were creatures that ate insects, but on that day, I learned spiders can become insect larva food instead.

Standards

NGSS—Life Science: Interdependent Relationships in Ecosystems

Life Science Disciplinary Core Idea 2.A: Interdependent Relationships in Ecosystems

"The food of almost any kind of animal can be traced back to plants. Organisms are related in food webs in which some animals eat plants for food and other animals eat the animals that eat plants...."

Develop a model to describe the movement of matter among plants, animals, decomposers, and the environment. (In this lesson the model format will be a nonfiction story.)

CCSS/ELA—Reading, Writing, Speaking & Listening, Conventions of Standard English

Reading Standards for Informational Text:

3. Explain the relationships or interactions between two or more individuals in a scientific text based on specific information in the text.

7. Draw on information from multiple print or digital sources, demonstrating the ability to solve a problem efficiently.

9. Integrate information from several texts on the same topic in order to write or speak about a subject knowingly.

Writing Standards: (development for oral presentation requires same standards; however the putting pen to paper action is optional in this project)

    2. Write information/explanatory texts to examine a topic and convey ideas and information clearly.
- b. Develop the topic with facts, definitions, concrete details, quotations, or other information and examples related to the topic.
- c. Link ideas within and across categories of information using words, phrase, and clauses (e.g., in contract, especially)
- d. Use precise language and domain-specific vocabulary to inform about or explain the topic.

    3. Write narratives to develop real or imagined experience or events using clear event sequences.
- c. Use a variety of transition words, phrases, and clauses to manage the sequence of events.

    4, 5, 6 (depending upon teacher's requirement for conveying the story.)

    7. Conduct short research projects that use several sources to build knowledge through investigation of different aspects of a topic.

    8. Recall relevant information from experience or gather relevant information from print and digital sources; summarize or paraphrase information in notes and finished work, and provide a list of sources.

Speaking and Listening Standards:

    1. Engage effectively in a range of collaborative discussions with diverse partners.

    4. Report on a topic, sequencing ideas logically and using appropriate facts and relevant, descriptive details to support main ideas; speak clearly at an understandable pace.

    5. (optional, if project integrated with Media Arts) Include multimedia components (e.g., graphics, sound) and visual displays in presentations when appropriate to enhance the development of main ideas.

Conventions of Standard English:

    6. Acquire and use accurately general academic and domain-specific words and phrases, including those that signal contrast, addition, or other logical relationships (e.g., however, although, nevertheless, similarly, moreover, in addition.)

Objectives

Fifth Grade students will be able to say

- I can conduct research to identify how the life cycle of a specific insect connects with plants as a food source.
- I can write notes on my research findings and cite sources correctly.
- I can create a non-fiction story, based on my research, which explains how the life cycle of a specific insect connects with plants as a food source.
- I can share the story I created orally (Optional: written/digital formats.)

Materials

- The personal anecdote.
- Same anecdote revised to model a student created nonfiction story.
- A list of insects to be researched (suggestions included)
- Access to books and websites about insects

Instructional Plan

Rationale

This project integrates Science and English/Language Arts curriculums by using a true story as a starting point. Collaboration with the school librarian on research skills and citing sources will also prove useful. Should the teacher opt for digital presentation, this lesson also integrates Media Arts.

Preparation

Remind students of the science core idea that the food of almost any kind of animal can be traced back to plants. Also remind students that insects take different forms during their life cycles, and sometimes eat very different food or even no food at all during different parts of their life cycles. Tell them they will be researching insects with the goal of discovering how the life cycle of the insect connects with plants.

Activity

1. Share the first-person anecdote with your students. After the story, have them discuss in small groups the following idea and question: The

food of almost any kind of animal can be traced back to plants. How does the food of mud dauber larva trace back to plants?

After the discussion, ask each group (or each student) to write a brief written statement explaining the connection. (Review statements for formative assessment before making the research assignments in Step 3. Students/groups who readily perceived that they needed to consider the spider's food sources to make the plant connection are ready for the more advanced level research. Students who struggled to perceive the connection with the spider's food sources will benefit from additional instruction on food webs and may need to be assigned an insect which will not require researching an additional insect/animal to find the plant connection.)

2. Demonstrate for your students how the information contained in the story they heard and discussed earlier, along with what many of them will already knew about spiders and their food sources, can be reshaped into a story that begins, "There once lived a female mud dauber wasp that needed to lay eggs." and ends with "…that's how plants are important for future generations of mud daubers." (*Note:* If I had begun with the adult female cuckoo wasp instead of the mud dauber, there would be additional layers of information to include in the story because the mud dauber's life cycle would also be involved in the connection between cuckoo wasp eggs and plants as a food source.)

Here's a model:

There once lived a female adult mud dauber wasp. She needed to lay eggs. Before she could lay her eggs, she had to provide food for the larva that would hatch from them. She found a spider web near her nest. Next, she flew into the spider's web, and shook it pretending she was caught. The spider ran toward her to eat her. Instead the mud dauber caught, stung, and paralyzed the spider. Then, the mud dauber carried the paralyzed spider to her nest, stuffed it in, and laid her eggs on the spider. When her eggs hatched, the larva ate the spider.

So, how does this connect to plants? Before the mud dauber caught the spider, the spider had probably been a successful predator. Butterflies and other insects would have been caught in the spider's web, and become the spider's prey. Many butterflies sip nectar from flowers for food. Flowers are part of plants, so that's how plants are important for future generations of mud daubers.

3. Assign the following project:

Each student (or group of students) is to research an assigned insect to learn how that insect's life cycle connects with plants as a food source.

During research, students are to make written notes on facts gathered and cite the specific sources of those facts.*

Gathered facts are to be used to create a story with the beginning "There once lived a female adult (insect) who needed to lay eggs." and concluding with "…that's how plants are important for future generations of (insect)."

Suggested Insects & Research Notes:

Insects that eat plants or nectar from plants in either their larva or adult forms: grasshoppers, monarch butterflies, mole crickets, cicadas, stag beetles, honey bees (slightly more complex because a social insect).

Insects whose food sources eat plants or who otherwise connect to plants as food without detailed research needed on other creatures' life cycles: lady bugs, yellow jackets, leaf cutting ants, fireflies, ichneumon wasps, whirligigs, velvet ants, mosquitoes (*note:* some adult mosquitoes and fireflies do eat nectar, but students are starting stories with egg-laying).

Insects whose food sources may or may not eat plants, or who will connect to plants through researching the life cycle/origin of the food source: cicada killers (a type of wasp), robber flies, bot flies, fleas, tiger beetles, praying mantids/mantises, dung beetles, carrion beetles, house flies, dragonflies, silverfish.

(*Note:* Sometimes going from egg-laying to plants will require learning about the insect's entire life cycle, sometimes it will not. If you want your students to chart the entire life cycle of the assigned insect, please alter the assignment to include this additional requirement.)

4. Students research using text and digital resources. (*Note:* Correct citations vary in formatting. Instruct students in your school's accepted format before they begin research.) For resources, see the bibliography and visit your school library's 595.7 section. For a formative assessment of this step, see the Citing Sources part of the Assessment section.

5. Arrange student-to-student sharing of work in progress by having students do a trial run oral telling of their story in small groups. Use peer review for formative assessment by encouraging the small group listeners to ask questions about any aspect of the connections from insect to plants they did not understand. Have another student (not the researcher) write the questions, and give them to the researching student after the peer review conversation.* Have peer reviewers sign question page to document participation.

6. After additional research and revision based on information holes discovered in Step 5, students practice revised stories. (See Assessment, Science Vocabulary & Story Structure for possible additional instruction.)

7. Students share their finished product. Some may want to incorporate appropriate visuals as part of their presentation. Students could share the stories orally in small groups, or if you intend to also help them develop

oral presentation skills, you can help them share aloud to the entire class. (For an oral presentation, students should also be required to provide a written bibliography.) Optional: Written version with bibliography. Digital version with story as oral text paired with images, plus bibliography.

Secondary Activity

Predator, Prey, Parasitoid!
Science vocabulary used to describe interdependent relationships in ecosystems.

Students will be able to say:

- I can understand the defining characteristics of predators, prey, parasites, and parasitoids.

The same personal anecdote illustrates a very important distinction between predators and prey. Yes, the spider is a predator, but in this story it becomes prey. And yet the spider never stops being a predator because spiders are predators!

The mud dauber engages in predatory behavior, but not to catch prey and eat it. Instead the mud dauber engages in predatory behavior toward the spider because it needs the spider to become a host for its larva. This is a type of host/parasite relationship, but because the parasite, the mud dauber larva, does not just inconvenience the host or make it ill, but instead kills the host, it is called a parasitoid. Other parasites, head lice or fleas for example, do not kill their hosts.

If a butterfly flies into a spider's web, the spider will engage in predatory behavior; however if the butterfly manages to escape the web, the spider is still a predator, but the butterfly has not become prey.

Predator may be a thought of as a descriptive category or classification, but prey is a label that only applies based on what happens to the animal that becomes prey.

Host would be another label that depends on what happens to the animal that becomes a host. If you don't have a parasite living on you, you are not a host!

Parasites are a descriptive category like predator. Fleas are parasites whether they are lying in wait for a mammal to come by so they can jump on it and begin feeding or whether they are already feeding.

Parasitoids are also a descriptive category like parasite or predator.

Assessment

Fact-checking—Are the insect facts accurate?
For insects unfamiliar to you, a student's records of note-taking and citations will provide the information you need to fact check their oral reports.*

Citing Sources—Are sources cited accurately? (Spot check a few to be sure.)

Formative Assessment: Provide students with the opportunity to improve their source citing by using peer reviewers to check sources. Conduct this activity using the written notes page students are creating as they conduct their research. Require the student who checks citations to note which citations they checked by initialing them and marking them. Marking should designate no need for revision or revision needed because citation is incomplete (source could not be located based on citation) or inaccurate (source located but information based on source not found where noted).

Suggested markings: star/asterisk for no need for revision, × for incomplete, ? for inaccurate. Have peer reviewers sign the notes page to document their work.*

Benefits include:

1. Students with inadequate citations will learn their citations are lacking before the end of the assignment.

2. By checking the sources of others, students may end up discovering a source they need for their own research!

3. Citations you receive at the end of the project will be far better than what you would receive without this step.

4. While verifying another student's citations, the student will also learn about another insect.

Science Vocabulary—Were scientific terms used appropriately and accurately? Expected terms may include: insect, egg, larva, nymph, pupa, cocoon, prey, predator, parasite, parasitoid, complete metamorphosis, simple or incomplete metamorphosis, molt, scavenger. Please do not assess student work by counting the number of scientific terms used. Instead, value appropriate use of scientific terms like larva or nymph, not insect baby. (Instruction Idea: Have students circle scientific terms in the model story which include: larva, eggs, predator, and prey.)

Story Structure—Did student begin and end the story as assigned?
Were words and phrases used appropriately to help listeners clearly follow the chain of events? (Instruction Idea: Have students underline words that help clarify the sequence of events in the model story. These include: before, next, instead, when, then. Student brainstorming can lead to more

helpful words including; first, second, although, moreover, in addition, because, later, after.)

Note: If you are also requiring a written story, students can check their own drafts for words that clarify event sequences and for science terminology.

*These are items you should expect to receive from your students during this project. In addition, you should also receive a bibliography of all sources consulted, and, if required, a written or digital story.

BIBLIOGRAPHY

Many books on individual insects are also available, written at a wide, wide variety of reading levels, which allows for a successful research project for students with varied reading abilities. Books here cover multiple insects and were all found in the 595.7 section of public library children's departments.

Books

Arnosky, Jim. *Creep and Flutter: The Secret World of Insects and Spiders.* New York: Sterling Children's Books, 2012. (Includes fold-out illustrations of full-sized large insects and diagrams clearly indicating actual size of any enlarged illustrations).

Dourlot, Sonia. *Insect Museum: Describing 114 Species of Insects and Other Arthropods, Including Their Natural History and Environment.* Buffalo, NY: Firefly Books, 2009.

Johnson, Jinny. *Simon & Schuster Children's Guide to Insects and Spiders.* New York: Simon & Schuster, 1996.

Leahy, Christopher. *Peterson First Guide to Insects of North America.* Boston: Houghton Mifflin, 1987. (Peterson First Guides series includes guides for caterpillars and for butterflies and moths. Peterson Field Guides for Young Naturalists series include guides for butterflies and for caterpillars.)

McGavin, Dr. George C. *Insects of North America.* San Diego: Thunder Bay Press, 1995.

Mound, Laurence. *Insect.* (DK Eyewitness Books.) London: Dorling Kindersley Limited, 2004.

Murawski, Darlene, and Nancy Honovich. *Ultimate Bug-Opedia: The Most Complete Bug Reference Ever.* Washington, D.C.: National Geographic Kids, 2013.

Parker, Nancy Winslow, and Joan Richards Wright. *Bugs.* New York: Greenwillow, 1987.

Stewart, Melissa. *Maggots, Grubs, and More: The Secret Life of Young Insects.* Brookfield, CT: The Millbrook Press, 2003.

Websites

http://www2.ca.uky.edu/entomology/dept/youth.asp. A University of Kentucky, Department of Entomology website (not limited to Kentucky insects; lots of information and resources for teachers, parents, and students; widely recommended by others including National Geographic and the University of North Carolina at Chapel Hill School of Education.) The Critter Files section of this site allows for searching by insect name.

http://www.amentsoc.org/bug-club/. British website jointly supported by the Amateur Entomologists' Society and the British Entomological and Natural History Society. The Bug Club is the children's section of their site.

http://www.biokids.umich.edu/critters/Insecta/. BioKIDS is sponsored in part by the Interagency Education Research Initiative. It is a partnership of the University of Michigan School of Education, University of Michigan Museum of Zoology, and the Detroit Public Schools.

http://www.entsoc.org/public. The Entomological Society of America's list of resources for the public. This site is not for students, but may prove helpful to a teacher if students strike out on finding material.

http://insected.arizona.edu/info.htm. The University of Arizona Center for Insect Science Education Outreach.

www.insects.org. Includes articles and photos of many insects. Searchable by insect name, but please know this does not always lead to an article specifically about that insect.

http://urbanext.illinois.edu/insects/. This site, from the University of Illinois Extension Office Schools Online project, provides an overview of general information about insects, with narration available in English or Spanish. You can't look up individual insects here, but if your students have little knowledge of insects, this site will help them learn the basics before they begin their research.

"The Knee-High Man"
Adding Science to Your Animal Stories

Kevin Strauss

CCC topics: Patterns, Scale, proportion, and quantity, Structure and function

POSE topics: Developing and using models, Planning and carrying out investigations, Obtaining, evaluating, and communication information

The Story

"The Knee-High Man"

(African American)

A long time back there was a man who was so small that he only came up to your knee. And since that was how small he was, that's what everyone called him, the "Knee-High Man." He lived out in the woods at the edge of a swamp and one day, he got an idea.

"I don't want to be so small anymore. I want to be big. And since it isn't happening on its own, I should find out how to make it happen. I'm going to go find the biggest creature in the land and ask it how it got so big. Maybe then I can figure out how I can get bigger."

So he packed some food in a bag and set off down the road. The first creature he met was a deer in a grassy field.

"Hey there Mrs. Deer, how is it that you got so big?" said the Knee-High Man.

"Well.... I don't know," said Deer. "I just eat a lot of grass every day and I run around and run around. Why do you want to know?"

"Well I'd like to be big like you."

"Then all you have to do is eat a lot of grass and run 20 miles a day," said Deer.

So the Knee-High Man set to work eating grass and running and running and running. He never quite made it to 20 miles in a day, but he ate grass until his stomach hurt, he ran until his legs and his lungs hurt. And after a few days, he measured himself and he hadn't gotten any bigger at all.

"I don't think Mrs. Deer can help me. But maybe someone else can."

So once again, the Knee-High Man set off down the road and he came to the oak woods and saw a black bear eating acorns. The Knee-High Man sat down on a rock and explained his problem to the Bear.

"What do you think, Mr. Bear? You're so big, can you teach me how to get big, too?"

"Sure," grunted Bear. "Just eat a whole lot of acorns and then snort and bellow and climb trees. That's what I do every day and that's how I got so big."

"Great!" said the Knee-High Man.

He set to work eating acorns and snorting and bellowing until his stomach hurt and his throat hurt. He climbed to the top of trees every day, too. But after a week, he hadn't grown an inch.

"Hmmmf!" he snorted. "That bear gave me a bunch of bull."

The Knee High Man figured this was a serious problem. And he didn't know much, but he did know that when people or animals had a serious problem, they didn't keep it to themselves. They went and asked the wise Owl what to do about it. The Knee-High Man set off in search of Owl's nest deep in the forest. It was evening before he found it. He called up, "Mrs. Owl, Mrs. Owl, I've got some questions for you."

Owl flew down on silent wings and landed on a branch next to the Knee-High Man.

"Who—who's calling my name?" called Owl.

"It's me, Mrs. Owl, the Knee-High Man. I didn't know who else to talk to. I've been trying to get bigger so people would be more impressed with me. I've been asking animals how they got bigger. I tried doing what horses do to get bigger and what bears do to get bigger, but it doesn't seem to work for me. So I thought maybe you might have some advice."

"Wait a minute," said Owl. Why do you want to be bigger?"

"Well, I want to be bigger so that if I get into a fight, I can win."

"Has anyone ever threatened to pick a fight with you?" said Owl.

"Well, no."

"So if you don't have any cause to fight, then you don't have any need to be bigger, right?"

"Well … if I were bigger, it would be a lot easier to see a long way down the road," said the Knee-High Man.

"How do you see further down the road now?" said Owl.

"Well, I just climb a tree," said the Knee-High Man.

"Can you climb a tree being the size you are?"

"Yes, I can," said the Knee-High Man. "But, what about people taking me seriously. I'm so little that sometimes people don't think I know anything at all."

"Well how tall am I?" said Owl.

"About as tall as me," said the Knee-High Man.

"Yet people take me seriously all the time," said Owl.

"They do?" said the Knee-High Man.

"Yes, just like you're doing right now. You see, to be taken seriously, you don't need to grow your body, but you do need to grow your brain and that's where I can help you."

Before long, the Knee-High Man learned so much from Owl that everyone came to him for advice. Before long, they didn't call him the "Knee-High Man" anymore. They called him Clever Charlie.

And that's the end of the story.

Standards

NGSS—Life Science and Ecology

3rd Grade: Life Science—Interdependent Relationships in Ecosystems

5th Grade: Life Science—Matter and Energy in Organisms and Ecosystems

MS: Life Science—Natural Selection and Adaptations

CCSS—Reading, Writing, Speaking, Listening

3rd Grade: CCSS.ELA-LITERACY.W.3.2

Write informative/explanatory texts to examine a topic and convey ideas and information clearly.

4th Grade: CCSS.ELA-LITERACY.SL.4.4

Report on a topic or text, tell a story, or recount an experience in an organized manner, using appropriate facts and relevant, descriptive details to support main ideas or themes; speak clearly at an understandable pace.

ARTS Standards

3rd Grade, TH:Cr1.1.3

a. Create roles, imagined worlds, and improvised stories in a drama/theatre work.

5th Grade, TH:Cr.1.1.5

c. Imagine how a character's inner thoughts impact the story and given circumstances in a drama/ theatre work.

Objectives

Grade 3–5 Students will be able to say:

- I can identify whether an animal action is factual (non-fiction) or fictional in a story.
- I can describe how animals "sense" the world differently from humans.
- I can define the ecological relationships between two different animals.

Materials

- Copies of animal folktales with a least two different kinds of animals in each story
- Pencils, paper
- Copies of the *Creating Effective Animal Characters Animal Information Sheet* for each student

Instructional Plan

Rationale

Knowing more about the animals that appear in a story make it easier to present more interesting animal characters in a story. It also makes it easier for teachers to use stories to teach animal biology and ecology.

Preparation

Read the *Developing Effective Animal Characters* article and use the techniques described there in your learning and re-telling of the "Knee-High Man" story. Print copies of this or other animal folktale stories, along with copies of the *Creating Effective Animal Characters* chart for each student or each small group of students.

Activity

1. Tell "The Knee-High Man" or another story with several animal characters to your students.

2. Define fiction and non-fiction for your students. Ask students to describe factual (non-fiction) and fictional aspects of this story. List those elements on the white board.

3. Ask students to read another animal story and use the *Creating Effective Animal Characters* chart to identify factual and fictional aspects of their story.

4. Ask students to revise their story to add more factual aspects to the tale. Simple ways to do that involves asking them to describe how the animal sees, or smells, or hears its world, or using the ecological relationships between animals to explain animal behavior.

For example, if students are using "The Three Little Pigs," student writers could describe how the wolf uses his great sense of smell to smell the pigs hiding in the stick house. They could also describe how "He wasn't a mean wolf. He was just hungry. When pig farmers moved in and cut down his forest, the deer disappeared and all that was left were these pigs."

5. Have students either write or tell their re-written stories and describe why they made the changes they made to the original tale.

Assessment

Assessment Quiz:

1. Describe story elements that are factual and elements that were fictional in one of the stories that you read or heard as part of this lesson.
2. Describe how one animal's senses are different from human senses.
3. Describe the ecological relationship between two different animals that you've heard about during this lesson.

BIBLIOGRAPHY
- Kricher, John C. and Gordon Morrison. *Peterson Guide to the Ecology of Eastern Forests.*
  This guide gives background on the biology and ecology of animals in the eastern forest.
- Mercatante, Anthony S. *Zoo of the Gods: The World of Animals in Myth and Legend.*
  A description of both real and imaginary animals.
- Strauss, Kevin. *Tales with Tails: storytelling the wonders of the natural world.*
  The textbook for environmental and nature storytelling. This book includes nature stories and nature facts to help storytellers, teachers, parents and naturalists use stories to teach about the natural world.

Developing Effective Animal Characters

Kevin Strauss

How Animal Characters Are Different from Human Characters

Animal characters are different from human characters in a number of ways. Animal characters think differently from human characters. They often think about much more survival-level issues like finding food and avoiding predators. Esoteric ideas like "justice" or "beauty" are not often in the front of their minds.

Animal characters are often much more "down to earth" than human characters. Bodily functions like defecation, snot or devouring live prey aren't a big deal to them. Animal characters don't tend to be all that reflective about the world. They do what they need to do and then they move on. You won't see a wolf sulking over missing a deer on a hunt. In addition, animal characters see, smell and hear the world very differently from humans, so their perspectives of the world are very different from our own.

The Five Facets of Effective Animal Characters

1. A good animal character moves like an animal.

As I am working on an animal character, I first try to visualize how it moves. How an animal moves tells us a lot about what it is thinking and doing. While humans are far more isolated from the natural world now than at any time in our history, there are still some easy ways to watch live animals. Visit a zoo, park, nature preserve or pet store and have a look at the animals there. Ideally watch the same animal species that you have in your stories. If you can't do that, look for one that is related. If you can't find a lion at the zoo, look for a tiger, a leopard or a bobcat. As you are watching the animal, try to "get inside its head," to figure out what it is thinking. If you are feeling especially playful, imagine an interview with the animal. What would it tell you about itself?

When portraying animal characters, use body language and facial expressions to convey your characters. Crouching a bit for smaller characters, standing tall and straight for big animals can convey character in a nonverbal way. I get the most mileage out of facial expressions. Beavers are easy; I just take on an overbite. For owls I stoop and puff out my cheeks. Play around with animal charades to get a feel for what works for you.

Remember that you can also convey a character by using only part of your body. Using an arm for a snake or a hand for a swimming fish can show movement and character all at once.

2. A good animal character sounds like an animal (or its cartoon likeness). Real animals don't speak English, but they do communicate, often with some kind of vocalization. Work on developing a unique voice for the one or two main animal characters in a story. Watch animal cartoons or reruns of the Muppet Show® to get a sense for how cartoon writers and puppeteers convey character though voice.

Generally speaking, big animals have deep voices and small animals have high voices. You can also vary the pace that you speak. Big animals seem to have slower voices and smaller animals seem to speak more quickly. Biologically this makes sense since a mouse has a much faster heart rate and breathes much more quickly than a bear. In other cases, choose a speaking pace that fits the animal's movement (see 1. above); rabbits talk fast because they run fast. Turtles talk slowly because they move slo-wly.

In addition to using vocal tone and pace, you may also want to insert some animal vocalizations in an animal character's speech. When I am talking like a crow, I might insert an occasional "caw" into its speech. That way, without using changes in tone or pace, listeners get the signal that it is the crow that is still talking.

3. A good animal character uses its senses the same way the real animal does.

This step takes some research, but it is well worth the effort. Knowing how an animal senses its world will give you a real feel for how it thinks and how it reacts to problems. Most animals have at least one sense that is far superior to human senses. In many cases, animals can smell, hear or see us in the forest long before we ever see them. That's why most people don't see very many animals during a walk in the woods. Make sure that your animal characters reflect this ability.

Wolves, like many mammals, have an excellent sense of smell. Canines (wolves, dogs, foxes) "see" the world through their noses. A wolf can track a moose by smell up to a mile away. So when telling a story involving a wolf, rather than just saying "Wolf saw the Deer," I say "Wolf smell the air and caught the whiff of something good to eat. 'Mmmmm, deer, I love deer for dinner!'"

The animal facts pages in Chapter 4 include information about how many animals use their senses. Check out the wildlife books listed in the bibliography. Naturalists, zookeepers and the Internet can also help with information on a specific animal and its senses.

4. A good animal character has reasons for doing what it does.

Find out why your animal character acts the way it does in a story. This knowledge will help you develop your animal characters from the inside out. Is your animal character acting the way that it does in the story because of biology (predators are often portrayed as "evil" characters in stories)? Or is the animal acting a certain way because of a human-created archetype? Are your story owls always wise? Discover your animal character's motivation.

5. A good animal character will grow and mature over time.

You can work and develop animal characters now, but also realize that your animal characters, like other characters in stories, will develop over time. The more that you tell stories with animal characters, the more your animal characters will develop distinctive voices and movements all on their own. Don't be surprised when this happens.

Creating Effective Animal Characters
Animal Information Sheet
© Kevin Strauss 2006

Animal	*Physical Traits*	*Ecological Relationships*	*Symbolism*
Omnivores (eats animals and plants)			
Black Bear	Poor eyesight, good sense of smell, eats a lot of food in preparation for a six-month "hibernation" in winter, climbs trees	Eats mostly plants (berries, catkins, seeds), also eats ants, wasp nests and honey	Big bully, often portrayed as slow or stupid, other cultures saw bear as a healer and wise creature
Crow/Raven	Can see in color, very intelligent and adaptable, tool user,	Eat just about anything from fruit to carrion (dead ani-	Often portrayed as a trickster, other times portrayed as a sym-

Animal	Physical Traits	Ecological Relationships	Symbolism
	over 100 vocalizations	mals), often "clean up" dead animals, known to follow wolves to a kill site	bol of death or evil
Mouse/Rat	Good sense of smell and hearing, can chew through just about anything, only sees in black and white	Eaten by hawks, owls, snakes, foxes and other predators, consumes crops, reproduces very quickly	"Underdog" character, quick-witted, adaptable, social, sly
Turtle	Poor eyesight, deaf to airborne sound, shell is modified ribs, moves slowly, sleeps through cold winters buried in lake mud	Well-protected animal, some live on land, others in the water	Protection, endurance, longevity, patience, strength, stability, slowness
Herbivore (only eats plants)			
Rabbit/Hare	Poor eyesight, good hearing and sense of smell, fast runner, hares change color to white in winter	Reproduces very quickly (18 young per year), prey for wolves, hawks and other large predators	Trickster, fickle, clever, lucky, fertility symbol, swiftness
Butterfly/Moth	Color vision, tastes with its feet, powerful sense of smell, short-lived (two-weeks in some cases)	Nectar drinker, pollinates flowers; moths fly at night, butterflies fly during day, moth larvae (caterpillars) are destructive to plants and clothing	Resurrection, transformation, Spring, light-mindedness.
Deer	Good sense of smell and hearing, fast runner (35 m.p.h.), can defend itself with hooves, antlers fall off every winter	Prey for wolves and cougars, can damage forests if deer population is too high	Beauty, purity, grace, vanity, speed
Carnivores (only eats meat)			
Wolf	Good senses of smell, hearing and sight, hunts in family	Predator, kills deer, moose, farm animals (rarely), kills easiest	Portrayed as evil, helpful, foolish or wise by different cul-

Animal	Physical Traits	Ecological Relationships	Symbolism
	(pack) groups, sharp teeth, strong jaws	prey (often old, young, sick or injured), may curb prey populations	tures, symbol of ferocity, cruelty, courage, nourishing care, family bonds
Owl	Excellent sense of night sight and hearing, can detect prey in total darkness, no sense of smell, sharp talons (claws) and beak, wings are designed for silent flight	Predator, kills mice and other rodents, controls prey populations	Death, night, cold, evil, wisdom, powerful sight
Snake	Smells with its tongue, can't hear airborne sounds, decent eyesight, some snakes use a kind of "heat vision" to detect prey, needs to warm up on cold days before it can move, some snakes are venomous, sheds skin	Predator, eats mice, rats, birds, worms, insects, hibernates during cold winters	Healing, protection, evil, death, immortality, guile, intelligence, elegance, renewal

Republished with permission of ABC-CLIO, LLC, from Tales with Tails: Storytelling the Wonders of the Natural World, *Kevin Strauss, 2006; permission conveyed through Copyright Clearance Center, Inc.*

An Adventure Through a Cell
Using Plant and Animal Cells to Create an Adventure Story

JENNY MCCRERY

CCC topics: Structure and Function
POSE topics: Asking questions and defining problems; Developing and using models

The Story

"The Magic School Bus Inside the Human Body"
Synopsis from Goodreads.com

Talk about a change of plans! Ms. Frizzle and her class are on the Magic School Bus headed for a museum. They have been studying how the body turns food into energy, and now they are going to see an exhibit on the human body. Things seem fine until they stop for lunch. A strange mishap causes the bus to shrink and then be swallowed! Ms. Frizzle's class is suddenly inside a real human body!

Standards

NGSS

MS-LS1-1 Conduct an investigation to provide evidence that living things are made of cells; either one cell or many different numbers and types of cells.

CCSS for ELA

W.5.3 Write narratives to develop real or imagined experiences or events using effective technique, descriptive details, and clear event sequences.

Objectives

Fifth Graders will be able to say:

- I can distinguish between the basic structures and functions of plant and animal cells.
- I can write a first-person adventure story depicting the exploration of organelles found within a plant or animal cell and their functions.

Materials

- Cole, Joanna and Bruce Degen. *The Magic School Bus Inside the Human Body.* New York: Scholastic, 1990.
- Paper or writing journal
- Pencil
- Science notebook or class notes
- Chart paper, markers

Instructional Plan

Rationale

This lesson provides an opportunity for students to explore the function of cellular organelles and to write an adventure story while imagining how a character might think and/or feel as he or she ventures through a plant or animal cell. By the end of the lesson, students will use their knowledge and understanding of plant and animal cells as well as elements of an adventure story.

Preparation

Prior to class, create a three column graphic organizer on chart paper. Label one column "plant cells," one "animal cells," and the other "Function." This graphic organizer will be used for students to brainstorm organelles and their functions.

Create an additional chart prior to class for students to brainstorm elements of an adventure story.

Set aside one additional sheet of chart paper for brainstorming.

Activity

Read or tell *The Magic School Bus Inside the Human Body.*

Discuss what happens in the story, and how the authors used their imagination AND their knowledge of the human body to write the adventure story.

Explain to students that they are going to be chronicling their own adventure through a plant or animal cell. In order to create their adventure, they need to decide what organelles they are going to visit.

Have students brainstorm organelles found only in a plant cell. Write their responses on the graphic organizer.

Next, ask the student to brainstorm organelles found in an animal cell. Write their responses on the graphic organizer.

Complete the chart by having students describe the function of each organelle.

Example:

Plant Cell	*Animal Cell*	*Function*
Cell Wall		Thick cellular wall that supports the plant
Chloroplast		Uses photosynthesis to produce energy for the plant
Mitochondria	Mitochondria	Produces energy for the cell
Nucleus	Nucleus	Controls activities in the cell; contains DNA
Cell membrane	Cell Membrane	Allows food, water and gas to enter the cell

Ask students what an adventure story is. Write their responses on the second piece of chart paper.

Next, engage students in brainstorming elements of an adventure story. Some guided questions to use to elicit responses are:

- How does a writer set the scene, or open the story?
- How can a writer show readers the rising action and the high point, or climax, of the story?
- What is the literary term for the events of a story? (plot).
- What are some ways to create a successful ending to a story so readers know that it is over?
- Ask students how they think that they could incorporate their knowledge of plant and animal cells into an adventure story. Record ideas on chart paper.
- Explain to students that they will be the main character and that they

are to write an adventure in which they visit organelles found within a plant or animal cell.
- Finally, explain to the students they will use their understanding of plant and animal cells to write their own adventure story that they will play a starring role in.

Assessment

Student work will serve as the assessment. A rubric may be utilized.
Example:

	3	2	1
Organelles and functions.	Organelles and their functions are accurately represented in a creative manner.	Some of the organelles and their functions are accurately represented in a creative manner.	Organelles and their functions are inaccurate and may or may not be written in a creative manner.
Spelling and grammar	No spelling or grammar errors.	No more than three spelling or grammar mistakes.	Several spelling and grammar mistakes.

George Washington Carver
The Argument for Crop Rotation

BOBBY NORFOLK *with* SHERRY NORFOLK

CCC topics: Patterns, Cause and effect, Energy and matter
POSE topic: Developing and using models, Planning and carrying out investigations, Engaging in argument from evidence

The Story

"George Washington Carver: The Peanut Wizard"
By Bobby Norfolk

My first-person performance of George Washington Carver's amazing life story is divided into five distinct parts: One: Young George; Two: A Quest for Knowledge; Three: The Tuskegee Institute; Four: Carver as Scientist and the Wizard of Tuskegee; Five: Carver's Legacy. This excerpt from Story Three: The Tuskegee Institute, discusses how and why he became known as the Peanut Wizard.

When Booker T. Washington first approached me with a job offer in 1896 as Director of Agriculture at Tuskegee Institute I was very pleased! I arrived after finishing my master's degree, filled with zeal, believing that God had given me these special talents because of a divine plan for my life.

I was excited about seeing all the new plants and flora of Alabama. What a botanical paradise it would be for me—this was indeed a new world compared with Iowa! But once I arrived, I saw cotton, nothing but cotton. The scraggly cotton grew up close to the cabin doors; a few lonesome collard greens—the only sign of vegetables; stunted cattle, boney mules, fields and hillsides cracked and scarred with gullies and deep ruts. Not much evidence of scientific farming anywhere. Everywhere looked hungry—the land, the cotton, the cattle, and the people.

Now, the primary idea of all of my work was to help the farmer and fill the poor man's dinner pail. Looking at those sad Alabama fields, I realized that God had sent me to this place at this time for a purpose.

I devoted much of my time between the years of 1902 and 1905 to helping the poor farmers in the area find crops that would help improve their terrible soil conditions. Cotton—the chief money crop of the day—depleted the soil because it took nitrogen from the dirt and did not replenish it. That was causing the cotton crops to get steadily smaller and smaller and the soil to be less and less productive.

The answer to these problems was crop rotation, so I started experimenting with certain foods like peanuts, sweet potatoes, black-eyed peas and soybeans to find plants that would replenish the nitrogen-poor soil.

I found, for example, that peanuts pull nitrogen from the air and put it back into the soil. This became ever more urgent when the boll weevil infestation swept the South, destroying the cotton and wreaking havoc on the farmers. With the loss of the cotton, farmers needed quick remedies for their impoverished fields. I proposed that they plant peanuts or soybeans—quick ways to enrich the soil. I traveled the South, delivering lectures and providing graphic displays of my experiment stations, pinpointing the mysterious causes of the crop failures and the near-miraculous effects of planting peanuts or soybeans.

But the farmers rebelled. "How can we sell these useless crops? We'll lose even more money—we have to plant cotton. Cotton is King! It's the only way we can make a living!"

They were desperate, and they were adamant.

So I went back to my laboratory, and began to develop uses for those useless peanuts. It wasn't so hard! Soon, I had found more than 300 uses for peanuts—and 118 uses for sweet potatoes, 60 uses for pecans, and dozens more uses for soybeans, black-eyed peas, wild plum and okra. Once the people learned about the value of peanuts and those other soil-enriching crops, a demand was created—and the farmers responded to that demand by planting peanuts!

That's how I became the Peanut Wizard—and that's how peanuts revolutionized the economy of the South by liberating it from an excessive dependence on cotton.

Standards

NGSS—Life Science

    LS2.B: Cycles of Matter and Energy Transfer in Ecosystems

186   Part Two. Upper Elementary (Life Science)

George Washington Carver. **Painting by Betsey Graves Reneau, 1888–1964 (U.S. National Archives).**

CCSS for ELA—Reading, Writing, Speaking, Listening

  RI.5.1. Quote accurately from a text when explaining what the text says explicitly and when drawing inferences from the text.

  RI.5.2. Determine two or more main ideas of a text and determine how they are supported by key details; summarize the text.

  RI.5.3. Explain relationships or interactions between two or more individuals, events, ideas, or concepts in a historical, scientific, or technical text based on specific information in the text.

W.5.1. Write opinion pieces on topics or texts, supporting a point of view with reasons and information.

W.5.3. Write narratives to develop real or imagined experiences or events using effective technique, descriptive details, and clear event sequences.

W.5.9. Draw evidence from literary or informational texts to support analysis, reflection, and research.

SL.5.1 Engage effectively in a range of collaborative discussion (one-on-one, in groups, and teacher-led) with diverse partners on grade 5 topics and texts, building on others' ideas and expressing their own clearly.

NCAS

Create, Present, Respond, Connect

Objectives

Fifth Grade students will be able to say:

- I can explain why George Washington Carver was interested in peanuts
- I can use the Scientific Method Format to conduct a growing experiment with lettuce or radishes
- I can discuss soil depletion and the need to return nutrients to the soil

Materials

- Potting soil
- Lettuce or radish seeds (at least 6–8 per student)
- Suitable potting containers (16–18" deep with good drainage)
- Natural light
- Nutrient Testing Kit (optional—available at most garden supply stores)

Instructional Plan

Rationale

Reading a short paragraph about George Washington Carver is not enough to introduce students to this fascinating man, nor is the written word accessible to all students. The oral story creates an "on-ramp" for learning, allowing students of all capabilities to engage in and understand his story. Once we've explored his life together, students are ready to literally dig in—to conduct a growing experiment that helps them see the soil depletion process first-hand.

Following my performance, I set aside at least 20 minutes for a question-and-answer period, during which students demonstrate to their sometimes astonished teachers just how much detail they have retained and understood from the oral text! This is a chance to clear up any misunderstandings, and to review the material as needed. In a quiz-show style, I sometimes pose some questions myself, such as:

- Why did George Washington Carver stay with his owner after he was no longer a slave?
- Why did the freed slaves have trouble earning a living from the land they were working?
- How do peanuts improve the soil?
- Why did Carver have to find ways to use peanuts?
- How did the boll weevil persuade Southern farmers to start planting peanuts?

Preparation

George Washington Carver is a household name—second-graders learn it when they are exploring Famous Americans; it is on thousands of bulletin boards and posters during Black History Month. Countless biographies have been written about him; he is the namesake of elementary, middle and high schools from coast to coast. But who was George Washington Carver?

My goal in telling George Washington Carver's story is to bring the man to life for students so that he is not just a familiar name, but an inspiration. Through the oral telling, they follow his remarkable journey—enslaved, kidnapped, abandoned, and emancipated all before his first birthday. Dr. Carver went on to gain international fame, meeting with presidents and heads of state, and as "creative chemist," devised hundreds of uses for peanuts, soybeans, and sweet potatoes. He also revolutionized the processes of crop rotation and organic farming.

Activity

The teachers take it from there!

Begin by reviewing the life of George Washington Carver and his famous work with peanuts. Why did he get interested in peanuts? What problem was he trying to solve? How did people respond to his suggestion of planting peanuts? What did he do to address their concerns?

Divide the class into groups of three or four students and ask each group to write a skit about the problem George Washington Carver was trying to solve, what he discovered, what he learned, what he proposed, and how people responded. Provide access to print or online sources for students to check their facts (see suggestions in the bibliography below).

Each group should be allowed time to rehearse and perform their skit for the class. By telling and retelling the same story in several ways, students will be helped to understand and retain these concepts.

To help students experience the process of soil nutrient depletion, I recommend teachers follow up with a simple but effective lesson plan based on one developed by Oklahoma Ag in the Classroom, which provides a hands-on experiment using the Scientific Method to observe soil depletion and its impact. OAC has generously granted permission to share it here:

Provide seeds of radishes, lettuce or some other fast-growing plant. Explain that they will be planting and growing these seeds, then harvesting them and re-planting several times *without fertilizing the soil*. Before students plant the seeds in a potting medium, ask them to complete sections I, II and III of the Scientific Method form:

> I. Stating the Problem:
> What do you want to learn or find out?
> II. Forming the Hypothesis:
> What is known about the subject or problem, and what is a prediction for what will happen?
> What makes you predict that?
> III. Experimenting: (Set up procedures)
> This should include: materials used; dates of the experimental study; variables, both dependent and independent (constant and experimental); how and what was done to set up the experiment; what kinds of tests or record-keeping will be done (records, graphs, photos, measurements)?

Discuss what kinds of data will best help them determine whether or not their hypothesis is correct. How can they record their data (graph, chart, photos, etc.)? How often should data be collected?

As the plants grow, students water them, and collect and record data in section IV:

> IV. Observations:
> Includes the records, graphs, data collected during the study.

After completing the Observations for the first set of plants, students pull them up and plant again *without adding fertilizer*. Repeat the process several times over a period of several months, keeping track of plant quality through careful observations and record-keeping.

When the process is complete, discuss the results of the experiment. Were student hypotheses confirmed or negated? What evidence supports this conclusion? What do they explain these results?

Ask students to write Letters to the Editor (persuasive paragraphs) from the perspective of George Washington Carver, explaining the soil depletion process and arguing the need to return nutrients to the soil.

George Washington Carver worked throughout his career to help farmers in the South understand and overcome the difficulties they experienced due to soil depletion and the devastating impact of the boll weevil. His story can be the beginning of discovery and understanding for your students!

Assessment

Skits, Scientific Method Format forms, and Letters to the Editor can be assessed for accuracy and thoroughness.

BIBLIOGRAPHY

- Clopton-Dunson, Karen. *The Wacky Discoveries of George Washington Carver.* CreateSpace Independent Publishing Platform, 2011.
- Driscoll, Laura. *George Washington Carver: The Peanut Wizard.* New York: Grosset & Dunlop, 2003.
- *The National Peanut Board:* George Washington Carver. http://nationalpeanutboard.org/the-facts/george-washington-carver/
- *Oklahoma Ag in the Classroom*: The Peanut Wizard lesson plan. http://agweb.okstate.edu/fourh/aitc/lessons/intermed/pnutwiz.pdf
- *The State Historical Society of Missouri*: Historic Missourians. George Washington Carver. http://shs.umsystem.edu/historicmissourians/name/c/carver/index.html

"Monkey and Buzzard"
Animal Adaptations
FRAN STALLINGS with SHERRY NORFOLK

CCC topics: Patterns, Cause and effect, Energy and matter, Stability and change

POSE topics: Asking questions and developing models, planning and carrying out investigations, Constructing explanations and designing solutions

The Story

"Monkey and Buzzard"
Retold by Fran Stallings

It was summer in Africa, and it was hot. One morning the sun had barely come up, but it was already hot. Rabbit peeked out of her hole. What a hot day it was going to be!

She looked up in the sky and saw a dark speck ... circling ... coming lower ... flap ... flap.... It was Buzzard. Buzzard landed next to Rabbit. "Good morning, sister! How hot you look down here! Don't you know, it's cool and pleasant up in the sky. Wouldn't you like to come with me for a cool ride in the sky?"

Rabbit remembered that her mother used to say buzzards love to eat fresh rabbit for breakfast. But this seemed like such a *nice* buzzard! "Thanks, I'd love to come ride with you!"

Rabbit hopped onto Buzzard's back. Buzzard took off and soon they were high in the sky, enjoying the cool breeze. But after a while Buzzard said, "Rabbit, you're getting heavy. I need to go down for a landing." Buzzard dove almost straight down [*nyaooowww* sound effect) but swooped up at the last moment.

Rabbit had no seatbelt. *Splat!*

Buzzard ate fresh rabbit for breakfast.

It was noon, and the sun overhead made everything hot, hot, hot. Squirrel climbed as high as he could into the branches of a tree, hoping for a cool breeze. He saw a dark speck in the sky … circling … coming lower … flap … flap…. It was Buzzard. Buzzard landed next to Squirrel.

"Good day, brother Squirrel! How hot you look down here! Don't you know, it's cool and pleasant up in the sky. Wouldn't you like to come with me for a cool ride in the sky?"

Squirrel remembered that his mother always said buzzards love to eat fresh squirrel for lunch. But this seemed like such a *nice* buzzard! "Thanks, I'd love to come ride with you!"

Squirrel hopped onto Buzzard's back. Buzzard took off and soon they were high in the sky, enjoying the cool breeze. But after a while Buzzard said, "Squirrel, you're getting heavy. I need to go down for a landing." Buzzard dove almost straight down *nyaooowww* but swooped up at the last moment.

Squirrel had no seatbelt. *Splat!*

Buzzard ate fresh squirrel for lunch.

It was evening. The sun had set, but the day's heat lingered on.

A monkey stepped out of the jungle into the open grassland and began to dance around, arms extended like wings. "Monkey, what are you doing?" asked the other animals.

"I'm doing a buzzard dance," replied Monkey.

"Don't you know, buzzards like to eat fresh monkey for supper?"

"I know. But I have a plan."

They all saw a dark speck in the sky … circling … coming lower … flap … flap…. It was Buzzard. Buzzard landed next to Monkey.

"Nice dance," said Buzzard. "But I'll bet it's making you hot. Wouldn't you like to come with me for a cool ride in the sky?"

Monkey said, "Good idea!" and hopped onto Buzzard's back.

Buzzard took off and soon they were high in the sky, enjoying the cool breeze. After a while Buzzard said, "Monkey, you're getting heavy. I need to go down for a landing."

But Monkey said, "No thanks! I'm enjoying this cool ride!" She wrapped her tail around Buzzard's neck and pulled hard. Buzzard couldn't dive down!

Monkey steered Buzzard all over the sky. They did aerobatic tricks: figure eights, spirals, barrel rolls. The animals down below saw what was happening and laughed at Buzzard. "Look at that! He's got a monkey on his back! He can't control himself!"

Finally Buzzard choked, "Monkey, I'm really getting tired. You're so heavy! I've got to go down."

"Okay," said Monkey, "but go down slow and easy." Monkey steered Buzzard into a gentle landing.

The minute Monkey hopped off his back, Buzzard took off with the other animals laughing at him. He knew word of Monkey's trick would soon reach all the other animals. He could never fool them again! He warned the other buzzards.

So from then on, buzzards no longer tried to get fresh meat. They only ate meat that was safely already dead.

Story Notes:
My telling is based on a story told to me many years ago by the late African American storyteller Ayubu Kamau, over lunch in a Tulsa cafe. He didn't say where he learned it.

In the library I have found Diane Wolkstein's picture book version, *The Cool Ride in the Sky* (Alfred A. Knopf, 1973). She credits and quotes "Straighten Up and Fly Right," a 1943 song written by Nat King Cole and Irving Mills, based on a Black folk tale that Cole's minister father had used as a sermon theme.

The song, and the story as collected by folklorists ("Straighten up and fly right" collected from John Blackamore by Richard M. Dorson in *American Negro Folktales* [Fawcett, 1968] can be found reprinted in *My People: 400 Years of African American Folklore* [Norton, 2003, pp. 26–27] edited by Daryl Cumber Dance), mentions only Monkey and Buzzard. Rabbit and Squirrel may have been Wolkstein's contributions, but her time frames are different from Kamau's and she does not mention the mothers' warnings, which may have been his innovations. He also may have added the description of the speck in the sky, spiraling down (with gestures). Nor does she mention "a monkey on his back" (analogy to obsession or addiction). Kamau may have emphasized this because of his work with juvenile offenders.

Note: In the U.S., we commonly use "buzzard" and "vulture" interchangeably, for instance: "The turkey vulture (Cathartes aura), also known in some North American regions as the turkey buzzard (or just buzzard)...." However, African buzzards are raptors who prey on small rodents, rabbits, snakes—but readily take carrion when it's available, whereas African vultures eat only carrion, and are essential members of nature's clean-up crew (especially getting rid of the remains of diseased animals). In the African setting indicated by the presence of Monkey, perhaps we should say Vulture instead of Buzzard—but Cole's song lyrics clearly say Buzzard. Maybe the African birds got conflated along with the English names when the story came to America.

194 Part Two. Upper Elementary (LIFE SCIENCE)

Auger Buzzard photographed in Nairobi National Park by Lip Kee (Wikimedia Commons).

Standards

NGSS

LS4.C: Adaptations: For any particular environment, some kinds of organisms survive well, some survive less well, and some cannot survive at all.

CCSS for ELA

SL.3.1: Engage effectively in a range of collaborative discussions (one-on-one, in groups, and teacher-led) with diverse partners on *grade 3 topics and texts*, building on others' ideas and expressing their own clearly.

RL.2.2 Recount stories, including fables and folktales from diverse cultures, and determine their central message, lesson, or moral.

RL.2.3 Describe how characters in a story respond to major events and challenges.

RI.3.7 Use information gained from illustrations (e.g., maps, photographs) and the words in a text to demonstrate understanding of the text.

NCAS

Presenting, Responding

Objectives

Third Grade students will be able to say

- I can listen to and retell a story.
- I can define physical and behavioral adaptations and list two examples of each.
- I can describe how animals use adaptations, instincts, and learned behaviors to get food, find shelter, and provide protection;
- I can explain how natural and human influences on a habitat can impact an organism's ability to use adaptations to survive.
- I can participate in creating a story that demonstrates specific animal adaptations and the impact of natural and human influences on a habitat.

A Story About Something That Happened as I Told a Story—A Folktale Science Story

I had quite a morning working with my teacher friend's third graders! I was telling my version of "Cool Ride in the Sky" as a speaking and listening activity. For me the idea is to tell a stealth ecotale. After my telling, we outlined it orally, and the teacher divided the students into groups of three to practice retelling. Student A = Rabbit in the morning, Student B = Squirrel at noon, Student C = Monkey in the evening; then shift parts and repeat. The third graders did well with it.

Of course, we discussed buzzard's essential role in the ecosystem. "Circle of life!" was one student's spontaneous response to my mention that of course buzzards eat dead stuff now.

Their teacher said they had studied food webs months ago. We're pleased that they remember! In your classroom, this story could be used to *introduce* the subject of food webs and natural hygiene. Yech, why would any critter eat dead/rotten food—really? Worldwide, there are many other folktales that "explain" this diet.

Afterwards some of the students were already thinking about story variations they could create, using different animals in other habitats. Perhaps instead of Monkey, who used her tail to throttle Buzzard, they could substitute a big snake.

We also discussed the applications of "He's got a monkey on his back" to bad habits and addictions. Students commented that they know better than to go along with a suspicious stranger who seems to be acting "nice."

The most striking thing about the morning was an extra student in the classroom sitting solo at a table by teacher's desk, an in-school suspension. He looked young, maybe a 2nd grader. She explained he had been exiled from his own class because he had been terrifying them with detailed descriptions of his plans to shoot all his family members in their sleep.

He listened well like the third graders, and when it was time for our retelling exercise in groups of three, she didn't pair him with her own students but fetched one of his classmates from down the hall: a girl she knew to be not only smart but also good in people skills. This girl sat opposite the boy while he was given the responsibility to retell the entire story to her—solo. The boy stood calmly and told the story with poise and with the details of description and dialogue. He was still going while many of the third grade triads were in their second round! I didn't eavesdrop, but judging by behavior he did not belabor the gore in the story. The girl praised him, "That's a great story! I've got to tell it to someone!" and gave him a thumbs-up.

I had some qualms about telling such a gory story to third graders, but these Oklahoma kids are familiar with buzzards eating road kill, and perhaps a sweeter story might not have held the attention of the exiled student.

Materials

- Picture of a buzzard
- Picture of a monkey
- Print or online resources about the plants and animals of a variety of habitats

Instructional Plan

Rationale

Stories put otherwise theoretical, abstract concepts such as animal adaptations into graspable, accessible context—thus my reference to a "stealth ecotale." "Monkey and Buzzard" engages students in thinking about the adaptations of Buzzard and the other animals, and demonstrates some of the ways that changes in the environment impact survival. Similarly, children demonstrate understanding of these concepts when they write a fictional story that accurately incorporates these concepts.

Preparation

After students have heard and learned to retell the story as discussed above, introduce the concept of *adaptations*:

- An *adaptation* is a characteristic that makes a plant or animal more suited to its environment, improving its chance for survival. Most living things have a variety of adaptations. These are classified as either behavioral or physical adaptations.
- *Behavioral adaptations* include what an animal does and how it behaves in order to survive in a specific environment. Examples of behavioral adaptations include migration, hibernation, gathering and storing food, defense behaviors, and rearing young.
- *Instinctive behavior* is an unlearned, inborn tendency to behave in a way that is characteristic of a species, such as migration.
- *Learned behavior* is gained through observation, experience, or instruction, such as stalking prey.
- *Physical adaptations* are the body structures or forms that a plant or animal has that help it survive in a specific environment. These include body coverings, colors and patterns for mimicry or camouflage, and specific physical characteristics of body parts.

Ask students to look around the classroom—what human adaptations were required to make the classroom comfortable, to eat, to write, etc.? Analyze and demonstrate the value of human physical adaptations, such as feet, eyes, opposable thumbs, and brain. Discuss and list human physical, behavioral adaptations, and learned and instinctive behaviors.

Activity

Display a picture of a buzzard. Ask students to identify the physical adaptations that help buzzard survive and to scavenge successfully. Then think about the story—what behavioral adaptations were mentioned or implied? Were these learned or instinctive behaviors? (In the story, the behavior was learned—but is the story fiction or non-fiction?)

Now look at a picture of a monkey. What physical adaptation did Monkey use in the story? What prevented Squirrel and Rabbit from surviving in the same way?

Discuss *interdependence*: all forms of life are dependent upon nonliving components of the environment, such as water, oxygen, nutrients, space, and sunlight. The living and nonliving components of an ecosystem interact and are interdependent. Human practices and natural occurrences can influence both living and non-living components of an ecosystem. Pollution, litter, waste, as well as fires, floods, and erosion can drastically alter an ecosystem. Such changes can impact the ability of organisms to use their adaptations and threaten their survival. If any one component is damaged or lost, it can have far-reaching effects on the other living things in that web of life.

If pollution, pesticides, global warming, climate change, fire, flood, litter, or depletion of resources change a habitat, how could plants or animals survive? What negative impacts were threatening Buzzard and the other animals in this story? What was the threat? Were these natural or manmade threats? What human behaviors could impact buzzards' habitat?

Now move the story to a different habitat! In the new story, Buzzard will still be the main character, and he'll still be killing other animals in order to survive—but you'll develop a different way that the habitat is changed, and choose animals in the new environment that will try to use their physical and behavioral adaptations to survive.

To develop the new story, work with the class to answer the following questions. The *process* is the most important part of this activity, so allow plenty of time for the group to brainstorm, deliberate, and make decisions.

- What is the habitat?
- What is the nonliving component of the environment that is altered (water, oxygen, nutrients, space, and sunlight)?
- How is it altered (by humans [pollution, pesticides, global warming, climate change, fire, flood, litter, or depletion of resources] or by natural occurrences [fires, floods, and erosion])?
- What animals are being impacted and how?
- What are the first two animals that Buzzard encounters?
- What happens to these animals?
- What is the third animal?
- What physical or behavioral adaptation does the third character use in order to survive?

During the development of the new story, students will need to apply their understanding of animal adaptations and of interdependence. Students can then work within their groups of three to generate their own stories, which can be performed for the whole class.

Assessment

Formative assessment occurs in observation of students' contributions to discussion and the development of the story; the stories demonstrate the level of student understanding.

"Sausage Nose"
Food Spoilage and Preservation
GEORDAN STENSON *with* CY ASHLEY WEBB

CCC topics: Patterns, Cause and effect
POSE topics: Asking questions and developing models; Planning and carrying out investigations; Analyzing and interpreting data; Obtaining, evaluating, and communicating information

The Story

"Sausage Nose"
a folktale from Sweden

There was once an old woman, who was all alone one evening in her cottage, occupied with her household affairs. While she was waiting for her husband, who was away at work in the forest, and while she was bustling about, a fine, grand lady came in. The old woman began to curtsy and curtsy, for she had never seen such a grand person before.

"I should be so much obliged if you would lend me your brewing pan," said the lady, "for my daughter is going to be married, and I expect guests from all parts."

Oh, dear, yes! That she might have, said the woman, although she could not remember whether she had ever seen her before, and so she went to fetch the pan.

The lady took it, and thanked the woman, saying that she would pay her well for the loan of it, and so she went her way.

Two days afterwards the lady came back with it, and this time she also found the woman alone.

"Many thanks for the loan," said the lady. "and now in return you shall have three wishes."

And with this the lady left, and vanished so quickly that the old woman had not even time to ask her name or where she lived. But that did not matter, she thought, for now she had three wishes, and she began to think what she should wish for. She expected her husband back soon, and she thought it would be best to wait until he came home and could have a say in the matter. But the least they could wish for must be a fine big farm—the best in the parish, and a box full of money, and just fancy how happy and comfortable they would be then, for they had worked so hard all their days! Ah, yes, then the neighbors would have something to wonder at, for you may guess how they would stare at all the fine things she would have.

But since they were now so rich it was really a shame that there should be nothing but some blue, sour milk and some hard crusts of bread in the cupboard for her husband when he came home tired and weary, he who was fond of hot food. She had just been to her neighbor's and there she had seen a fine big sausage, which they were going to have for supper.

"Ah, deary me, I wish I had that sausage here!" sighed the old woman; and the next moment a big sausage lay on the table right before her.

She was just going to put it in the pan when her husband came in.

"Father, father!" cried the woman, "it's all over with our troubles and hard work now. I lent my brewing pan to a fine lady, and when she brought it back she promised we should have three wishes. And now you must help me to wish for something really good, for you're so clever at hitting upon the right thing—and it's all true, for just look at the sausage, which I got the moment I wished for it!"

"What do you mean, you silly old woman?" shouted the husband, who became angry. "Have you been wishing for such a paltry thing as a sausage, when you might have had anything you liked in the world? I wish the sausage were sticking to your nose, since you haven't any better sense."

All at once the woman gave a cry, for sure enough there was the sausage sticking to her nose; and she began tearing and pulling away at it, but the more she pulled the firmer it seemed to stick. She was not able to get it off.

"Oh, dear! oh, dear!" sobbed the woman. "You don't seem to have any more sense than I, since you can wish me such ill luck. I only wanted something nice for you, and then—, oh dear! oh, dear!" and the old woman went on crying and sobbing.

The husband tried, of course, to help his wife to get rid of the sausage; but for all he pulled and tugged away at it he did not succeed, and he was nearly pulling his wife's head off her body.

But they had one wish left, and what were they now to wish?

Yes, what were they to wish? They might, of course, wish for something very fine and grand; but what could they do with all the finery in the world, as long as the mistress of the house had a long sausage sticking to the end of her nose? She would never be able to show herself anywhere!

"You wish for something," said the woman in the midst of her crying.

"No, you wish," said the husband, who also began crying when he saw the state his wife was in, and saw the terrible sausage hanging down her face.

So he thought he would make the best use he could of the last wish, and said, "I wish my wife was rid of that sausage."

And the next moment it was gone! They both became so glad that they jumped up and danced around the room in great glee—for you must know that although a sausage may be ever so nice when you have it in your mouth, it is quite a different thing to have one sticking to your nose all your life.

SOURCES

Djurklou, Gabriel. *Fairy Tales from the Swedish*. Translated by H. L. Brækstad (Philadelphia and New York: J. B. Lippincott, 1901), pp. 27–32.

Yolen, Jane, ed. *Favorite Folktales from Around the World*. New York: Pantheon, 1986, pp. 185–187.

Standards

NGSS

LS1.B: Growth and Development of Organisms: Reproduction is essential to the continued existence of every kind of organism. Plants and animals have unique life cycles.

LS2.C: Ecosystems Dynamics, Functioning and Resilience: When the environment changes in ways that affect a place's physical characteristics. temperature. or availability of resources, some organisms survive and reproduce, others move to new locations, yet others move to the transformed environment, and some die.

LS4.C: Adaptation: For any particular environment, some kinds of organisms survive well, some survive less well, and some cannot survive at all.

CCSS

RI.3.7: Use information gained from illustrations (e.g., maps, photographs) and the words in a text to demonstrate understanding of the text (e.g., where, when, why, and how key events occur).

SL.3.5: Create engaging audio recordings of stories or poems that demonstrate fluid reading at an understandable pace; add visual displays when appropriate to emphasize or enhance certain facts or details.

Objectives

Third to Fifth Grade students will be able to say

- I can experience and think about the relationship between story and science
- I can follow the scientific method in a long term experiment

(Note that more complicated long-term studies can be accomplished by older students)

Materials

- 26 slices organic bread
- Plastic sandwich bags
- Toaster
- Knife
- Sharpie marker
- Tablespoon
- Salt
- Lemon Juice
- Notebook
- Magnifying glass

Instructional Plan

Rationale

Preserving has always been a way for people to keep foods from spoiling. And sausage-making is one sort of preserving. The constant advance of bacteria, forever multiplying, eats our food before we can. The fresh stuff seems to go so fast and the stages of deterioration always move forward. Straight from healthy soil, a carrot can never taste more carroty. An egg has a more orange hue and deeper flavored yolk, the younger it is, turning yellow as time passes. A pig's meat, a few days from slaughter, will have its cleanest flavor and deepest red muscle color. Also, when ground into a sausage, arguably the best taste. Over time, people have developed many ways of trying to save our food before the bacterial encroachment becomes too great for healthy eating. Salting, pickling, smoking and refrigeration are all ways of limiting bacterial growth so the food and nutrients can last longer than the food could alone.

People have kept their food supply safe by limiting the favorable environment for bacteria to grow. Bacteria, like all living things, need a few things to multiply. First, they need a food source, namely the food that people want to preserve. Second, they need water; water helps the transfer of food and nutrients on the cellular level which transfers the food to the bacteria. Third, they need the proper temperature. Normally, bacteria need a temperature between 68° F and 80° F for the best possible growth. At 45° their growth rate slows and at 140° most bacteria start breaking down and decomposing. By keeping foods below 40°F or above 145°F, bacterial growth is controlled. Lastly, bacteria need a balanced pH level—or an environment that doesn't have too much acid or too much alkaline. On the pH scale, which goes from 1 to 14, any number below 7 is considered an acid. If the number is higher than 7 it is an alkaline. Bacteria can grow and reproduce anywhere between 4.5 and 10 on the pH scale. All these criteria need to be balanced for the bacteria to breed and, in turn, spoil the food.

Meat is especially important to preserve. The protein meat provides to people is vital, especially during the winter months when protein containing plants like legumes and nuts cannot grow. In the time when "Sausage Nose" was created, the amount of labor and the cost of raising meat, prior to refrigeration and subsidized grain, was something a farmer would not want to waste. So making sure the pork, beef, chicken or fish could last as long as possible was paramount. Temperature couldn't be controlled that well. People were subject to the seasons and the daily amount of sunshine. There were storage cellars but even these had limits. People instead curtailed the bacterial environment with salt to dry out the water in the meat and acids in the form of an acidic plant or fruit (lemons, wine, juniper, laurels/bay leaf, to name a few) to make it more acidic. Sausage helped in that regard greatly. By grinding the meat, one can put salt and acid not just on the outside of the meat, but on the inside as well. Then by smoking the meat, thus burning off some of the bacteria, and hanging it in a dry place for longer storage, one can dry out the sausage even more, keeping the meat even longer.

"Sausage Nose," a Swedish folktale, comes from an environment where long winters demanded long preservation times for food so people could eat while waiting for spring. By asking for a "fresh, fat sausage," the woman in the story is probably near the end of winter and wanting a fresh *ground* sausage. The sausages then would have a softer texture as opposed to the firmer ones she had recently been eating—something closer to a hard salami, due to the drying out of the past few months. She's wishing for what she would've eaten closer to autumn and closer to the harvest when the animals are slaughtered.

For elementary students, preservation without refrigeration might come as a complete surprise. If there is not a package date on the side, they might not know how to identify what is safe and healthy to eat and what is not. The following experiment highlights other ways people have preserved food by limiting the bacterial environment, and also what spoiled food looks like.

Activity from Cy Ashley Webb
"Comparing Spices, Salt and Dehydration in Food Preservation"

Research questions:

- Why does salting work to preserve food?
- Why does dehydrating food work to preserve food?
- Which works better—dehydration, salting or acid?
- What other preserving methods might be useful?

Be sure to follow directions to correctly set up the experiment!

Place 12 slices of bread in separate sandwich bags. Seal the bags.

Toast the other 12 slices to dryness. This may take ten minutes on medium heat in a toaster oven. Be careful to dry the bread and not to burn it. Place each toasted piece in a separate bag.

Keep two of the fresh slices and two of the toasted slices aside. Label them "fresh control" and "smoked control."

Take 6 of the fresh slices and 6 of the toasted slices and cut them into small pieces with a knife. Put these into separate bags.

There are now six remaining bags of fresh, untoasted, uncut bread.

(a) Open two of these bags and sprinkle one tablespoon of salt over one side of the bread. Label these "Salt/Fresh."

(b) Open another two of these bags and pour one tablespoon of lemon juice over the surface of the bread. Label these "Lemon/Fresh."

(c) Open the remaining two bags and sprinkle one tablespoon of salt and one tablespoon of lemon juice on each side. Label these "Salt & Lemon/Fresh."

With the six remaining bags of toasted bread, treat them as with the fresh bags, and label them "smoked" rather than "fresh," e.g., Salt/Smoked, Lemon/Smoked, Salt & Lemon/Smoked.

With the cut slices of fresh bread, open two of these bags and sprinkle one tablespoon of salt over one side of the bread. Label these "Salt/Fresh/Cut." Open another two of these bags and pour one tablespoon of lemon juice over the surface of the bread. Label these "Lemon/Fresh/Cut." Open the remaining two bags and sprinkle one tablespoon of salt and one tablespoon of lemon juice on each side. Label these "Salt & Lemon/Fresh/Cut."

With the six remaining bags of cut, toasted bread, treat them as with the fresh cut bags, albeit label them "smoked" and not "fresh."

Examine your bags with your magnifying lens every day for six weeks. Record in words and pictures in the note book the progress and what types of spoilage occurs. Determine which bag became contaminated first and whether the contamination grew at the same rate in each bag. Determine which treatment provided the most protection from spoilage.

Incorporate the story into your log by explaining the relationship of the story and the observation. Tell the story.

BIBLIOGRAPHY

Ruhlman, Michael, and Brian Polcyn. *Chaucuterie, the craft of salting smoking and curing*. New York: W.W. Norton, 2005.

Webb, Cy Ashley. "Comparing Spices, Salt and Dehydration in Food Preservation." www.education.com/science-fair/article/food-preservation/ Jan 2015.

Nimrod and His Animal Teeth
Exploring Physical Structures, Functions, Life Cycles and Connections

Ingrid Nixon

CCC topics: Cause and effect
POSE topics: Asking questions and defining problems; Constructing explanations and designing solutions

The Story

"Nimrod"
by Ingrid Nixon

This is a tale about a very inventive man who lived up near Eagle, Alaska, on the Yukon River. His name was Erwin A. Robertson, but everyone knew him as "Nimrod." He had been a jeweler before coming north in 1896 for the Klondike Gold Rush. He eventually traveled down the Yukon River to Eagle, Alaska. He staked a claim on Flume Creek, a tributary of the Seventymile River. He loved to hunt and trap. He loved making and inventing things. Perhaps his greatest invention—the one that made him famous—came about after he got scurvy and all his teeth fell out.

Nimrod needed some dentures and to get those, he needed to see a dentist. But it had been years since he had seen a dentist traveling through Interior Alaska.

One day he got the idea that he should make some dentures out of animal teeth. He used Dall sheep teeth for the front teeth, caribou teeth for premolars and bear teeth for molars. He used his training as a jeweler to melt down an aluminum pot and make two metal plates that fit his gums. Then, he carefully placed the teeth in the plates for the top and the bottom so they would work together. They were a sight to behold. But the important thing is that they worked. He could chew again!

He seemed to enjoy seeing the look on people's faces the first time they saw him eat with his animal dentures. You might say he was the first and only man to eat a bear with the bear's own teeth!

Standards

NGSS

LS2.D: Social Interactions and Group Behavior: Being part of a group helps animals obtain food, defend themselves, and cope with changes. Groups may serve different functions and vary dramatically in size. (3-LS2-1)

LS4.C: Adaptation: For any particular environment, some kinds of organisms survive well, some survive less well, and some cannot survive at all. (3-LS4-3)

LS4.D: Biodiversity and Humans: Populations live in a variety of habitats, and change in those habitats affects the organisms living there. (3-LS4-4)

CCSS for ELA

SL.3.1 Engage effectively in a range of collaborative discussions (one-on-one, in groups, and teacher-led) with diverse partners on *grade 3 topics and texts*, building on others' ideas and expressing their own clearly.

SL.3.1.B Follow agreed-upon rules for discussions (e.g., gaining the floor in respectful ways, listening to others with care, speaking one at a time about topics and texts under discussion).

SL.3.1.C Ask questions to check understanding of information presented, stay on topic, and link their comments to the remarks of others.

SL.3.1.D Explain their own ideas and understanding in light of the discussion.

SL.3.6 Speak in complete sentences when appropriate to task and situation in order to provide requested detail or clarification.

Objectives

Third Grade students will be able to say:

- I can explain how teeth structures serve different purposes in our mouths.

- I can explain how the teeth of different animals influence what they can eat.
- I can the basic elements of a food web: plants, animals and connections between them all.

Materials

- Story of Erwin A. "Nimrod" Robertson.
- Whiteboard or flipchart.
- Markers.
- Skull stations labeled #1, #2 and #3 featuring the skulls of a bear (omnivore); wolf (carnivore); Dall sheep, caribou or moose (herbivore).
- Measuring tape to go with each skull.
- Copy of student worksheet for each student.
- Sharpened pencil for each student.
- Selection of photos of Alaskan animals, with a short list of what each one eats, such as:
  - Bear: other animals, sedges, grasses, flowers, berries
  - Wolf: caribou, moose, fish, ground squirrels, fish
  - Lynx: a variety of small animals (hares, birds, rodents)
  - Caribou: grasses, sedges, willow, mushrooms, lichens
  - Dall sheep: grasses, flowers, sedges
  - Moose: willow, aspen, tree bark
  - Golden Eagle: a variety of small animals like ground squirrels, hares and ptarmigan
  - Wolverine: a variety of meat, including carrion
  - Marmot: grasses, sedges and flowers
  - Ground Squirrel: grasses, sedges, flowers, bird eggs
  - Red Squirrel: spruce seeds, bird eggs, small birds and hares
  - Short-tailed Weasel: small rodents and shrews, small birds, insects, and fish
  - Mountain Goat: grasses, flowering plants and shrubs
  - Ptarmigan: willow buds and twigs, birch, berries, seeds
  - Snowshoe Hare: green vegetation and willow bark

Create a worksheet to record information at each skull station. Sample:

Skull Station #1: This is the skull of a _____.

It is _____ inches long, _____ inches wide and _____ inches tall.

There are _____ total teeth on the top jaw.

There are _____ total teeth on the bottom jaw.

Number of incisors: _____ Number of canines: _____

Number of premolars: _____ Number of molars: _____

Instructional Plan

Rationale

In our modern world, the majority of people live in urban areas, buy most (if not all) of their food from supermarkets, and get what they need from stores (or by just going to the dentist). Students should be encouraged to think about our connection to the natural world by exploring how one man made dentures out of animal teeth in order to help with his own survival. Through these activities, students will discover how plants, animals (including humans) rely on one another. Students will also glean insights into how clever and creative humans can be when we really need something that is not within easy reach.

Preparation

In this lesson, students will use the story of a man who made dentures out of animal teeth to launch exploration of Alaska animals' physical characteristics and traits. Through discussion and small work groups, students will complete a worksheet and create a simple food web as they explore and develop an understanding of the physical structures, functions, life cycles and connections between Alaska's wildlife species.

The lesson begins with the storyteller or teacher sharing the story of Erwin A. "Nimrod" Robertson who made a set of dentures out of animal teeth.

DISCUSSION

What might that feel like to put animal teeth in your mouth? Expect: "Oo-oo-oo, yuck!"

Let's review Nimrod's dentures: According to the story, what animals did he get his teeth from?

Answers:
- Dall sheep
- Caribou
- Bear

According to the story, where did each kind of teeth go?

Answers:
- Dall sheep—front
- Caribou—sides
- Bear—back

Teeth are tools used to get the job done. What's the job? Eating!

INTRODUCTION TO HERBIVORES, CARNIVORES AND OMNIVORES

Let's take a minute here to figure out just what animals eat: What DO animals eat?

- List what students say, grouping their answers so plants (e.g., flowers, berries, grasses, willow) are on one side and meat products (e.g., birds, fish, squirrels, caribou) are on the other side.
- Introduce the words *herbivore, carnivore* and *omnivore*.
- Create Venn diagram and label herbivores, carnivores and omnivores.
- As humans, what are we?

If teeth are tools, then should animals that eat different things have different kinds of teeth?

- Turns out they do!

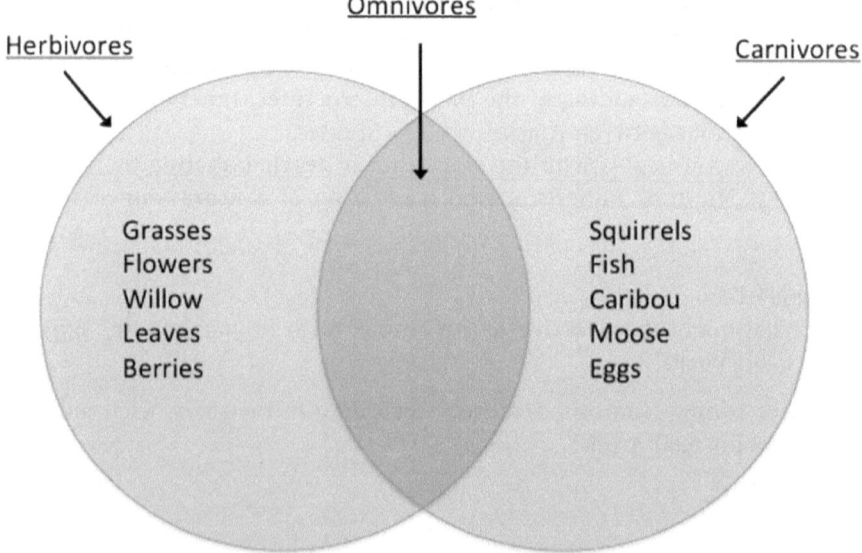

Kinds of eaters.

Getting Back to the Story

To make his dentures, Nimrod used the teeth from what three animals?
- Dall sheep
- Caribou
- Bear

Dall Sheep Teeth/Incisors

Does anyone know what a Dall sheep eats?
- Students will likely say plants.
- So is a Dall sheep a carnivore, herbivore or omnivore?

Nimrod put the Dall sheep teeth in front to function as teeth we call incisors.
- They are for snipping things off.
- Why do you suppose that it might be helpful for a Dall sheep to have incisors?
- Students will answer some variation of "grazing."

Caribou Teeth/Pre-Molars (Also Called Bicuspids)

Does anyone know what a caribou eats?
- Kids will likely say plants.
- So is a caribou a carnivore, herbivore or omnivore?

Nimrod put the caribou teeth on the sides to function as pre-molars.
- They assist the molars in grinding up food.
- Why do you suppose that it might be helpful for a caribou to have premolars?

Bear Teeth/Molars

Does anyone know what a bear eats?
- Kids will likely say plants.
- Kids will likely say fish, caribou calves, moose calves, ground squirrels, etc.
- So is a bear a carnivore, herbivore or omnivore?

Nimrod put the bear teeth in the back part of his mouth to serve as molars.
- Molars grind up food.
- Why do you suppose that it might be helpful for a bear to have molars?

Wolf teeth/Canines: One type of tooth Nimrod did not use is a sharp tooth called a "canine," nor did he use any teeth from a wolf.

Does anyone know what a wolf eats?

- Students will likely say fish, caribou, moose, squirrels, etc.
- So is a wolf a carnivore, herbivore or omnivore?
- We do have pointed teeth called canine teeth. In wolves they are longer and sharper. What do you suppose canine teeth do? (Canine means "dog.")

Activity

EXPLORING TEETH WITH ANIMAL SKULLS

If teeth are tools that animals use to eat, should we expect all animal teeth to look alike?

- Have labeled skulls placed at three different locations around the classroom.
- Make sure there is room for kids to move around to view the skull from all angles.

Instructions:

- Divide students into groups of three.
- Each student gets a sharpened pencil and a student worksheet.
- Each student group is to go to their skull station and answer the questions on the student activity sheet.
- Monitor progress at each table and have groups switch when they have answered the questions.

When groups are done, bring everyone back together. Ask probing questions, such as:

- Did you notice the differences between the skulls?
- Did you find canine teeth on the moose/caribou/Dall sheep skull?
- Did any of the jaws have just one kind of teeth?

MAKING A SIMPLE FOOD WEB

We've been talking about Nimrod's teeth and how he used the teeth of Dall sheep, caribou and bear to make his dentures.

Why do you suppose he didn't use the teeth of a snowshoe hare? ("Too small!")

Why do you suppose he didn't use the molars of a moose? ("Too big!")

Right! Still, a moose has molars and so does a hare. What do molars do? ("Grind!")

- Animals may be very different sizes, but you may see similarities in their teeth and their function.

- It's not a perfect match, but herbivores will typically have incisors for snipping off plants and molars for grinding them up.
- Omnivores will have teeth that allow them to accomplish everything.
- Carnivores will have teeth that are good for ripping.

Let's take a look at Alaska's animals to see who is a herbivore, carnivore and omnivore:

Follow these steps: (be ready with the tape dispenser to give each student a piece)

　　1. Distribute the animal pictures with the information of what each animal eats to the class.

　　2. Have each student introduce his or her animal, read what the animal eats and suggest the appropriate category the animal fits into. Make sure the class agrees. Some animals may generate discussions.

　　3. After each brief discussion, have the student come up and tape his/her animal under the right heading.

- When birds are put on the board, ask if they have teeth? No, but we are using them here to show they are part of the ecosystem. (An extension of this lesson would be to examine types of bird beaks by comparing them to common tools such as a wrench, pliers, et al, and determining what the bird eats.)
- Definition of ecosystem: A community of living things (such as plants, animals and people) together with their environment (like water, soil, climate) functioning as a unit.

Once all the animals have been distributed, spend a little time brainstorming plants that animals may like to eat. Students may come up with the following:

- Berries
- Flowers
- Grasses
- Willow
- Bushes

Draw lines between plants, animals that may eat them and animals that may eat those animals. This creates a simple food web. Points to make:

- Animals and plants live together in communities called ecosystems.
- In order for one animal like a wolf to live in an area, the animals it feeds upon need to be present, too.
- Humans are part of the ecosystem.
- Everything is connected.

Assessment

Students will demonstrate sorting Alaskan animals using physical characteristics and behaviors, and be able to describe how characteristics (teeth) have helped them survive as a species.

Through discussion and observation, students will compare external features of animals (teeth) that may help them grow, survive, and reproduce.

Students will be able to describe links in a simple food chain.

BIBLIOGRAPHY

Alaska animal info: www.adfg.alaska.gov/index.cfm?adfg=educators.notebookseries
"Out in Alaska in 1905, he made his own dentures." *Bushcraft U.S.A.*, 03 Mar. 2010. n.p. Web. 7 Jan. 2015.
Scott, Elva R. *Jewel on the Yukon Eagle City.* Eagle: Eagle Historical Society and Museums, 1997.
Skulls and animal parts suppliers: For real and artificial materials, check with the Interpretation/Education division of nearby national and state parks, and local museums.

EARTH AND SPACE

"The Wave"
Tsunamis

ANNE SHIMOJIMA *and* SHERI LUCTERHAND

CCC topics: Patterns, Cause and effect, Energy and matter, Stability and change
POSE topics: Asking questions and defining problems, Constructing explanations and designing solutions, Obtaining, evaluating and communicating information

Synopsis

In ancient Japan, an old man, the beloved headman of a village, views the ocean from his veranda high up on the mountain. It is earthquake weather. When the quake comes, it seems odd—a shaking deep in the earth that stills. Then he sees the water in the ocean move away from the land. The people are gathering at the shore in wonder, but the old man remembers that this means great danger is coming. He has no time to run down the mountain to warn the people, so he chooses to burn his own rice fields to get their attention. The people see the smoke and flames and run up the mountain to help him, but he points to the ocean and they turn and witness the great waves destroy the village where they had been standing. He has sacrificed his wealth to save the people.

In the final line of the story, after the villagers have witnessed the destruction of the great wave and realized the old man's sacrifice, he tells them to come, and he leads the way. The old man is the moral center of the village and the story. He continues to lead the way through the disaster, to hope and to the future. He shows us an example of generosity and optimism in the face of tragedy, an example that lifts us all.

Standards

NGSS—Earth and Space Science—earthquake and tsunami

ESS2.B: Plate Tectonics and Large-Scale System Interactions

The locations of mountain ranges, deep ocean trenches, ocean floor structures, earthquakes, and volcanoes occur in patterns. Most earthquakes and volcanoes occur in bands that are often along the boundaries between continents and oceans. Major mountain chains form inside continents or near their edges. Maps can help locate the different land and water features areas of Earth.

4-PS4-1 Waves: Waves and Information

Develop a model of waves to describe patterns in terms of amplitude and wavelength and that waves can cause objects to move.

PS4.A: Wave Properties

Waves, which are regular patterns of motion, can be made in water by disturbing the surface. When waves move across the surface of deep water, the water goes up and down in place; there is no net motion in the direction of the wave except when the water meets a beach.

Waves of the same type can differ in amplitude (height of the wave) and wavelength (spacing between wave peaks).

CCSS—Speaking, Listening, Language

CCSS.ELA-Literacy.SL.4.1.c: Pose and respond to specific questions to clarify or follow up on information, and make comments that contribute to the discussion and link to the remarks of others.

CCSS.ELA-Literacy.SL.4.1.d: Review the key ideas expressed and explain their own ideas and understanding in light of the discussion.

Fine Arts Anchor Standards:

VISUAL ARTS—Creating: Generate and conceptualize artistic ideas and work.

VISUAL ARTS—Presenting: Organize and develop artistic ideas and work.

VISUAL ARTS—Responding: Refine and complete artistic work.

VISUAL ARTS—Connecting: Select, analyze, and interpret artistic work for presentation.

Objectives

Fourth Grade students will be able to say:

- I can demonstrate understanding of the consequences and damage created by the earthquake, tsunami, and release of radioactive contaminants in Fukushima, Japan in 2011.
- I can listen attentively to a story and make connections with the tsunami in Fukushima, Japan in 2011.
- I can explain what a collage is and how to create one.
- I can create a collage with various papers to illustrate the theme and feeling of the story.

Materials

- Tagboard, cut 9" × 12"
- Colored drawing pencils
- Gluesticks
- Scissors
- Assorted construction paper
- Assorted vellum matte finish transparent colored paper
- Assorted colored paper, thinner than construction but thicker than origami paper

Instructional Plan

Rationale

During the fourth grade's study of earthquakes and tsunamis, Anne (the library media specialist) and Sheri (the art teacher) collaborated on an activity to expand the student learning with storytelling and art. The 2011 Fukushima, Japan, earthquake, tsunami, and nuclear disaster have made this unit much more impactful as students can witness through photographs, videos, and news accounts the devastation brought about by such natural disasters. The Japanese legend, "The Wave," collected by Lafcadio Hearn in the late 1800s, describes a tsunami and an old man's sacrifice that saved the people of his village. We used storytelling to open the students' hearts and minds to the emotional truths of the story and the art project to give them a way to express their understanding of what the story's theme meant to them.

Preparation

Assemble art materials for easy student access. Remind students that paper can be torn as well as cut.

218   Part Two. Upper Elementary (Earth and Space)

Activity

1. As students study earthquakes and tsunamis in their earth science unit on how processes shape the earth, show photographs, videos, and news accounts of the Fukushima, Japan natural disaster of 2011. Have the students discuss the effects of the tsunami on the people.

2. Show students a copy of Japanese artist Hokusai's woodblock print "The Great Wave off Kanagawa" and tell them about the series, "Thirty-Six Views of Mount Fuji (1826–1833). Describe how a woodblock print is made. Mention that Claude Monet was influenced by Hokusai.

3. Explain that they will hear the Japanese legend "The Wave" and create a collage to illustrate the story.

4. Tell the story "The Wave."

5. Review the plot of the story and discuss the main character and theme of the story. Have the students discuss the relationship of the old man and the villagers before the tsunami. What characters change and how? What was the most powerful moment of the story for you? What do you think the most important idea of the story is? What will happen after the story ends?

6. Give the students a moment to close their eyes and try to remember images from the story. Have the students describe in detail what they saw. What did the village look like before and after the tsunami hit? What did they see the old man do?

7. Model the creation of a collage: How to tear the paper, how to use the glue sticks, how to use transparent papers. The construction paper is for the background, the transparent paper is for the water and waves, and the solid thin paper is for other details such as the village or the people.

8. Discuss the use of cool colors versus warm colors and the feeling each conveys.

9. The students choose their own colored solid and transparent papers and create their own collages to illustrate the story.

Assessment

Students show proper listening behavior during the story.

Students participate in a discussion of the Fukushima disaster and aftermath.

Students participate in a discussion of the story's plot, characters, and theme.

Students create a collage, organizing and using appropriate materials.

Students fill out a self-evaluation sheet on which they elaborate:

What was the main theme of the story?
How does your collage express the theme of the story?
Why did you choose the colors and papers that you did?

BIBLIOGRAPHY

Hearn, Lafcadio. *Gleanings in Buddha-Fields; Studies of Hand and Soul in the Far East.* Houghton Mifflin, 1897, pp. 16–26. http:// http://sacred-texts.com/bud/gbf/gbf02.htm
Hodges, Margaret. *The Wave.* Boston: Houghton Mifflin, 1964.
Kajikawa, Kimiko. *Tsunami!* New York: Philomel Books, 2009.

"The Making of Whirlwind"
The Cyclone Applied to a Dyson Vacuum Cleaner

Jane Stenson

CCC topics: Cause and effect, Systems and systems energy, Energy and matter, Structure and function, Stability and change

POSE topics: Asking questions (for science) and defining problems (for engineering), Developing and using models, Planning and carrying out investigations, Constructing explanations (for science) and designing solutions (for engineering)

The Story

"The Making of Whirlwind"
(Kiowa)
From *Earthmaker's Tales* by Gretchen Mayo

Hot summer lay upon the people like a heavy moist blanket. Not a leaf moved. No whisper of a breeze lifted a strand of hair. The people gathered around an old medicine man. "Tell us what we can do. There is hardly a breath in this hot, stuffy air," they said.

The old man sent some women to the river bank to gather red mud. When they returned, he told the people to watch carefully. Then he shaped the mud into the form of an animal. It looked something like a horse with four legs and a tail.

"Watch me, and do what I do." said the old man to the people who were gathered around. Then the old man blew into the nostrils of the horse and the horse began to grow.

"Blow hard!" the old man commanded. They blew at the horse as hard as they could and it grew larger still until four people were needed to hold it, then twelve, then twenty. As they held the red mud horse, it began to stretch and twist.

"RED HORSE, I name you RED WIND!" called out the old man. "Now show us what you can do to cool the people!" With that the Red Horse tore away from the people holding it. It whirled into the air, stirring it and laughing and blowing dust from the ground widely into the air.

At first the people cheered and lifted their arms to the cooling gusts. But the wind snatched the feathers from their hair and the bracelets from their wrists. Red Wind twisted and jumped round and round like a wild thing. Trees snapped as if they were twigs.

"Now look what you've done, Old Man," shouted the people. "Red Wind will tear up the earth and blow us all away."

So the old man called out again, "Red Wind! I made you. I named you! Now I give you a home. From this time on, you will live in the sky."

Ever since that time, Red Wind, the whirlwind, has lived in the sky among the black clouds. And, on days when the earth is very hot, he begins to roar and twist and stretch down ... because he does like to kick things up on earth again.

Standards

NGSS—Earth and Space—weather system applied (engineering) to a vacuum cleaner.

ETS1.A: Defining and Delimiting Engineering Problems—Possible solutions to a problem are limited by available materials and resources (constraints). The success of a design solution is determined by considering the desired features of a solution (criteria). Different proposals for solutions can be compared on the basis of how well each one meets the specified criteria for success or how well each takes the constraints into account.

ETS1.B: Developing Possible Solutions—Research on a problem should be carried out before beginning to design a solution. Testing a solution involves investigating how well if performs under a range of likely conditions.

At whatever stage, communicating with peers about proposed solutions is an important part of the design process, and shared ideas can lead to improved designs.

Tests are often designed to identify failure points or difficulties, which suggest the elements of the design that need to be improved.

ETS1.C: Optimizing the Design Solution—Different solutions need to be tested in order to determine which of them best solves the problem, given the criteria and constraints.

CCSS.ELA-LITERACY.W.5.2: Write informative/explanatory texts to examine a topic and convey ideas and information clearly.

CCSS.ELA-LITERACY.W.5.2.A: Introduce a topic clearly, provide a general observation and focus, and group related information logically; include formatting (e.g., headings), illustrations, and multimedia when useful to aiding comprehension.

CCSS.ELA-LITERACY.W.5.2.B: Develop the topic with facts, definitions, concrete details, quotations, or other information and examples related to the topic.

CCSS.ELA-LITERACY.W.5.2.C: Link ideas within and across categories of information using words, phrases, and clauses (e.g., *in contrast, especially*).

CCSS.ELA-LITERACY.W.5.2.D: Use precise language and domain-specific vocabulary to inform about or explain the topic.

CCSS.ELA-LITERACY.W.5.2.E: Provide a concluding statement or section related to the information or explanation presented.

Objectives

Third Grade through Fifth Grade students will be able to say:

- I can understand the principle of a vacuum and of a cyclone.
- I can explain and apply the principles of a cyclone to the vacuum cleaner.
- I can take apart and put the vacuum cleaner back together.
- I can retell the story "The Making of Whirlwind" and explain the story from a science viewpoint.

Materials

- three Dyson or Shark vacuum cleaners
- a traditional or filter vacuum cleaner
- instructions for assembly and disassembly
- eventually, a pile of dust

Instructional Plan

Rationale

In order to have students experience that creating/learning is a series of gradual steps where a problem leads to a solution that leads to another problem, I present two teaching stories to augment "The Making of Whirlwind," the origin story. The first is the story of how Dorothy got to Oz, and the second is of James Dyson, inventor. He was annoyed that his vacuum cleaner lost suction as the bag began to fill.

A cyclone is formed when great wind pressure is exerted on a center spot (in this case where Dorothy's house stood) and that air becomes still. The focused air pulls air away from the center and forms a whirlwind around the center point. Any object in the center is forced upward, rising albeit twirling, until the cyclone winds diminish and the whirlwind blows itself out. In Dorothy's situation the cyclone forced the house higher and then set it down gently in the Land of Oz. Showing the beginning of the movie to students will help them visualize the problem before them.

While a traditional vacuum cleaner filters the air and dust before it goes into the bag, the "cyclone dust extractor" has no filter to clog the sucking motion found in older vacuums, causing diminishing returns. Dyson's idea was to create a vacuum cleaner that used a cyclonic or forced air extraction method instead of sucking dust and air through a filter.

Dyson made over 5000 prototypes constructed over 5 years ... he employed the "make, break, make, break" method to construct his vacuum cleaner. The question before him was always, "Why doesn't it work?"

Preparation

Research and understand the story of James Dyson, inventor of the vacuum that works on the principle of the cyclone and purchase/seek donations of at least three Shark (much less expensive) or Dyson vacuum cleaners that work on the principle of "cyclonic dust extraction."

Activity

1. Students will work in small teams, preferably no more than three per team. Each team will examine and diagram a filter vacuum. Then, they will take apart and put back together a "cyclonic" vacuum cleaner. Each team will have a set of directions provided with the cleaner and demonstrate the efficiency of the vacuum.

2. Students will document their vacuum work with photos, drawings and text that accurately defines a cyclone and a hurricane, as well as their work with the cyclonic dust extractor.

3. Students will research and report on famous cyclones or hurricanes that occurred on the earth, defining the path of the storm, the damage, and the effort to rebuild.

Assessment

Students should design the rubrics for this activity in each of the following categories: literacy, science, engineering and social studies, and conclude their papers with a statement about the integration of knowledge demonstrated.

NOTE

1. Kevin Ashton. *How to Fly a Horse*. He elaborates upon Dyson's dilemma with his traditional vacuum cleaner and how he created the cyclonic vacuum.

Embodied Storytelling
Using Voice, Body, Visual Images and Writing to Clarify a Pattern or Process

ARIANNA ROSS

CCC topics: Patterns, Cause and effect, Energy and matter, Stability and change
POSE topics: Asking questions and defining problems; Developing and using models; Constructing explanations and designing solutions; Engaging in argument from evidence

The Story

"The Ancient One"

A long, long, long, long, long, long, long time ago, deep in the heart of the Amazonian rainforest of Brazil, there lived an old tree that they called "Ancient One." This tree was so huge around that it was estimated that it had been alive for as long as the forest had existed. The only way to find out accurately how old this tree would be was to chop it down and count his rings or stick a tool called an "increment borer" inside to pull a piece out so that the rings could be counted. Of course no one wanted to perform either of these options.

They did know one thing: all the forest animals, the tall thin trees and even the little bushes heeded his wisdom. He could feel the wind on his leaves and know what weather was coming. Actually, all of the forest listened, except for one young tree called the Little One. She was tall and thin, as she had only been alive for a decade. Whenever the Ancient One spoke, she refused to pay attention for she wanted to dance the samba.

Whenever there was a shift in the weather, the Ancient One would call out saying, "Hold on tight the wind or rains are coming." While all the others would dig down deep with their roots into the ground, the Little One would have none of it. She would have a blast, her slim trunk would sway and leaves would shake in the wind. The Ancient One tried to reason with her and explain that when the Great Wind comes you have to hold on to the ground with your roots, or you could become injured or worse.

She would shout back, "I'm not listening to you. You may be great but you are old, stiff and no fun. The wind only wiggles the tips of your leaves and your trunk never moves. I am young, beautiful and flexible so when the winds comes I am going to dance." It was as if she was sticking the branches in her ears and singing "NaNaNa." The Ancient One paid her insults no mind because he hoped that by the time the Great Wind came she would listen.

One day it seemed as though the wind stopped moving. The Ancient One unfurled his leaves and felt the air. His eyes opened ever so slightly as dark clouds slid into place. In his all-knowing wisdom, he knew a huge storm was coming that could harm the forest. He called out to the animals and trees: "Hold on tight. This storm will be bigger than any of us have ever experienced." The Ancient One knew that trees only fall when the forces of wind are so great that it uproots the tree, or the ground becomes so soaked with water that the tree is easily toppled over.

Soon the storm began with a gentle breeze and a drizzle of rain. Quickly the wind began to pick up speed, the thunder rolled in like a drum-line, and suddenly the skies lit up with lightning. The wind blew fast and rain started to tumble from the sky. The Ancient One had time to tell the forest again, "Hold on tight!"

The Little One chanted "I'm not listening, I'm not listening…" She loved how the rain made the ground soft and her roots could soak up the endless water. Moreover, she did not notice the strength of the wind because she was simply dancing.

The Ancient One tried to lean over and tell her to be still. He tried to protect her but she refused to stop and bow down to what she called the "old ways." Instead she kept dancing until the wind came upon her so fast that she was knocked over with one push-pull of the wind. She fell to the ground with a loud crack. The Ancient One peeked down and saw the little tree had completely fallen over. In vain, he tried to help her stand up, but she could not move.

After many hours the wind finally died down to a gentle breeze and the rain slowed to a drizzle again. The Ancient One reached out to the little tree softly with his words, "Are you ok, Little One?"

At first she didn't respond, but when she did you could barely hear her voice, "I can't move but I'm ok. I know that when a tree falls in the forest it feeds the ground, it gives the earth energy, it decomposes. In my spot a new tree will grow, and I will make sure to tell it that it needs to listen to the Ancient One."

Standards

NGSS—Earth and Space (weather), Life Science

3-ESS2-1. Represent data in tables and graphical displays to describe typical weather conditions expected during a particular season.

3-ESS2-2. Obtain and combine information to describe climates in different regions of the world.

ESS3.B: Natural Hazards: A variety of natural hazards result from natural processes. Humans cannot eliminate natural hazards but can take steps to reduce their impacts.

5-ESS2-1. Develop a model using an example to describe ways the geosphere, biosphere, hydrosphere, and/or atmosphere interact.

3-LS4-3. Construct an argument with evidence that in a particular habitat some organisms can survive well, some survive less well, and some cannot survive at all.

PS2: Motion and Stability: Forces and Interactions: Each force acts on one particular object and has both strength and a direction. An object at rest typically has multiple forces acting on it, but they add to give zero net force on the object. Forces that do not sum to zero can cause changes in the object's speed or direction of motion.

CCSS/ELA

CCSS.ELA-LITERACY.RI.3.3—Describe the relationship between a series of historical events, scientific ideas or concepts, or steps in technical procedures in a text, using language that pertains to time, sequence, and cause/effect.

CSS.ELA-LITERACY.W.3.2—Write informative/explanatory texts to examine a topic and convey ideas and information clearly.

CCSS.ELA-LITERACY.W.3.5—With guidance and support from peers and adults, develop and strengthen writing as needed by planning, revising, and editing.

CCSS.ELA-LITERACY.SL.3.1—Engage effectively in a range of collaborative discussions (one-on-one, in groups, and teacher-led) with diverse partners on *grade 3 topics and texts*, building on others' ideas and expressing their own clearly.

CCSS.ELA-LITERACY.SL.3.4—Report on a topic or text, tell a story, or recount an experience with appropriate facts and relevant, descriptive details, speaking clearly at an understandable pace.

CCSS.ELA-LITERACY.L.3.6—Acquire and use accurately grade-appropriate conversational, general academic, and domain-specific words and phrases, including those that signal spatial and temporal relationships.

Fine Arts Anchor standards:

TH:Cr1 Creating—Process Component: Envision, Conceptualize
TH:Cr1.1.3

    a. Create roles, imagined worlds, and improvised stories in a drama/theatre work.

    b. Collaborate to determine how characters might move and speak to support the story and given circumstances in drama/theatre work.

TH: Pr4.1 Performing—Select, analyze, and interpret artistic work for presentation.
TH:Pr4.1.3

    a. Apply the elements of dramatic structure to a story and create a drama/theatre work.

    b. Investigate how movement and voice are incorporated into drama/theatre work.

Objectives

Third through Fifth Grade students will be able to say:

- I can create and present from a written text a physical and voiced exploration that demonstrates the group-selected science topic on the Amazonian rainforest.
- I can work effectively in an ensemble to create dynamic tableaux.
- I can create and present a monologue with all the elements of a strong paragraph included.
- I can perform in front of an audience.

Materials

- pencils
- colored pencils
- rulers
- drawing paper

Instructional Plan

A. The following activities occur within the larger habitat study of the Amazonian rainforest:

1. research on the interrelatedness of its biosphere, hydrosphere, geosphere, atmosphere
2. students will generate questions and areas of research
3. working groups will select questions and topics for inclusion in a report and for the following artistic activities/understandings.

B. Building a Small Group Machine that demonstrates the story.

Rationale

Embodied Storytelling uses the body and voice to initially tell the story which leads directly into the comprehension of the story they have "Embodied." In the classroom the teacher/teaching artist will use a combination of movement-based strategies as well as oral presentations to effectively demonstrate comprehension.

- Become better readers and writers by having them move their words, draw their story, verbally re-tell what they intend to write, and then finally write the text.
- Develop critical thinking and problem solving skills.
- Bring student ideas to life and make the whole body the tool for learning.
- Follow a sequence of directions.
- Build inference skills and basic comprehension of a text.
- Write a strong statement of understanding that uses evidence from the text.
- Build self-confidence, body awareness, and vocal strength.

C. Relating the text, the telling, and the embodied understanding

Step One: Reading the Passage

1. TELL the story (after reading it) out loud, in the most boring voice possible, sentence by sentence. Do not discuss the passage before you read it as a class.
2. TELL the story (after reading it) in the most dramatic voice possible, sentence by sentence.
3. Identify the important words with a visual cue like a red circle and create Power Phrases for the words that we want to emphasize as important. Power Phrases: The students with the teacher's support should decide how to say the word as well as create specific choreography that demonstrates what each word means.
4. Stand up and act out the passage using the Power Phrases to mark the sequence of events.

Step Two: Creating the Machine

1. Use the Group Outline (handout) which follows this article. (handout on tableaux also follows article) to plan your tableau and written work requirements.

2. Each person will create a non-locomotor movement using their whole body to represent their step in the process. A non-locomotor movement is movement in one spot. They will be repeating this motion over and over again.

3. Each person needs to cite evidence in the text and develop one line, explaining their job in the scientific process (in defining their role in the biosphere or atmosphere or hydrosphere or geosphere for example). They will say their line one time loudly and then they will be whispering it over and over again.

4. Next, the group will put the machine together, by deciding where each person is going to stand, and if the entirety of their project is adequately represented. Collectively, they create a machine: each person should be connected to the rest of the ensemble.

5. Practice presenting the machine to the class ... getting into the machine, the actual machine and getting out of the machine ... while remembering to allow each person a moment in the spotlight.

Step Three: Writing a Brief Statement of Understanding Explaining Your Job

The statement serves as a short story or monologue. Each student will write out his/her character in the tableau/scientific process—a short statement or story (1–7 sentences). The writing should contain the main idea and 3 supporting details ending with a concluding sentence. It should tell the story of the role or part of the scientific process.

It is assumed that paragraph structure has been taught/reviewed: main idea, supporting details, and conclusion. Questions to consider: Who are you? What is your role in the sequence of events? What happens before you and what happens after you? Why are you an important part of this process?

Step Four: Cartooning: Developing the Paragraph/Story Through Cartooning

1. Students will make a cartoon or graphic representation of their paragraph that explains each element, focusing on main idea and supporting details. They will draw a simple cartoon of the main idea and then two of the supporting details of their role in the sequence.

2. Students will label each cartoon with a sentences that explain the cartoon. (They are really just writing the rough draft of their paragraph using their drawings as a guide.)

3. In partners or small groups have students close eyes to visualize

the story (what they read, what they performed in the machine, what they drew and what they ultimately wrote).
4. Students tell their story with partners listening. (two minutes)
5. Partners can offer appreciations and suggestions; each students shall tell his story twice being conscious of vocal dynamics and power words.

Step Five: Final Presentation: Students Will Share Their Writing
1. Practice reading their writing to the small group. They will have the opportunity to read their statement to their working group as an embodied storyteller. The team will offer them appreciations and suggestions for what they hear.
2. Select 2–3 students to share their paragraph with the class.
3. Returning to their original group, practice the machine for performance:

- Getting into the machine
- Freeze the Machine
- Each individual steps out one at a time to perform their monologue/paragraph

4. Have students perform for the class.
5. Audience Serves to assess the machine and the monologues: Did they include?

- All of the elements of the criteria
- Textual Evidence
- Have clear comprehension of the cycle
- Audience can also use the attached rubric.

Assessment

Criteria for building the machine (handout follows article)
I must....

- Freeze the final moment of my machine thereby creating a tableau.
- Write, practice and perform a statement of understanding.
- Stay in my personal space bubble and the group bubble.
- Use my body to tell the story complete with a range of levels, motion and facial expression.
- Use vocal dynamics to demonstrate the meaning of the words and the changes in the story.

HANDOUT 1: Elements of Embodied Storytelling
Emotion: Reflections of Inner Attitude

- **Facial Expression:** How we use our face to reflect the emotions in the story (smile, frown).
- **Body Language:** How we use our body to tell the inner feelings of the characters in the story (open body, closed body).
- **Word Choice:** How we choose colorful and clear words to explain what we read.
- **Dynamics:** How we change the volume of our voice to reflect a specific emotion. Dynamics also indicate the intention, the need of the character or narrator of the story (e.g., to escape, to excite, to lie, to...).

Movement: Physical Expression

- **Non-Locomotor Movement:** To move in one space around and across the body's axis; feet do not move from the spot (e.g., bend, twist, stretch, wiggle).
- **Locomotor Movement:** To move across space (e.g., walk, run, turn, kick, jump).

Inflection: Voice Variation

- **Dynamics:** Change in volume (loud or soft).
- **Character voices:** Changing the sound in the voice to become anything or anyone (e.g., an old man, a tiger, a snake, a baby, etc.).
- **Word Stress:** Emphasizing or stressing one part of the word over another part.

Body: Physical Expression

- **Shape:** A frozen pose (curved, straight, angular, large, small).
- **Part:** Body parts (torso, head, eyes, shoulders, arms, fingers, etc.).
- **Tableau:** A frozen pose that tells a story.
- **Mountain Position (Actor's Neutral):** Stand with your hands to your side.

Space: Where you perform, where the action occurs

- **Personal Space:** Space immediately around the body.
- **General Space:** Space throughout the room, shared with others.
- **Levels:** High, Medium, Low.
- **Focus:** Direction of the gaze.
- **Size:** Big, Small, Narrow, Wide.

Language: Use of the Words

- **Word Picture:** A sequence of words that create a visual image of what is happening in the story as well as move the action of the story forward.
- **Sensory Language:** What does something look, sound, feel, and taste like?

- **Narrative:** Referred to as the story line or sequence of events.
- **Literal:** The word or phrase means exactly what is written down on the paper.
- **Non-Literal:** The figurative language or phrase could be interpreted to mean something different.

HANDOUT 2: *Group Outline to Break Down the Text*
What is happening in this process?

Write down step-by-step what happens in this process?

1. _____
2. _____
3. _____
4. _____
5. _____

Decide who is acting out which step in the process

1. _____
2. _____
3. _____
4. _____
5. _____

HANDOUT 3: *What Is Tableau?*
   Definition: A **tableau** is a frozen picture or a still image created by one individual or members of the class on stage.
   Share with students the definition for tableau twice and say:
   This dramatic image is designed to tell a specific story to the audience. Today we'll be creating group tableaus in class.
   Here are the rules or guidelines for creating successful tableaus.
   Rules:

   a. Stay frozen.
   b. Use your whole body including your face.
   c. Choose a point of focus.
   d. No props.
   e. Create a title for the tableau

HANDOUT 4: *Assessment*

"How Dragon Lost His Tail"
Shaping Landforms

SHERRY NORFOLK

CCC topics: Patterns, Cause and Effect, Scale, Proportion and quantity, Energy and matter
POSE topics: Developing and using models, Planning and carrying out investigations, Obtaining, evaluating, and communicating information

The Story

"How Dragon Lost His Tail"
Retold by Sherry Norfolk

In ancient times, before people lived on Earth, there lived a huge dragon. He slept a lot, always curled in the shape of a perfect circle, always lying at the place where the land we now call China meets with the China Sea. His body formed the land, and only a tiny bit of his long tail trailed out into the sea.

Now, Dragon had children, and those dragon children were like children everywhere—when they were not being watched, they got into trouble! They splashed in the China Sea and made huge waves, they fought together and made small typhoons, they breathed out smoke that covered the sea in clouds.

And they got bored.

"I'm bored," whined a little dragon.

"Me, too," sulked another little dragon.

"BORED!" agreed a third little dragon.

"Let's wake up Daddy and get him to play with us!" they shouted. And they tried to wake up the sleeping dragon.

"Daddy!" they shouted together. "Wake up, Daddy!"

But Dragon snored on. He didn't even twitch.

"DADDY!" they tried again, much louder. But Dragon did not wake up.

"Oh, phooey!" whined the first little dragon. "I wanted him to make a huge storm."

"And cover the sky with tall black clouds," sulked the second little dragon.

"Or blow up a ginormous TYPHOON!" yelled the third little dragon.

They splashed loudly and huffed out steam.

"I know how to wake him up," said the first little dragon, and he raced over and BIT Dragon right on the tail. He bit so hard that he made a tiny dent on Daddy Dragon's tail! Then he raced away and waited for Dragon to wake up. But Dragon snored on.

The other two little dragons had been holding their breath, eyes wide and fearful, waiting for Daddy Dragon to rise up roaring and angry, but when he didn't even twitch, they crept closer.

Suddenly, they both raced over and nipped at Daddy. Then all three were snapping and biting and chomping and gnawing on Daddy Dragon's tail and back. They gleefully spit the bites into the water, until...

"RRRRROOOOOOOOOAAAAAR!" Daddy Dragon woke up! He shook himself like a wet dog, and the three little dragons were tossed off his back. He thrashed his tail in anger—but the little dragons' bites had weakened it so much that the tip of it flew off and fell into the China Sea. SPLASH!

The tip of Daddy Dragon's tail fell right on top of one of the little dragons and trapped him there forever.

Daddy Dragon was furious with the little dragons. He rolled over and went back to sleep with his back to them, stretched out with his head far, far to the west and his cut-off tail to the east. He has stayed there ever since.

That's why, if you look at a map today, you can see the tip of Daddy Dragon's tail just off the coast of China—it is called Taiwan. The mountain range down the middle of the island is the little dragon that is still trapped underneath. Across the Straits of Taiwan, you can see the raggedy coast of China, showing where the little dragons bit and snapped at their daddy that day, and to the south and west you can see the huge curved mountains called the Himalayas, which is that angry Daddy Dragon, fast asleep.

But look at the map again. Between the island of Taiwan and the coast of China is a narrow strip of water called the Straits of Taiwan. You won't see them on the map, but the little dragons still play there, splashing in the water and making huge waves, fighting together and making small typhoons, and breathing out smoke that covers the sea in clouds.

236   Part Two. Upper Elementary (Earth and Space)

Standards

NGSS

4-ESS2-2. Analyze and interpret data from maps to describe patterns of Earth's features.

CCSS for ELA

RL.4.1. Refer to details and examples in a text when explaining what the text says explicitly and when drawing inferences from the text.

RL.4.10. By the end of the year, read and comprehend literature, including stories, myths, and traditional literature from different cultures.

RI.4.7. Interpret information presented visually, orally, or quantitatively.

W.4.2. Write informative/explanatory texts to examine a topic and convey ideas and information clearly.

W.4.3. Write narratives to develop real or imagined experiences or events using effective technique, descriptive details, and clear event sequences.

SL.4.4. Report on a topic or text, tell a story, or recount an experience in an organized manner, using appropriate facts and relevant, descriptive details to support main ideas or themes; speak clearly at an understandable pace.

NCAS

Create, Present, Respond, Connect

Objectives

Fourth Grade students will be able to say

- I can analyze and interpret data from maps to describe patterns of Earth's features.
- I can write a How and Why story about a specific landform.
- I can research and write an informative text.

Materials

- "How Dragon Lost His Tail," in Cheney, Cora. *Tales from a Taiwan Kitchen.* New York: Dodd, Mead, 1976.
- Topographical map or globe clearly showing Taiwan, the Himalayas, the Straits of Taiwan, and the South China Sea

- "Plate Tectonics for Kids" 5 minute video at www.makemeagenius.com or https://www.youtube.com/watch?v=tcPghqnnTVk (optional)
- Student access to print or online topographical maps and research materials

Instructional Plan

Rationale

"Scientific Inquiry refers to the diverse ways in which scientists study the natural world and propose explanations based on the evidence derived from their work."(National Research Council) How and Why stories (also called pourquoi) are perhaps the earliest form of scientific inquiry, representing man's attempts to answer the most common questions still posed by scientists today: How? and Why?

Preparation

Before telling this story, review the ways that landforms are shaped: volcanic explosions and earthquakes, erosion of rocks by wind and/or water, etc., then look at a topographical map or globe clearly showing Taiwan, the Himalayas, the Straits of Taiwan, and the China Sea. Ask students to hypothesize what forces formed the island of Taiwan, the Straits, and the Himalaya Mountains. Discuss what makes them say that. What evidence can they point to that supports their hypothesis?

Activity

The island of Taiwan was actually formed at the intersection of two tectonic plates which pushed against each other to raise the land up out of the sea. You can demonstrate that very simply by pushing two interlocking puzzle pieces together—they will pop up or one will slide over the other. Tectonics!—or by watching the "Plate Tectonics for Kids" video on MakeMea Genius.com.

Did anyone hypothesize this kind of force? Probably not—and the people who lived long ago didn't think of it, either! Explain that long ago, there weren't scientists to explain the world to people, so folks often made up stories that *pretended* to explain how and why things were the way they were—why the sky is blue, why evergreen trees don't lose their leaves, or how particular landforms were created. Like this one...

Tell "How Dragon Lost His Tail."

Discussion: How did the story explain the formation of Taiwan, the Himalayas, and the shape of the coast of China? Look at the map to compare and contrast the story to the reality.

Why did people make up this story? Curiosity: the need to explain the fascinating shape of their world.

Ask the class to look at a map and identify other interesting landforms.

Discussion: What questions do you have? What makes you curious?

Choose one of the landforms and develop a class How-and-Why story by answering the following questions:

- What landform are we going to talk about?
- What will you explain about it?
- How does the land look in the beginning of the story?
- What happens to change the way it looks? (Think about why it gets changed, who might do it, and how it gets done)
- How does it look at the end of the story? Why?

You will need to TELL the resulting story to the kids, complete with characters voices and actions and sound effects, modeling the transition from an outline to a narrative. Then students can work individually to develop their own landform pourquoi stories.

After editing and illustrating these stories, children should be curious to learn how the landforms they wrote about were *really* formed. Time for research! Provide access to print and online sources for kids to research this information and write informative/explanatory essays on the topic. Publish the resulting fact-and-fiction stories and have the kids perform them, too! Students may also wish to create dioramas that depict before-and-after images from their story.

Assessment

- Assess student analysis and interpretation of data during class discussions, especially answers to "what makes you say that?"
- How and Why stories can be assessed against a rubric that includes the logic of the how and why "explanation" as well as effective technique, descriptive details, and clear event sequences.
- Informative text can be assessed for accuracy and clarity.

BIBLIOGRAPHY

"Plate Tectonics for Kids" 5 minute video at www.makemeagenius.com or https://www.youtube.com/watch?v=tcPghqnnTVk

Study Jams: Landforms, Rocks and Minerals. http://studyjams.scholastic.com/studyjams/jams/science/rocks-minerals-landforms/landforms.htm

Van Gorp, Lynn. *Investigating Landforms: Earth and Space Science (Science Readers)*. Teacher Created Materials, 2008.

Pele, or a Volcanic Trip
Tectonic Plates, Sulfur Gases, the Rock Cycle and Art

Jeff Gere

CCC topics: Patterns, Cause and Effect, Scale, Proportion and quantity, Energy and matter
POSE topics: Developing and using models, Planning and carrying out investigations, Obtaining, evaluating, and communicating information

The Stories

"Pele, Goddess of the Volcano"

By the time Pele came to Hawai'i from southern Polynesia, her sister, the goddess of sea, was already her enemy. Pele would put her o'o digging stick into the earth, and the lava would bubble up. Ahh! She liked it like this! But just when things were nice and hot and comfortable for Pele, the ocean would rise up and attack, flooding her craters, cooling her lava beds, putting out her fires, containing her expansion. Then Pele, upset, would move on, and dig in another spot. Kauai is the oldest island, with lush deep valleys and wet mountain tops. Next Pele created O'ahu (Waikiki and Pearl Harbor, and the map shows what is left: the land where two volcanoes touched. The rest of both volcanoes has been washed away by the sea). Then come Molokai and Lanai, and Maui (which still has the figure 8 shape of its two volcanoes, and the spaces between her and Lanai are so shallow that whales come from Alaska in the winter to breed and birth their babies). Finally, Pele's new home, the "Big Island" of Hawai'i (in Halema'uma'u Crater) where lava has been running and oozing continually in large and small eruptions for 30 years.

Some Hawai'ians can trace their family back to Pele. And people in the islands tell stories of meeting Pele.

"An Encounter with Pele"
told to Jeff Gere

I (Jeff) am now aware of her face, ... the woman telling of the encounter ... things are slowing down, the room falls away, and I know what is coming, "Sure, Pele.... Ummm, do you have a story you want to tell me?" And now everything stops as she starts.

"My brother and his friend, they told me this. Happened to them. On the Saddle Road...."

Now Saddle Road is the only road on the Big Island passing between Hilo (east) and Kona (west) directly. It goes over the "saddle," the low-place, the mountain hump between Mauna Kea (White Mountain, because it snows on top where all the planetary observatories are) and Mauna Loa (the Long Mountain). It is an old road, one land in each direction, but largely paved in the middle. It is small, winding, climbing with the curves of the topography through forests and clouds (heavy fogs), pastures to a desolate plateau on top, with some areas covered with barren lava flows. It can feel really spooky. There are LOTS of stories. Driving it is a rite of passage.

"Dark, late at night—they was driving that road. Spooky, you know?" I nod.

"So he say it was slow going—fog would come an' go, no moon. Said it felt like a night with no end, like driving in another world, with their headlights stabbing into the blackness. Just weird! Gives you chicken skin, you know?" I nod again.

"So they follow the headlights again, plunging down into a valley, and the fog goes away.

"At the end of the coming straight-away, they see her: a skinny old lady, can see the white hair, a dark face (Hawai'an?), the lava lava (simple wrap-around cotton cloth) 'round her skinny body, the bare feet, and the thumb stretched out for one ride.

'It's Pele!' says my brother's friend. 'She like ride! You better STOP!'

'It IS Pele!' says my brother. 'She like ride. But I no stop for NOTHIN'!' and he jams his foot down on the gas. 'Go go go GO!'

"My brother and his friend, they both say they see this—no foolin.' They say the car stay speeding by the lady, fast fast. But, you know how when you pass something by your car, the headlights hit what you be passing as you fly bye, yeah? So both of them say they can see the lady, clear, in the headlight, as they went fly by, right? Both their eyes is LOCKED on this lady standing there with her head down, thumb out, white hair.

"And as they go speeding by, she look up, just a little, and they both see her face.

"Framed by that gray-white hair, that face.... or what should be a face ... except, in that flash of headlight, clear as day, they saw what should not be. Her face ... it had no eyes.

"No eyes, no nose, no mouth. Nothing ... just darkness, with little holes all over ... like lava. Her face was lava.

"ZZZzzoommmmm.... and it was gone, leaving them both screaming.

"And what they saw they told me. In fact, they could not stop telling it to me. And now I told it to you."

"Thanks alot," I said. "Gotta go. Talk Story, talk story..."

"The Fire Pit"
(indigenous art in the fire pit)

Tim's Pit Fire Party at the Kilauea Iki Crater: We landed in Hilo, bought food, and drove an hour up up up the slope of Mauna Kea to the mountain-top village of Volcano, to join our friend Tim for his Pit Fire Party. My French wife Dominique and philosophy professor/potter Tim are old friends. Both are volcano nuts. This occasional backyard, all-night celebration attracts the colorful creative characters from the woods of Upcountry Hawai'i to cavort around a huge bonfire, inside of which sit three dozen of Tim's burnished clay pots of all sizes. Hand-built, wheel thrown and altered vessels, they are already stone-hard when pit-fired. The pit-fire is just for color—scarred by the licking flames.

We helped Tim assemble wood, line a pit, big enough for a man to lie in, with stones and helped him load in each pot. Each one is built and shaped of clay, thin at the bottom, swelling wide and convening on a craggy mouth. Rough clay at the base turns into a shiny curve in the swelling edge, rubbed with polished stone until it shines. Each has already been bisque-fired in an electric kiln then waiting for this baptism of fire to create the smokey molten hues. Tim carefully embeds each into sawdust and sprinkles the top with jade green copper, which will create the amber umber colors amidst the white and dark stains of the fire. It's slow and careful work. We mound split wood small to large on top of the pots, a huge flammable mound.

At one point we go over to a 15-foot tree that's lying on its side. "Oh, the stake gave way in last night's wind," says Tim. I could see the roots at the base of the trunk in a ball, with tendrils still spreading off into the earth. A floor of lava stone a foot down into the soggy earth prevents deeper penetration. We stand the tree up and Tim reties the rope to the stake holding it upright. Only in Volcano!

Standards

NGSS

ESS2.A: Earth Materials and Systems: Earth's major systems are the geosphere (solid and molten rock, soil, and sediments, the hydrosphere (water and ice), the atmosphere (air), and the biosphere (living things including humans). These systems interact in multiple ways to affect the Earth's surface materials and processes. The ocean supports a wide variety of ecosystems and organisms, shapes landforms, and influences climate. Winds and clouds in the atmosphere interact with the landforms to determine patterns of weather.

5-ESS2-1: Develop a model using an example to describe ways the geosphere, biosphere, hydrosphere, and/or atmosphere interact. [Clarification statement: Examples could include the influence of the ocean on ecosystems, landform shape, and climate; the influence of the atmosphere on landforms and ecosystems through weather and climate; and the influence of mountain ranges on winds and clouds in the atmosphere. The geosphere, hydrosphere, atmosphere and biosphere are each a system

CCSS

CCSS.ELA-LITERACY.RL.5.2 Determine a theme of a story, drama, or poem from details in the text, including how characters in a story or drama respond to challenges or how the speaker in a poem reflects upon a topic; summarize the text.

CCSS.ELA-LITERACY.RI.5.3 Explain the relationships or interactions between two or more individuals, events, ideas, or concepts in a historical, scientific, or technical text based on specific information in the text.

CCSS.ELA-LITERACY.RI.5.4 Determine the meaning of general academic and domain-specific words and phrases in a text relevant to a *grade 5 topic or subject area.*

CCSS.ELA-LITERACY.RI.5.9 Integrate information from several texts on the same topic in order to write or speak about the subject knowledgeably.

CCSS.ELA-LITERACY.W.5.2.A Introduce a topic clearly, provide a general observation and focus, and group related information logically; include formatting (e.g., headings), illustrations, and multimedia when useful to aiding comprehension.

CCSS.ELA-LITERACY.W.5.2.B Develop the topic with facts, definitions, concrete details, quotations, or other information and examples related to the topic.

CCSS.ELA-LITERACY.W.5.2.C Link ideas within and across categories of information using words, phrases, and clauses (e.g., *in contrast, especially*).

CCSS.ELA-LITERACY.W.5.2.D Use precise language and domain-specific vocabulary to inform about or explain the topic.

CCSS.ELA-LITERACY.W.5.6 With some guidance and support from adults, use technology, including the Internet, to produce and publish writing as well as to interact and collaborate with others; demonstrate sufficient command of keyboarding skills to type a minimum of two pages in a single sitting.

CCSS.ELA-LITERACY.W.5.7 Conduct short research projects that use several sources to build knowledge through investigation of different aspects of a topic.

NCAS: creating, responding, presentation, connecting

Objectives

Fifth Grade students will be able to say:

- I can research the Earth's major systems demonstrated in Hawai'i.
- I can create and write about the creation of a clay pot as an expression/reflection the geosphere, biosphere, hydrosphere, and/or atmosphere of Hawai'i.
- I can tell a Pele story and how it relates to the Earth's major systems.
- I can synthesize the various ideas (plate tectonics, myth, art) present in this project.

Instructional Plan

Rationale

Not only is Hawai'i exotic to mainland Americans, it offers wide possibilities to study the earth's systems in a contained place. Plus, the applications of the study transfer easily to other locales. Braiding ideas of Pele, goddess of the volcano, the creation of the islands, with the creation of a clay pot, and with the science of the earth's systems is a holistic way of looking at man's relationship to the Earth—as mythographer, artist, and scientist.

Preparation

For each of the understandings there are different preparations. Activity #2, the rock cycle—observe and action: A. Breaking apart rocks to form gravel/sand. B. Applying downward pressure to a mixture of sand and gravel and mud. Activity #4: With the art teacher and in the studio, have purchased enough clay, tools, glazes for the class so each student can create a meaningful art object.

Activity

Activity #1: Put your hands on your scalp. Feel the crack running across the middle of the top of your skull? There's another about your hair line, and at your temples, the crack reaches back to your ears, right? Feels good to rub those cracks. Our earth has cracks in it too, called *tectonic plates*. Next, put your hands together, palms down, fingers pointing away from you, so the length of your pointing fingers touch sides from above thumb to fingernail. Now move your fingers back and forth in opposite directions. Feel the heat as they rub each other?

The earth's plates (and oceans) are like scabs on top of a molten lava sea. They rub, grind and chew on each other as they float back and forth. This creates mountain ranges, pours out to make huge flat plains, and in some cases cracks, where the lava breaks out and builds up along the edge of these big plates and cools. Eventually, they build up and break above the surface of the ocean, and slowly continue to make islands (Hawai'i). Think of this: these seven islands are among the most remote places on the planet: six hours on a plane to California in the east, six hours on a plane to reach Japan in the west (another chain of volcanic islands). But the Hawai'ians have another way of telling this story....

Activity #2: The Rock Cycle. Raised cross-section mismatch: This shifting earth also lifts one side of the crack a bit, which begins the dissolving of the earth into smaller rocks and eventually soil. There wasn't much "dirt" on the lava pour; give it another 1000 years. The exposed uneven cross-section of the earth showed several layers of pour, each type and time with a different texture. You can see the different periods of lava on top of one another ... 1979, 1974, etc. You are looking at glacial time, earth's sense of time; the oozy, the explosive, unreported, unaffected by human witness, the continual living process of the earth breathing in a timeframe of hundreds of centuries, beyond our lifetime or timeframe of history, before Christ, Buddha or cave men...

Activity #3: Research and writing: Working groups of students will choose one of the Earth's systems as demonstrated in Hawai'i to establish in greater depth, including the sphere's relationship to the formation of the islands; the volcanic rock cycle; the significance of PELE, the fire goddess, and other mythologies—how and why they developed and are maintained.

Use precise vocabulary: volcano, crater, lip of the crater, lava pit, sulfur dioxide gas, caldera, volcanologist, sunken caldera, tectonic plates, Ohia bushes.

Activity #4: Clay Pots: Working with the art teacher, each student will create a clay expression, perhaps a pot that signifies their understanding of Hawai'i—perhaps a pot in the shape of a volcano, perhaps relief icons, colorful glazes, or statues of Pele—something that reflects the work they pursue in their study of the biosphere, atmosphere, hydrosphere, or geosphere. Imagery activity: Students will imagine a photo of smoke wrapping around their earthen clay skins. In contrast, itself vacillating between crispy white and ghostly gray, and varying shades of earthy red tan rock, an elegant shape, thin below, swelling to convene around a hole, a pit, an empty opening. Caldera! Often that smooth, shiny, smoky rising skin grows rough, crusty, pitted and uneven, molten perhaps near the edges of the hole. Students will make an artistic statement.

BIBLIOGRAPHY

Nordenstrom, Michael. *Pele and the Rivers of Fire*. Bess Press: Honolulu: 2002.

Carroll, Rick (collector). *True Encounters with Hawaii's Fire Goddess: Mme Pele*. Honolulu: Bess Press, 2003. (Carroll wrote a series of five books collecting Hawaii's "Spooky Lore." He also collected/published *Hawaii's Best Spooky Tales, Vol. 2—More True Local Spine-tinglers*.)

Kane, Herbert. *Pele, Goddess of Hawaii's Volcanoes*. Honolulu: Kawainui, 1996. An excellent narrative with excellent illustrations. Kane is well regarded as one of the top Hawaiian painter/illustrators of early Hawaii.

Varez, Dietrich, and Pua Kanakaole Kanahele. *Pele the Fire Goddess*. Honolulu: Bishop Museum Press, 1991. With woodblock illustrations by Varez.

Wichman, Frederick B. *Pele Ma: Legends of Pele from Kauai*. Honolulu: Bamboo Ridge Press, 2001. A must for anyone interested in the pre-contact period. Wichman is the authority/author on all Kauai folklore rendered as literature.

To See Below the Surface
A Story of Folklore and Fossils

DARLENE J. NEUMANN *and*
LARRY C. NEUMANN

CCC topics: Patterns, Cause and effect, Systems and System models.
POSE topics: Asking questions, Planning and carrying out investigations, Analyzing and interpreting data, Engaging in argument from evidence, obtaining, evaluating and communicating information.

Short Text of Story

To See Below the Surface

Have you ever looked at something really, really closely? Have you ever wondered why this beautiful something was the way it was? William Smith wondered! Who would guess that someone with such an ordinary name could change the face of scientific thinking for the future?

William was born in 1769 in the village of Churchill, Oxfordshire, England. His father was a blacksmith who died when William was 8, and he was sent to live with an uncle on a dairy farm, where he was treated cruelly.

Perhaps as a defense mechanism, William began a lifelong habit of asking himself questions and looking carefully at what was around him. He and his friends would play marbles with pretty little roundish rocks. To William's friends they were marbles, nothing more, but William knew they were called fossils. He called them pundibs, but they had long been known as lampshell fossils. There were living versions of these little pundibs found on shallow sands and in the estuaries of rivers. William picked up other fossils—white, dome-shaped rocks in the fields around Oxfordshire. He saw the dairymaids casually using them on their butter scales but William noted the delicate patterns with five segments on the tops. He studied and collected them and perhaps compared them with pictures of modern sea urchins that he found in his schoolbooks. What were such sea creatures doing in a pasture a hundred miles from the sea?

Even though people didn't really know what fossils were or where the fossils came from, collecting them was all the rage.

Long before people understood that fossils had once been living plants and animals that turned to stone, stories developed across different cultures that explained what these strange rocks might be:

> Long, long ago, in the middle of the 18th century it was, a servant girl named Molly was off to the Suffolk market on the English coast. She was well prepared. She had put out small, white Fairy Loaves, made of stone, by the hearth in the master's kitchen. She also carried her long pound measuring stone which was a bit larger and more rounded than her fairy loaf.
>
> Of course, her fairy loaf had been baked by fairies! Because Molly kept these fairy loaves in the kitchen, the fairies would make sure the real loaves of bread that the cook made were always perfectly formed and would rise properly, and so it was that Molly had beautiful brown loaves of bread to sell. But if she let the house remain without these white stone loaves for a week, then the kitchen would lose the protective powers of the fairies. Finding fairy loaves and pound stones was easy. They were just lying about in the Oxfordshire fields. They had come out of the white chalk cliffs.
>
> Molly held her white poundstone in her hand. It was dome-shaped, almost round, with a 5-pointed star imprinted on its upper side. All of Molly's friends carried stones just like hers, weighing almost exactly the same. The sellers would use them to measure sweet butter.

William had little chance for schooling, but he loved books. When he found *The Art of Measuring*, it changed his life by teaching him the basics of surveying. When he saw a man carrying surveyor's tools, William struck up a conversation. The man was looking for an apprentice, and William fit the bill. His surveying work would take him not only across the fields, but also down into the coal mines, since the owners had hired his master. As he went deeper and deeper, William noticed how the layers of rock changed.

Of course the miners noticed the layers, too. They had names for the layers and veins like Farrington Red Formation, Mangots Field, Temple Cloud, or Warkey Course. "Check out the Firestone today," they might say, or "You work Little Course, and I'll do Dungy Drift."

William enjoyed the names, but he was curious about what the order of the layers meant. How did they become arranged that way? William noticed different fossils in different layers. He started to collect and carefully record the fossils he discovered. He moved beyond collecting easily found fairy loaves called Echinoids, like the Micraster or heart urchin. Or the pretty marbles, the brachiopods, he'd played with as a child. His desire to collect and understand fossils became insatiable.

This was the beginning of the Industrial Age, the end of the 18th century, and England's industries had an insatiable need for coal, but where could it be found? Could William predict where the coal might be? Could he draw a map somehow that would show what lay under the earth, fossils and coal both? That would suit his need for finding fossils and suit others' need for coal. That is how he could be paid while pursuing his passion for fossils!

All the mine owners began building canals to transport their coal to market as quickly and efficiently as possible. William himself was hired to survey and plan for a canal to carry the local coal, and his success led to surveying for many coal canals. As William walked across thousands of miles of the English countryside, he studied the rock layers exposed by canal excavations and his fossil collection grew.

Among the rock layers, William noted something odd. Between strata they called Millstone and Pennant Stone was a dramatic change in the kinds of fossils found in the rocks. In the Millstone layer, plant fossils dominated. Fossils such as *Annularia* and *Lepidodendron* were found and recorded. In the Pennant Stone layer, marine mollusk shells dominated. Here were the brachiopods such as *Carbonicola*, *Anthracosia* and *Lingula*. William assumed that at various times throughout the history of the world, different types of sediments must have filled the "then" ocean basins and entrapped animals living during those times.

> Molly's cousin Sarah didn't believe in fairy loaves. She called them thunderstones, because they had descended from the heavens during thunderstorms. Sarah had heard thunderstones called snakes' eggs! If balls made from froth of snakes were stolen during Midsummer's Eve and kept on a piece of cloth, the balls could protect people from deadly poisons. Sarah much preferred to call them thunderstones!
>
> Molly's Uncle Phillip was a shepherd on the downlands of southern England, and he said that Molly's fairy loaves were properly called shepherds' crowns. These stones gave prosperity, power, and protected homes from all types of misfortunes and calamities.
>
> As Molly passed the old church, she thought about the stones that were kept inside. Christians believed that if tonguestones were dipped into a poisonous drink, they would remove the poison. How could a girl like Molly possibly have known that these were teeth of sharks that lived so long ago?
>
> Molly holds her place in folklore as she holds her fairy loaves. The beliefs of Molly and her family are myths. What Molly holds are fossils of sea urchins, perhaps Micraster or Conulus, but there were many strange stones in Molly's area of Lyme Regis. When the devil clipped his toenails, Molly believed the clippings turned to stone. Today we call them Devil's Toenails, *Gryphaea*, extinct fossil oysters.
>
> Molly's family was not alone in their beliefs. In Britain and Ireland, ammonites were said to be snakes turned to stone by St. Hilda or St Patrick, and trilobite tails were butterflies turned to stone by Merlin. In Sweden, legend tells that belemnite fossils were candles used by gnomes. In China they were swordstones, and in Greece they were thunderbolts. The ancient Greeks also believed that the large bones of mammoths and dinosaurs were human bones, relics from a time when people were giant-sized.

How could William show the wonders that lay beneath the earth? Other maps used color to designate landforms on the earth's surface. Could he use colors to show what hid below the surface? Using all of his notes and fossil records, he began to draw a geologic map of the entire country of England and Wales. William realized something that no one had seen before. Certain fossils always appeared in certain layers and in a special order. This became known as faunal or fossil succession, and it became a keystone to understanding the true nature of earth's history. William could now locate valuable coal seams for a fuel-hungry nation, and scientists would have to acknowledge his new ideas. Publishing the map would be expensive, but he was sure that once people saw the map's value, he would be properly recognized and rewarded. He tried to get the support and recognition of the newly formed Geological Society by inviting them to his newly purchased estate, but they dismissed his incredible fossil collection which he had arranged in relative time order and carefully classified. They turned up their noses at his map and treated him like a lower class nobody. Unfortunately, the Geological Society was made up of cultured and well-bred gentlemen who would not even consider William Smith for membership in their elite group.

With no help at all from the Society, William gathered 200 investors and even mortgaged all his properties and finally published his map in 1815. The map measured 6 feet by 8 feet, 6 inches. His map was hand-colored to show the rock strata. William's map would eventually change how people thought about the age of the earth. It would spark new thinking like that of Darwin and others who wondered how life had evolved. It was quite simply one of the greatest scientific advances of his age!

The Geological Society soon recognized the importance of William Smith's map. Without his permission, they copied William Smith's map, sold it for a lower price than William could, and drove William into financial ruin. Instead of receiving fame and fortune, William landed in debtors' prison. Even selling his precious fossil collection was not enough to pay off his mortgages. After getting out of prison in 1819, he left London. He lived in obscurity, taking small surveying jobs to support his family that now included an orphaned nephew. In 1831, one of his odd jobs landed William on the estate of a wealthy gentleman in the North of England.

This wealthy gentleman, recognizing what William had accomplished, presented him again to the Geological Society. Although they had refused him membership twelve years earlier, the Society awarded him the first Wollaston Medal, their highest honor. In 1845, his nephew John Phillips received the same medal; in 1859, it was awarded to Charles Darwin. William Smith also received an honorary Doctorate of Letters from Trinity College, Dublin. And perhaps most practical, he received a lifetime pension from King William IV. Looking closely and wondering had finally earned William Smith the fame and fortune he deserved!

William Smith's final eight years were happy. He was to be known long after as "Strata" Smith and the Father of Modern Geology.

Copyright and all rights reserved by Larry and Darlene Neumann. Permission granted for classroom use. For other purposes please contact Larry and Darlene Neumann.

Standards

NGSS—Earth & Space Science—fossils

LS4-1 Analyze and interpret data for patterns in the fossil record that document the existence, diversity, extinction, and change of life forms throughout the history of life on Earth under the assumption that natural laws operate today as in the past.

CCSS

ELA-LITERACY.SL6.2 Interpret information presented in diverse media and formats (e.g., visually, quantitatively, orally) and explain how it contributes to a topic, text, or issue under study.
English Language Arts Standards: Science & Technical Subjects: Grade 6–8
CCSS.ELA-LITERACY.RST.6-8.8 Distinguish among facts, reasoned judgment based on research findings, and speculation in a text.

Objectives

Sixth grade students will be able to say:

I can distinguish between fact and folklore.
Using a fossil guide, I can identify individual fossils by common and scientific name.
I can place fossil specimens in relative order in reference to the geologic timeline.

Materials

- Fossils or pictures of individual fossils from the story's list
- Printouts of Geological Time Scale http://geographyclassroom2014.weebly.com or https://geogeek1726.files.wordpress.com/2014/04/geological-time-2.jpg (Permission granted for noncommercial use.)

- Fossil resource guide or web resources
- Story of "To See Below the Surface"
- List of Fossils in Groups for "To See Below the Surface" (Most, but not all, of these fossils are included in the story.)

Group A
Archaeopteris
Trilobites
Calamites
Ammonites
Annularia
Lepidodendron

Group B
Micraster
Conulus
Gryphaea

Belemnites
Echinoids
Brachiopods
Lingula

Group C
Shark's tooth
Mammoth
Tyrannosaurus
Triceratops
Stegosaurus

Instructional Plan

Rationale

This lesson would serve as an excellent introduction to a fossil unit or as a culminating activity. Using the story of a real scientist as well as the prevailing fossil folklore of his time, students can explore the identification of fossils as well as practicing relative time ordering.

Preparation

Fossil identification: Using books or websites, copy images of fossils related to the story "To See Below the Surface."

Make a worksheet that includes List of Fossils in Groups for "To See Below the Surface."

Familiarity with geological time scale—print copies for student use.

William Smith's contribution to geology—read the NASA site information on William Smith.

Activity

Begin the lesson by telling the "To See Below the Surface" story. It is set up so that it can be told in tandem as one story or by an individual as two separate stories. The teacher will ask students to briefly write down info gleaned from the story; expect at least three insights or facts from William Smith's life and three examples of fossil folklore. Discussion follows. Give them a list of fossils related to the story.

Students will select three fossils; each fossil must be from a different group. Using reference books or websites, they will answer these questions for each fossil:

1. Is it a plant, marine or terrestrial animal, vertebrate or invertebrate?

2. In what period of the geologic time scale did it first appear? Lay each fossil on the chart.

3. After studying the fossils or photos, students will form their own bit of folklore about how people might have explained one of these fossils. (e.g., When you look at the fossil, what does it remind you of in your own experience? How might you use this special object?) Share the fossil folklore with a partner.

4. What observations can students make about how fossils appear on the scale? (e.g., What do you notice about the order in which the fossils appear? Fossils occur in order from simple to complex).

Assessment

In partners, students will identify and order three fossils on a copy of the geological time scale according to their first appearance in the fossil record.

Evaluate observations made by students about how fossils appear on the scale.

BIBLIOGRAPHY AND RESOURCES

- Hull Museums Collections. "Fossil Myths and Folklore." 2008. http://www.hullcc.gov.uk/museumcollections/collections/storydetail.php?irn=242
- *National Audubon Society Field Guide to Fossils.* New York: Alfred A. Knopf, 2013.
- Natural History Museum. "Fossil Folklore." London, 2015. http://www.nhm.ac.uk/nature-online/earth/fossils/fossil-folklore/index.htm
- Other Worlds Educational Enterprises, LLC. http://www.otherworlds-edu.net. Click on the fossils link.
Excellent, affordable, and reliable source of fossils, kits, and lesson plans. Other Worlds Educational Enterprises, LLC, specializes in Earth and Space Games, Resources and Activities for the Classroom, Academic Science Competitions, Clubs, and Homes.
- *Prehistoric Life: The Definitive Visual History of Life on Earth.* New York: Dorling Kindersley Limited, 2009.
- Shuker, Karl P.N., Dr. "Sea Dragons, Fairy Loaves & Serpents of Stone." 2010. http://www.darkdorset.co.uk/the_dorsetarian/0/fossil_folklore

- Walker, Cyril, and David Ward. *Fossils*. New York: Dorling Kindersley, 2002. (DK Smithsonian Handbooks)
- "William Smith" (1769–1839). http://www.ucmp.berkeley.edu/history/smith.html
- "William Smith." NASA Earth Observatory. NASA Goddard Space Flight Center. http://earthobservatory.nasa.gov/Features/WilliamSmith/page2.php
- Winchester, Simon. *The Map That Changed the World: William Smith and the Birth of Modern Geology.* New York: HarperCollins, 2002.

"Skunny Wundy and the Stone Giant"
Crystallization

MARILYN A. KINSELLA *and* LARRY KINSELLA

CCC topics: Systems and system models, Structure and function, Energy and matter.
POSE topics: Developing and using models; Analyzing and interpreting data.

The Story

"Skunny Wundy and the Stone Giant"
Abridged by Marilyn A. Kinsella

Long ago there was a famous Indian by the name of Skunny Wundy. He was very clever, but such a braggart. He told everyone that he was not afraid of anything—not even the Stone Giants, who were also called the Flintcoats. The Flintcoats with skin as tough as stone; the Flintcoats with faces carved from granite; the Flintcoats whose eyes blazed of yellow quartzite. His people were so tired of hearing Skunny Wundy brag, but they wouldn't say anything because he was also a trickster. And no one wanted to be at the end of one of Skunny Wundy's tricks.

One day, a runner came to the village. "Run!" he cried. "There is a Stone Giant on the other side of the river we must run and hide!" Everyone ran, but not Skunny Wundy. "Stone Giants! I do not fear Stone Giants!" The old sachem, the chief, looked at Skunny Wundy, "Even you, Skunny Wundy, must fear the Stone Giants."

"Skunny Wundy and the Stone Giant" (M. Kinsella & L. Kinsella)

"I fear no one and I fear nothing!" His people walked away from him and into the council house. When they returned, the sachem said that they chose him to fight the giant. Skunny Wundy was actually very frightened but he said, "Well then, I'm off ... off to fight the Stone Giant."

He ran into the woods and cried, "How am I, little Skunny Wundy, going to fight a Stone Giant?" Then, he had an idea. "Is it not true that I, Skunny Wundy, am very clever, and the Stone Giants ... are not? I shall trick that Stone Giant!"

He ran to the river's edge. There was the Stone Giant with skin as tough as stone; a face carved from granite, but it was his eyes that Skunny Wundy couldn't help but look at, for they blazed of yellow quartzite. Skunny Wundy was scared, but when the Stone Giant looked at him, he said, "Hey, are you that Skunny Wundy?"

"Yeah, and what are you going to do about it?'

"Well, I'm coming over to fight you." The Stone Giant picked up a huge log, put it over his head like a war club and began to cross the river. But, the river was very deep, and before long he was submerged under the water. And, everybody knows, Stone Giants cannot swim.

Skunny Wundy knew this. He saw some logs banked across the river. He ran for all he was worth to the other side. When he got there, the Stone Giant emerged and said, "Skunny Wundy, where are you?"

Skunny Wundy yelled back, "I'm right here waiting for you. Oh, you Stone Giants have no sense ... including no sense of direction. You must have got turned around. Now get over here and fight."

The Stone Giant threw down his war club and began to cross back over. But, when he was submerged, Skunny Wundy ran back to the other side. He was running so fast that he didn't even notice that his stone ax, the one he wore at his waist, the one with his own special markings, had fallen to the ground, and he had no way to get it back.

When the Stone Giant emerged, he did not see Skunny Wundy, but he did see his stone ax. "What's that, some kind of toy?" He picked up that tiny ax. "I wonder how sharp it is?" So, he licked the very edge of the ax. "I think I'll break this toy ax against the huge, stone boulder." But, when he threw the ax, the stone boulder burst into a million pieces. (You see, everyone knows that a stone implement that touches the tongue of a Stone Giant becomes very powerful. But, the Stone Giants don't know this for they indeed have no sense.)

Then, the Stone Giant saw Skunny Wundy on the opposite shore and yelled, "Don't come over here and hurt me!"

"Do you promise to never hurt my people again? Do you promise to tell the story of the great and wonderful Skunny Wundy every night around the fire? Do you?"

"I promise, Skunny Wundy, we will go off to the high country. You will never see us again. And, uh, I promise to tell your story over and over ... but please don't come over here."

"All right then, be off with you, but never let me see your ugly face again!" Since that time that Stone Giant and all the others have never been seen. But, when Skunny Wundy could see that the coast was clear, he ran back over to the opposite shore, picked up his ax and said, "Now I can go back to my people. I can tell them how brave I was. I can tell them how clever I was!"

And, do you know what? That's exactly what he did. The people put their fingers in their ears because they didn't want to hear. But no one ever complained about all that bragging. Because not only was Skunny Wundy a braggart, he was a braggart with a very powerful stone ax.

Standards

NGSS

MS-ESS2-1 Earth's Systems. Students who demonstrate this understanding can develop a model to describe the cycling of Earth's materials and the flow of energy that drives this process.

CCSS for ELA

W.6.3. Write narratives to develop real or imagined experiences or events using effective technique, relevant descriptive details, and well-structured event sequences.

W.6.4. Produce clear and coherent writing in which the development, organization, and style are appropriate to task, purpose, and audience.

SL.6.1. Engage effectively in a range of collaborative discussions (one-on-one, in groups, and teacher led) with diverse partners on grade 6 topics, texts, and issues, building on others' ideas and expressing their own clearly.

W.6.3. Write narratives to develop real or imagined experiences or events using effective technique, relevant descriptive details, and well-structured event sequences.

SL.6.4. Present claims and findings, sequencing ideas logically and using pertinent descriptions, facts, and details to accentuate main ideas or themes; use appropriate eye contact, adequate volume, and clear pronunciation.

SL.6.5. Include multimedia components (e.g., graphics, images, music, sound) and visual displays in presentations to clarify information.

NCAS

Create, Connect

"Skunny Wundy and the Stone Giant" (M. Kinsella & L. Kinsella)   257

Objectives

Middle School students will be able to say:

- I can conduct an experiment that allows me to observe the process of crystallization.
- I can embed accurate, appropriate scientific facts into a fictional story.
- I can create a graphic model describing the crystallization process represented in my fictional story.

Materials

- Bruchac, Joseph. *Heroes and Heroines, Monsters and Magic: Native American Legends and Folktales.* New York: Crossing Press, 2000.
- For science experiment, each student will need:
  - A heatproof glass jar (a mason jar is excellent)
  - A measuring cup
  - One cup of boiling water
  - A spoon
  - ½ cup of salt
  - A paperclip
  - A pencil
  - Cotton string

Instructional Plan

Rationale

Evoking curiosity is the job of the story—satisfying that curiosity is the job of the scientist. Larry takes over at that point to demonstrate, explain and involve the students in hands-on discovery.

Preparation

Tell "Skunny Wundy!" The story engages students' curiosity, evoking a barrage of questions. The questions always include, "How did licking the ax make it stronger?" and "What is yellow quartzite and how does it blaze?"

Activity

Larry Kinsella is an experimental archaeologist, and I (Marilyn A. Kinsella) am a storyteller. Since 2002, we have worked to produce informative, entertaining, hands-on storytelling-and-demonstration programs for schools, libraries and museums. After I tell the story, Larry shows the class a variety of stones, including yellow quartzite, and discusses the various materials and how they are classified by the way in which they were formed. After a general discussion, he focuses on the quartzite.

Quartzite is mineral that has been converted into a solid quartz rock by precipitation of silica from water that flows or drips through pores and cracks below the Earth's surface or by recrystallization under high temperatures and pressures.

A mineral is an inorganic naturally occurring crystalline solid. This means that minerals form as crystals. Some mineral crystals, like halite (table salt when it's in your kitchen cupboard) are created by precipitation. The minerals precipitate out of a solution and collect into their crystal forms. With a few collected items, you can use this process to grow your own crystals.

To Prepare a Supersaturated Solution
- Tie the paperclip to one end of the string, and the pencil to the other end. When the pencil is placed across the top of the jar, the string should be just long enough to let the paperclip touch the bottom. Set the string, pencil, and paperclip aside.
- Boil about 1 cup of water, either in the microwave or on the stove. Pour the boiling water into the jar.
- Add the salt one teaspoonful at a time. Stir until each teaspoon is completely dissolved. Don't add all the salt at once—the experiment won't work as well! Be patient. Eventually, a small amount of salt will not dissolve but will collect at the bottom of the jar. The solution has reached super saturation. Once the solution is supersaturated, stop adding salt.
- Next, put it all together and find out what to do with that string and the paper towel:
- Lower the paper clip and string into the water and rest the pencil across the top of the jar. Cover the jar lightly with a paper towel. This will keep dust out of the jar. Place the jar where it won't be disturbed for a couple of days.
- Rock salt (halite) crystals form as cubes. After about 12 hours, small crystals begin to visibly form at the bottom of the jar, on the paper clip, and along the string. Some may even form on the surface of the water, like a wreath around the string. After 24 hours, definite crystal forms should be visible.
- After one or two days, cubes of salt crystals will be visible. Some may form alone and grow larger, while others may form clusters.
- To make a completely different shape, try using 1 and 1/2 cups of

Epsom salts (magnesium sulfate) instead of 1/2 cup of salt. The Epsom salt crystals will tend to form on the bottom of the jar and are generally shaped like stubby prisms.

After observing the crystallization process, pair students and ask them to discuss the outcome and journal their findings. What happened? What caused this outcome? What makes you say that? Compare and contrast the two different crystal structures. What patterns can be perceived? In nature, where would the water come from? What natural phenomena might disrupt or contribute to the process? How can this process be represented graphically?

Review the story of "Skunny Wundy and the Stone Giant." Ask the pairs to theorize about how the Stone Giant got his crystallized eyes. Where was he (at the beach, in the mountains, in a cave…)? What materials surrounded him (salt water, sand, trees, dirt…)? What happened to him? How long did it take? Were any other characters involved? How well does he see now? Do the crystal eyes have any special abilities?

Ask the pairs to collaborate in writing a story about how the Stone Giant got his quartz eyes. Explain that while the story itself will be fiction, the process of crystallization must be accurately described, as well as be represented in a graphic format.

Have a Stone Giant Storytelling Festival, allowing students to share their stories with the class using character voices, body language, and their graphic representations.

Assessment

- The crystallization activity can be assessed through observation; use a rubric to assess the journal entries for accuracy, completeness, and evidence of critical thinking.
- The Skunny Wundy story can also be assessed by a rubric for accurateness, appropriate scientific facts, and creative thinking.
- The graphic model can be assessed for accuracy in representing the crystallization process.

BIBLIOGRAPHY
- Kids Love Rocks.com. http://www.kidsloverocks.com/html/crystals.html
- Rocks for Kids.com. "How Rocks & Minerals are Formed." http://www.rocksforkids.com/RFK/howrocks.html
- Tomecek, Steve. *National Geographic Kids Everything Rocks and Minerals: Dazzling gems of photos and info that will rock your world.* Washington, D.C., National Geographic, 2011.
- Zoehfeld, Kathleen Weidner. *Rocks and Minerals.* Washington, D.C.: National Geographic, 2012.

PART THREE

Conclusions and Possibilities
Storytelling and the National Aeronautic and Space Administration

"Whoever these Beings are, I think they want to Dance."—
From *Forged in the Stars*, Jay O'Callahan

Childhood fascinations with how the world and space work have propelled Nobel winners and graduate students into NASA's program since 1958. Their work was a story waiting to be told.

Storytellers Beth Horner and Jay O'Callahan were commissioned by NASA to create stories, some for internal use, some external, about the work of the National Aeronautic Space Administration. The stories tell the "ups and downs" of NASA in ways understandable to non-scientists, and to the people of NASA.

The tales of tools and scientific processes created by engineers and scientists are even more amazing when we note that all of technology is manmade. People did these things! People created what nature didn't, thus beginning a new chapter in the human story. It is the joyous combination of the science and technology *and* our stories that frame our existence—our human and earthly history and our present lives, ... and our future—brought to us by dreams and passions and courage and intelligence and wisdom—and love.

An Interview with Beth Horner

On and off from 2006 to 2010 Beth Horner provided storytelling workshops for NASA (the National Aeronautic and Space Administration), specifically at the Jet Propulsion Lab (in conjunction with the International Storytelling Center) and for NASA's FameLab Astrobiology program. In 2009–2010, she worked with the Johnson Space Center's StoryMining Project, a project designed to collect stories from the scientists who worked in JSC's Lunar Receiving Laboratory (LRL) during the Apollo Missions of the 1960s and 1970s. Her assignment/contract was to interview and videotape the scientists and create a series of vodcasts for the inner–NASA website. The purpose of the project was to initiate new NASA staff members into the scientific history of the LRL, and to inform scientists of lunar samples still available for research in JSC's Pristine Lunar Sample Laboratory.

Jane: You were hired to create science stories, not cultural or personal journeys like Jay, and the late Syd Lieberman.

Beth: I was contracted to do both. The difference between the StoryMining project and Syd's and Jay's projects was in the final format of the information. Syd and Jay were hired to collect information and then create a story/narrative for live performance. I was hired to collect stories of the science and the scientists and then, to create a series of stories in vodcast format and in which the scientists themselves tell the stories.

The 1960s/70s was an amazing time for space exploration. President John F. Kennedy had made the public statement on May 25, 1961, "I believe that this nation should commit itself to achieving the goal, before the decade is out, of landing a man on the Moon and returning him safely to Earth." This was a high-profile effort in the United States' technological race with Russia. NASA created an engineering team ... originally exclusive of geologists ... to get a man up to the moon and back. Geologists looked at such a mission as an opportunity for what geologist Ross Taylor dubbed "A Big Giant

262 Part Three. Conclusions and Possibilities

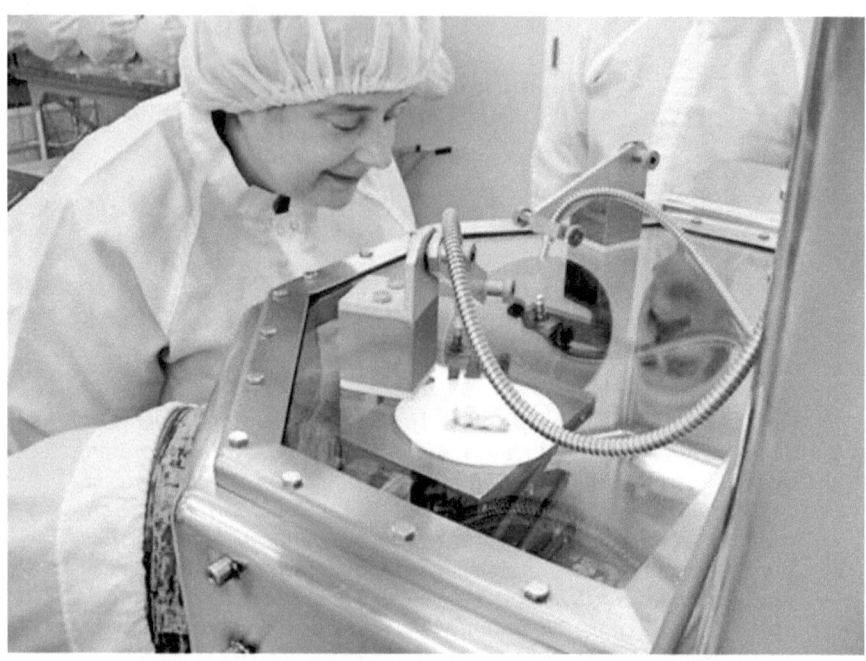

Beth Horner exploring at Lunar Receiving Lab.

Field Trip in the Sky" and lobbied for bringing back lunar samples to study. When NASA agreed to the idea, a team of geologists was gathered to train the astronauts on what type of lunar samples to gather and how to gather them, to work with engineers on designing procurement instruments and storage containers, to design protocols for handling and storing lunar samples for future scientific research, to create a building of laboratories for containing and providing initial scientific information on the lunar samples as well as protocols for readying and making available lunar samples for the world's scientists to study. The building was called the Lunar Receiving Lab (LRL). It was a heady time for this team that included both Nobel Prize winners and young graduate students who worked under great pressure with the world watching every move. The stories of the science and the scientists are riveting.

Jane: Those vodcasts—how did you decide to tackle that work? It is storytelling, but not in the traditional way of doing the research and creating a story for performance.

Beth: My interviewees did not necessarily understand the story. Therefore, in order to create the vodcasts, I had to create a series of questions that would elicit answers from the scientists so that they would be telling the stories in their own words.

Before I could create the questions and conduct the interviews, I had to already know the story of the LRL, a building which no longer exists as it did then—its history, its funding, its multifaceted function and multifaceted laboratories, the conflicts behind the scientific and political ramifications of its existence, the duties of its large and varied staff ... its story. I also sifted through hundreds of archival photographs and rare videotapes in order to provide visual images to accompany the story. I then created the story's structure and the interview questions that would elicit the answers that told the overall story at different points along the overall "plot line."

After the interviews were completed, my job then was to make editing decisions on the videotaped interviews so that at each step along the "plotline" of the overall LRL story, several scientists were telling the story from their specific points of view—all overlaid with images and edited into a series of short vodcasts.

Just like preparation for the first Apollo mission to the moon, preparation for these interviews was time limited and intense. I was to interview a series of geologists, astrogeologists, geochemists and astrobiologists whom I had not met before arriving at the Johnson Space Center. Before this project, I had never heard of the LRL, did not know the definition of a geochemist or astrobiologist and had never edited video. The scope of this project was also new to me because rather than my usual process of creating and presenting an oral story to an audience whom I could see, it was about creating vodcasts for NASA staff viewers to help them understand what it was like in the amazing and extraordinarily rare times of the Apollo missions, how each interviewee fit into the story and the remarkable science that resulted AND can still be discovered today.

In the very short and rather crazed prep time, I worked with the Story Mining team of Kay Tobola (JSC StoryMining Project Visioner/ Director and NASA Astromaterials Research and Exploration Science Directorate Education Specialist) and Judith H. Allton (Geologist, NASA Genesis Solar Wind Sample Curator and LRL historian who had compiled large amounts of the LRL documents, history and stories).

When I arrived at JSC, I had researched the LRL and each scientist I was to interview, but because Kay and Judy knew the scientists personally, their "coaching" was essential. At breakfast and lunch each day, Kay and Judy crammed information into my brain and made important suggestions: "The story of Elbert King, the first Lunar Sample Curator, is key. Ask several of the guys about him." "Be sure to ask Don Bogard why he calls the LRL *The Complicated Beast* and how he did gas analyses on the lunar samples." "Ask Gary Lofgren about being in a back room sawing through lunar rocks for study and going home with lunar dust in his hair while in another part of the LRL, as demanded by various government entities, lunar dust was being fed to cockroaches and mice and sprinkled onto plants to determine if it was poisonous and would harm the earth." "Ask Everett Gibson, who was right out of school at the time, about sharing an office with Nobel Prize winner Harold Urey. Oh, and Everett has some hysterical stories about working within the quarantine. Ask him about the notorious *No Pest Strip*." My favorite: "Jack Warren is reluctant to be interviewed. Take him to breakfast tomorrow, charm him and see if he'll agree to an interview. He was the technician who opened the first box of lunar rocks as all the photographers took thousands of photos from the other side of the quarantine glass and the world's scientists lined up to look inside the box. So, charm him Beth. He knows things no one else knows!" I would quickly scratch down these questions and bits of information on a yellow pad and then, the three of us would go to Jacobs Technology where I'd meet the scientist to be interviewed and, with my mind spinning with this new information and focused on the arc of the overarching LRL story, launch into an interview recorded by a videographer.

The scientists and technicians I interviewed were excited to tell their stories and more than once responded to questions with: "I've never told this to anyone"; "What we as a scientific community would never otherwise have discovered is…"; "Wow, no one has ever asked that"; "It's difficult to explain in lay terms, but I'll try"; "We decided to proceed with research in this manner because … and it set the protocol for … that is still being used today."

At the end of each interview I had a set of five questions that I asked each scientist. Two were:

- What path would a lunar sample take from the ship to the LRL to the scientists' research labs? What was your work in the process?
- If you could relive one moment from your work at the LRL, what would it be?

Some selected a moment in which they were absolutely astonished by a discovery and described the scientific process in fascinating detail; some selected a moment in which they would have taken a different direction and explained why; some simply reveled in a moment that touched them deeply. I learned to keep tissues nearby.

For example, one geologist recalled a late night in which he had been communicating with the astronauts while they were walking on the moon. He was instructing them on which type of samples to collect, to look for a specific crater, etc. Afterwards, he walked out of the LRL to go home and was halted by the beauty of the night sky's full moon looking down on him. At that moment, he realized that he'd just been talking with people walking on that moon and was suddenly awestruck with the absolute marvel of that fact and the absolute beauty of the moon. He simply stood and stared up at the wonder of the moon for a long time.

Jane: Beth, I think of you as a storyteller—an hilarious storyteller—and I think of some of our crazy antics. Yet, there you were working with scientists—geologists. Why did Kay Tobola seek a storyteller for the project and why did she select you specifically?

Beth: That's an excellent question and one that I continually asked Kay Tobola and Judy Allton. "I'm not a scientist," I would explain. "I'm not sure that I can understand what they are talking about and make it into a set of stories. Why me?" They explained that they had heard me tell "The Pipeline Blues" (a true story that I had created about sewage, science and community) and felt that as a storyteller, I understood the essential ingredients in the project: dynamic narrative, dynamic story.

When I see a cemetery, I immediately want to know who is lying under those stones and what those gravestones reveal about the people, how they lived, the culture, the society. What story does this cemetery tell? The geologist feels the same way about a rock. Why was it found here and not there? What is its composition? What does it say about what existed in the past or what will happen in the future? What can this particular rock tell us about science, culture, the past and the future? *What story does this rock tell?* Every aspect of scientific study is the unfolding of a suspenseful mystery. What better way to convey science than through story?

Beth Horner, a storytelling performance and teaching artist since 1983, is a National Storytelling Network Circle of Excellence Oracle Award recipient. She has performed at the National Storytelling Festival, on Live from National Geographic, *and at the International Art of Storytelling Festival, and conducted seminars and workshops for the National Conference of Agencies Serving Troubled Youth, the National Council of Teachers of English and NASA's FameLab Astrobiology.*

An Interview with Jay O'Callahan

From Jay O'Callahan's website where you can hear excerpts from Forged in the Stars: *"O'Callahan's ... work features the stories of three prominent NASA personalities: J.C. High Eagle, a NASA engineer of Cherokee Indian heritage whose childhood dream was to help men land on the moon; astronaut Neil Armstrong in the 1969* Apollo *moon landing; and the poignant story of New Hampshire teacher Christa McAuliffe, who died in the space shuttle* Challenger *disaster. Further, the story explores the wondrous journey of the twin* Voyager *spacecraft, launched in 1977 with the goal of exploring Jupiter and Saturn, and continuing on to this day to places no other spacecraft has ever explored."*

Jane: How did you come to be commissioned by NASA to create this story?

Jay: One of my former students, Jessica Fox, knew that I'd been commissioned to create a story about the immigrants who work at Bethlehem Steel Company. It was those immigrants who built much of this country. Jessica Fox worked with Dr. Ed Hoffman, who directs a leadership program at NASA. Hoffman was interested in my creating the story that would capture the "ups and downs" of NASA over fifty years. For me this was an extraordinary challenge. I did not know a lot about space science and I would be entering a new world. That's exactly what happens when one is commissioned to create a story.

I worked with a team and we interviewed engineers, scientists, managers, astronauts, NASA historians and professionals who dealt with food, clothing and so on. We began our interviews at the Johnson Space Center in Houston, Texas. Initially I wanted to do the interviews alone but being part of a team proved to be invaluable. Ed Hoffman was part of the team as was Jessica Fox and Don Cohen (Don Cohen edited a NASA engineering magazine, *ASK*). Hoffman and the others knew NASA so well they asked questions I would not have thought of and since putting a man on the moon and landing rovers on Mars is a team effort, it was good to be part of a team.

268   Part Three. Conclusions and Possibilities

I would begin the interviews asking about the childhood of those being interviewed. What did they wonder about? What did they like to do? Were they interested in space? Did they have special memories about nights under the stars? I found with many of them that they were interested in space from very early childhood. As I interviewed, threads began to appear. All of the astronauts were drawn to engineering and mathematics and all of the early astronauts were pilots.

The poet Wordsworth said, "The child is father of the man." So it was with Gary Flandro. Gary Flandro was a Caltech graduate student also working at NASA. When Flandro was a boy his mother gave him a book about the planets. He opened the book and there was a drawing of the sun and all of the planets were lined up on one side of the sun. That image came vividly back one morning when Flandro was in his office at the Jet Propulsion Laboratory in Pasadena, California. He suddenly realized that the gas giants, Jupiter, Saturn, Uranus and Neptune, were going to be lined up on one side of the sun in a way they have not been lined up for one hundred and seventy-six years. They would not be lined up that way for another one hundred and seventy-six years. In a flash Flandro thought this was the time for a Grand Tour of the outer planets. Many scientists thought this was impossible.

Gary Flandro's insight was the beginning of the *Voyager* Mission and the beginning of the long journey that has led *Voyager I* to leave our solar system.

Jane: As you thought about the story you were to craft, how did you approach the enormity of the fifty years, the remarkable developments in technology and physics?

Jay: In all of the interviews I looked for threads that made NASA's accomplishments possible. The threads were risk, vision, mathematics, communication, a pioneering spirit, perseverance, failure and learning from failure.

Communication was crucial. It took 600,000 people working together to put men on the moon. I discovered when communication breaks down not only do projects fail but people die. As I studied the *Challenger* disaster I saw there was a failure of communication that led to the deaths of the seven crew members.

Failure. One scientist told me that he and his team worked for two years on a Mars mission and it failed. He said, "Not only was I discouraged, but my family and all of my friends were discouraged and yet we persevere and learn from failure."

Risk. NASA's whole adventure is filled with risk. Scientists and engineers did not know initially how to land on the moon. They did not know if the *Voyager* spacecraft could reach Uranus and Neptune and did not know that *Voyager I* would actually leave the solar system.

Passion. Almost all of the scientists, engineers and astronauts I interviewed had passion for their work. Many of them had a passion for mathematics and science from their high school days and younger. They had a passion for being part of something far bigger than themselves, a passion for discovering more about the universe.

Pioneering Spirit. In Oklahoma I interviewed astronaut Tom Stafford, who flew a lunar lander above the moon a few months before Neil Armstrong landed on the moon. I learned that Stafford's mother came to Oklahoma when she was six in a covered wagon. Her son, Tom, grew up in Oklahoma with that pioneering spirit. As I continued my interview in Oklahoma I discovered many of the NASA astronauts, managers and engineers had grown up in Oklahoma and brought that pioneering spirit to NASA with them. That included J.C. High Eagle, a Native American, who worked as an engineer for forty years at NASA.

Dreams. NASA welcomed those who dream. President Kennedy had a dream of landing people on the moon at the end of the 1960s. J.C. High Eagle had a dream when he was only five years old that he would help people get to the moon. NASA helped him make that dream come true. Christa McAuliffe dreamed of being the first teacher in space.

The NASA commission made me dream again about outer space. I began once again to look at the stars. NASA's whole dream is one of turning our gaze to the stars.

Interconnectedness. Edgar Mitchell, an astronaut who also got a PhD from MIT, had an experience coming back from the moon that changed his life. He had an awareness that all things were interconnected. It was such a powerful awareness it changed his life.

As I told my story *Forged in the* Stars at space centers in the United States and at scientific conferences abroad, scientists and engineers could step back and see what they had accomplished. It gave them a new perspective and pride of accomplishment.

Jane: With so much technical information, how do we get to an interesting and understandable story? How do you decide what/how to deliver the science?

Jay: My challenge was to make the listeners care about the characters in the story. Ed Hoffman said he wanted me to make a love story about NASA. I thought he was joking but realized one day that was the key to the structure of the story. I would invent two characters, Jack and Kate, whose struggles would mirror the struggles of NASA. The threads in Jack and Kate's lives are the same threads that ran through NASA: risk, vision, mathematics, communication, a pioneering spirit, perseverance, failure and learning from failure. Jack and Kate are good in mathematics and love science, both intend to work for NASA and both of them struggle with taking a big risk. They have trouble communicating. If you care about Jack and Kate you care about the true stories they tell about NASA and all of the threads become important because you care about the characters. You care about the risks they take, the dreams they have and you hope that their communication will get better.

My story *Forged in the Stars* ends with Jack, a PhD. candidate at MIT going off on a riff about the Golden Record and the *Voyager*. The thread I didn't mention was imagination. *Voyager I* has left the solar system and is carrying a Golden Record with music of people around the earth. That's imagination. Nothing NASA accomplished could have been done without imagination.

What follows is the "Voyager Chant" an excerpt from *Forged in the Stars*, a synthesis of storytelling art and science:

In 1977, August, the first of the Voyagers *shoots up, September the 2nd the* Voyagers *shoot up with fifty-five "hellos." Bonjour, Nehow, Cho, Shalom.*
   Hello, hello, we want to say hello
   We want to say hello to you.
In 1979, one of the Voyagers *makes a flyby Jupiter and the scientists are fascinated. One of the moons of Jupiter, Io, looks like it's covered with a pizza. We discovered it is exploding. It is the most volcanic body in the solar system. Nobody had any idea. This is fascinating! And another moon of Jupiter, Europa, has got a crust of ice but underneath that crust of ice there may be a salt sea bigger than the Atlantic and Pacific put together. There may be life, life.*
   Hello, hello, we want to say hello
Saturn, and then January 1986, one of the Voyagers *is taking pictures of Uranus. We have never been near it. The scientists at JPL, leaping around for four days. The fourth day, January 28th, and that fourth day they're leaping around, and on the east coast, the* Challenger *is burning up.*
   Hello, hello, we want to say hello.
The Voyagers *go on. February 14th, 1990, one of the* Voyagers *is beyond Pluto and takes a photo of the planets of our solar system. And in that photo the earth is no bigger than the eye of a goldfish. It's a speck and on that speck is everything we love, and the* Voyagers *sail on.*
   Hello, hello
The Berlin Wall falls. The Voyagers *sail on.*
   Hello, hello
Nelson Mandela is released from prison after twenty-seven years and the Voyagers *sail on.*
   Hello, hello
One American and two Russians, they live in the International Space Station, one hundred and thirty-six days. Living in space has begun.

Hello, hello
The Clinton years, Princess Diana dies, the Voyagers *sail on. The year 2000, my dad, he's crossing the street in Portland, collapses and he is dead. We had hard times and wonderful times with my dad and I'm shaken as I've never been shaken in my life. And the* Voyagers *sail on.*
Hello, hello
9/11 comes.
Hello, hello
In 2003 I get here to MIT wondering can I make it? Am I good enough to get a Ph.D. at MIT? I'm scared to death and I meet a young woman, she's an engineering student and we fall in love. We're space nuts. And the Voyagers *sail on.*
2004 the Mars Rovers, two of them, set down, Spirit *and* Opportunity *and they're built to last three months. Solar panels, they're going to be covered with dust. The surprise is the wind blows the dust free and* Spirit *and* Opportunity *are going at this moment.*
Hello, hello
I get engaged. My sweetheart calls it off because I'm a stuffed shirt and breaks my heart. And the Voyagers *sail on. And now in six or seven years the* Voyagers *are going to leave our solar system. I'm sure you all know about the solar wind. The sun sends out a wind that's really particles streaming at a million miles an hour, sometimes, much more, and that forms a great bubble and the whole solar system is in the bubble. They call it a heliosphere but a bubble is a much better term. Well the* Voyagers *are going to leave the solar system, go right through the bubble. Here is the sun, here is Mercury, here is Venus, here is the Earth, ninety-three million miles from the sun. Well the* Voyagers *are ten billion miles from the sun. They're going to go through the bubble and they're going to reach the Ort Cloud in the year 26,000. They'll make the closest approach to Sirius in the year 296,036 and they will pass the twelve nearest stars in the year 1,000,000. And who knows, maybe some civilization will find one of the* Voyagers *and play the Golden Record and they'll hear Kesar Bai Kerkar, Melanisian panpipes, and Louis Armstrong and his trumpet. They'll hear Beethoven, Stravinsky and Bach and they'll heard Blind Willie Johnson singing "Dark is the Night." And maybe those beings up there will listen and say, "Whoever these beings are, I think they want to dance." And I think that would be just right because I think in the last fifty years we've been dancing our way into the universe.*

Science and Storytelling Online Resources
Compiled by KAREN CHACE

"Science and stories are not only compatible, they're inseparable."—Roald Hoffmann

Science resources to add to your curriculum; a few of the sites include folktales, pourquoi stories legends and myths. In addition, in most sections you will find stories to share with your students to complement the specific topic.

Animals

Discovery Education—Polar Bears Lesson Plan, Extensions, Reading Materials, etc. for grades 9–12.
http://www.discoveryeducation.com/teachers/free-lesson-plans/bears.cfm

Education World—*Why Polar Bears Are White.* Science and Art for grades K–2.
http://www.educationworld.com/a_tsl/archives/00-1/lesson0002.shtml

Electronic Zoo—Resources and various links to the study of the animal kingdom as well the environments in which some they live. For example, the link to whales has lesson plans developed by both educators and students to be interactive and interdisciplinary.
http://netvet.wustl.edu/ssi.htm

The Elephant Sanctuary—Two units focusing on the study of elephants offering teaching and learning activities for children grades K–8; 72 pages of instruction, background information, charts and graphs, activities, etc., for science, literature, math and social sciences.
http://www.elephants.com/curriculum.php

Feathers, Fins, Fur, Scales and Skin—Science lesson plan for K–1; students will identify animal groups by their appearance. The students will move through

animal centers looking for similarities and differences of birds, fish, mammals, reptiles, and amphibians.
http://www.learnnc.org/lp/pages/3304?ref=search

How Elephants Got Their Trunks
http://etc.usf.edu/lit2go/79/just-so-stories/1299/the-elephants-child/

How the Elephant Got His Tusks—Africa
http://www.travelbutlers.com/safari/wildlife-guide/folklore-tusks.asp

How the Leopard Got His Spots
http://etc.usf.edu/lit2go/79/just-so-stories/1304/how-the-leopard-got-his-spots/

Why the Bear Is Stumpy Tailed—Norway
http://www.ency123.com/2014/01/why-bear-has-stumpy-tail-norwegian-folk.html

Why the Fish Has Scales
http://folktales.webmanila.com/folktales/water/?fish-scales

Why the Fish Laughed
http://www.worldoftales.com/Asian_folktales/Indian_folktale_24.html

Birds

Arlington Echo Outdoor Education Center: Feathers in the Forest—Science and literacy lesson plan for Kindergarten students.
http://www.arlingtonecho.org/images/woodlands/Feathers_in_the_Forest.pdf

Beyond Polar Bears and Penguins—Hands-on Science and Literacy lesson plans that meet NCTE/IRA standards, about birds for K–5.
http://beyondpenguins.ehe.osu.edu/issue/arctic-and-anarctic-birds/hands-on-science-and-literacy-lessons-about-birds

King of the Birds
http://www.pitara.com/fiction-for-kids/folktales/king-of-the-birds/

Nature Story—Six adapted folktales about birds from storyteller Kevin Strauss.
http://www.naturestory.com/birdstories4,env.html

Earth and Sky

Beakman and Jax's Place—Interactive demos, news about the Beakman's World TV show, and Hubble Telescope pictures. Shockwave plug-in required for interactive demonstrations.
http://www.beakman.com/index.html

Earth and Mars Education Modules—Interactive student activities geared towards planet exploration. Best suited to upper elementary. Can serve as a link for teacher to other science activities. Activities linked to national benchmarks and standards teacher/student 2–3.
http://www-k12.atmos.washington.edu/k12/modules/index.html

For Kids Only—Earth Science Enterprise—Includes activities for young students to learn about various earth science concepts. Interactive online coloring book is a unique feature of this web site.
http://kids.mtpe.hq.nasa.gov/

Greatest Hits from the Hubble Telescope—Unique space photographs.
http://oposite.stsci.edu/pubinfo/BestOfHST95.html

Greek Mythology and the Forms of Energy—The ancient Greeks used myths to make sense of natural phenomena. This unit integrates literature and science, "to capture the student's interest using mythological explanations for phenomena we recognize as forms of energy." Includes some short myths to use at the end of the guide.
http://www.need.org/files/curriculum/guides/GreekMythology.pdf

How the Moon Was Created
http://www.pitara.com/fiction-for-kids/folktales/how-the-moon-was-created/

How the Rainbow Was Made—Native American
http://americanfolklore.net/folklore/2012/10/how_the_rainbow_was_made.html

How the Stars Got Into the Sky
http://www.families.com/blog/how-the-stars-got-into-the-sky

Literature Based Teaching in Science: What's in the Sky?
http://www.readingrockets.org/article/literature-based-teaching-science-whats-sky

NASA's Planetary Photojournal—A NASA database with over 1200 space images.
http://photojournal.jpl.nasa.gov/

Planet Pals.com—This is a colorful, fun and information filled website on all things Earth: Lesson plans and activities for both teachers and parents, the history behind Earth Day, coloring pages, puzzles, clip art and so much more.
http://www.planetpals.com/index.html

Sci4Kids—The science behind agriculture is presented as a series of interactive stories based on research projects featured in "Agricultural Research". Web site includes photos, graphics, trivia, and classroom connections.
http://www.ars.usda.gov/is/kids/

The Sun and the Moon
http://www.mindfueldaily.com/livewell/the-sun-and-the-moon-a-filipino-folktale

Weather WizKids: Volcanoes—Although volcanoes are natural disaster situations, nor weather phenomena, the website offers simply worded but useful information, a vocabulary list, and links to lesson plans, experiments, and science fair projects.
http://www.weatherwizkids.com/weather-volcano.htm

When the Earth and Sky Were Married
http://www.pitara.com/fiction-for-kids/folktales/when-the-earth-and-sky-were-married

Windows to the Universe—Six stories, including a link to Native American Starlore.
http://www.windows2universe.org/art_and_music/storyfolk.html

Why the Sun and Moon Live in the Sky
http://www.worldoftales.com/African_folktales/African_Folktale_10.html

The Young Maiden Who Saved Guam
http://www.guampedia.com/how-the-young-maidens-saved-guam-folktale/

Ecology

Folktales and Ecology: Animals and Humans in Cooperation and Conflict—Intended for grades 3–5 but it can be easily adapted for K–1. There are story suggestions and a useful website of folktales to help you make the most of this lesson plan.
http://edsitement.neh.gov/lesson-plan/folktales-and-ecology-animals-and-humans-cooperation-and-conflict

FOSS (Full Option Science System)—A research-based science program for grades K–8 developed at LHS with support from the National Science Foundation.
http://lhsfoss.org/index.html

"Goodall" Africa: Geography, Science and Folk Tales—Integrated Kindergarten for Science, Language Arts and Geography. A rubric is also included for assessing students' understanding. This lesson plan uses two folktales, *The Tug of War* and *How Many Spots Does a Leopard Have by Julius Lester*.
http://ronanmagalong.blogspot.com/2012/08/tug-of-war-bantu-folktale-of-east-africa.html and http://coreknowledge.org/mimik/mimik_uploads/lesson_plans/924/Goodall%20Africa%20Geography%20Science%20and%20Folk%20Tales.pdf

Fire

How Fire Came to Be
http://www.firstpeople.us/FP-Html-Legends/HowFireCameToTheSixNations-Mohawk.html

How Raven Brought Fire
http://www.worldoftales.com/Native_American_folktales/Native_American_Folktale_59.html

The Origin of Fire
http://www.worldoftales.com/Native_American_folktales/Native_American_Folktale_1.html

Teaching Activity: Teaching Guide for First Fire: A Cherokee Folktale—Comprehensive and cross cultural activities aligned with all of the State Standards. Arbordale Publishing offers and amazing array of activities and lesson plans based on the Cherokee folktale.
http://www.arbordalepublishing.com/documents/TeachingActivities/FirstFire_TA.pdf

Flowers

Indiana Expedition: Lesson Plan for Parts of a Flower: Life Science for grades 4–7.
http://media.wfyi.org/IndianaExpeditions/IDEXSeason2_2009/IDEX204/IDEX204PartsofaFlowerLesson.pdf

The Legend of the Water Lily
http://folklore4u.blogspot.com/2009/11/legend-of-water-lily-folklore-from.html

The Story of Clytie or The Girl Who Was Changed Into a Sunflower
http://www.mainlesson.com/display.php?author=bailey&book=hour&story=clytie

Insects

5 Resources to Teach About Metamorphosis—Science resources for grades Pre K–12; movies, text, worksheets, activities and more from the National Education Association.
http://www.nea.org/tools/lessons/55353.htm

How Butterflies Came to Be—Philippines
http://folktales.webmanila.com/folktales/animals/?butterflies

Why We See Ants Carrying Bundles Bigger Than Themselves
http://www.heritage-history.com/?c=read&author=barker&book=folktales&story=bundles

Magnets

Brain Pop—Lesson plans, activities and more.
http://www.brainpop.com/educators/community/bp-jr-topic/magnets/

Magnus Gets Stuck
http://eteamscc.com/wp-content/uploads/2014/10/Magnus-Gets-Stuck.pdf

Myth Lesson Plans by Raymond Huber
http://www.raymondhuber.co.nz/wp-content/uploads/MythLessons.pdf

Science Facts: Fun Magnets Facts for Kids
http://www.sciencekids.co.nz/sciencefacts/magnets.html

Natural World: Using Pourqoui Stories

Environmental Storytelling.com—Storyteller, teacher and author Kevin Strauss shares stories to teach lessons on the environment, including insects, trees, plants, birds and more.
http://www.naturestory.com/database,environ.html

Teaching with Pourquoi Tales—Activities that explore other cultures and integrate science and language arts. "Children are naturally curious about the wonders of nature. To feed this interest in the natural world—as well as inspire great

imaginative writing—you can use pourquoi tales!" Five folktales are offered along with extension plans for the classroom.
http://www.scholastic.com/teachers/lesson-plan/teaching-pourquoi-tales

Writing How & Why Stories—A unit for second through sixth grade students using pourquoi stories to enhance Science, Writing and Literacy lessons.
http://beautyandthebeaststorytellers.com/pdf/howAndWhyUnit.pdf

Trees

Arbor Day.org—The official site with everything to help you support and share this important day.
http://www.arborday.org/

Arlington Echo Outdoor Education Center: Tree-Cycle—Lesson Plan for Kindergarten with emphasis on science and environmental literacy.
http://www.arlingtonecho.org/images/woodlands/Tree_Cycle_.pdf

From the Mango Tree and Other Folktales from Nepal—Useful classroom guide to complement the book and integrated curriculum. Science areas include Subsistence Farming, Deforestation, Environment Effects of Tourism and more.
http://www.sarahlamstein.com/MangoStudyGuide.pdf

Spirit of Tree—Curricular resources, essays, organizational links, poetry and folktales from some of our leading storytellers and scholars. Rest in the cool shade of its branches and let the spirit of the trees nourish your soul.
http://spiritoftrees.org/

Trees for Life—"Award winning conservation charity dedicated to restoring the Caledonian Forest in the Highlands of Scotland." From Alder to Yew, this site is offers an array of myths and folklore of the Caledonian Forest that will surely complement an Arbor Day storytelling program.
http://treesforlife.org.uk/forest/mythology-folklore/

Water

The Crab That Played With The Sea
http://etc.usf.edu/lit2go/79/just-so-stories/1297/the-crab-that-played-with-the-sea/

ExplorA-Pond—Experience a simulated pond, take a virtual tour of an outdoor classroom, pond math and pond science activities, publish your adopted pond online, and chat with other K–6 students interested in pond stuff.
http://www.uen.org/utahlink/pond/

Flood Stories from Around the World
http://www.talkorigins.org/faqs/flood-myths.html

MathMol Hypermedia textbook for elementary school—Includes an online textbook for grades 3,4 and 5 to learn about water, matter and energy, and atoms and molecules.
http://www.nyu.edu/pages/mathmol/textbook/elem_home1.html

Measure It Up! Explore the various states of water, accompanied by activities for water measurement and conservation. Handouts, academic standards are included.
http://learningtogive.org/lessons/unit370/lesson3.html

Save That Water! Water conservation and environmental stewardship, including handouts, academic standards are included.
http://learningtogive.org/lessons/unit370/lesson4.html

SEED (Schlumberger Excellence in Educational Development)—Begun in 1998, SEED is a global non-profit education program serving students ages 10–18. The main site at http://www.seed.slb.com/en/index.htm is ripe with resources and provides access to "technological and knowledge resources for under-served students and teachers.... These include a range of project-based activities provided through an extensive multilingual web site, hands-on science education workshops, and collaborative international projects." There are also activities http://www.planetseed.com/page/teacher-center to complement an *Ocean of Stories* from Algeria to Yemen, adapted and retold by storyteller Laura Simms.
http://www.seed.slb.com/en/things_to_do/projects/ocean_of_stories/index.htm

Storytelling and Science: What a Concept—Judy Sima, Storyteller, author and librarian shares scientific information and stories to connect them with the water cycle and other areas, including astronomy, fire, frogs and more.
http://www.judysima.com/pdfs/Storytelling%20and%20Science.pdf

Teacher Plus—Magical Folklore Meets Logical Science—Activities that integrate language arts and sciences; specific folktales are suggested with links to other sites with appropriate folktales.
http://www.teacherplus.org/resources/magical-folklore-meets-logical-science

Water, Glorious Water—Identify the uses of water and its importance to the world. handouts, academic standards are included.
http://learningtogive.org/lessons/unit370/lesson1.html

Where Does Our Water Come From? Understand the water cycle, create a tactile model, and relate it to the importance of water conservation. Handouts, standards and activities are included.
http://learningtogive.org/lessons/unit370/lesson2.html

Why the Sea Is Salty
http://folktales.webmanila.com/folktales/water/?saltysea

Why the Sea Moans—A folktale from Brazil.
http://www.worldoftales.com/South_American_folktales/South_American_Folktale_21.html

Wind

Chinook Wind—Native American/Yakima
http://www.firstpeople.us/FP-Html-Legends/Chinook-Wind-Yakima.html

The Origin of the Winds—Native American
http://www.ilhawaii.net/~stony/lore91.html

Traditional Stories About the Wind—Stories and lesson plans for grades K–4. Includes the Native American tale, *Raven Makes the Wind*.
http://www.arcticclimatemodeling.com/lessons/acmp/acmp_k4_Wind_TraditionalStoriesAboutWind.pdf

The Wind and the Moon—India
http://www.culturalindia.net/indian-folktales/jataka-tales/wind-and-moon.html

Wonders of Wind Teacher's Resource Guide—Students learn about the wind through reading and activities; for grades K–8.
http://www.need.org/files/curriculum/guides/Wonders%20of%20Wind%20Teacher%20Guide.pdf

Yaponcha the Wind God—Native American/Hopi
http://www.firstpeople.us/FP-Html-Legends/Yaponcha_The_Wind_God-Hopi.html

Science Concepts; Science and Math Integration

Chem4Kids—This site speaks directly to the young scientist. It's an excellent tutorial for children learning scientific concepts and how math is integrated into science. There are no hands-on activities and the student has to have genuine interest in topic because it's encyclopedic in its approach.
http://www.chem4kids.com/

Cool Science for Curious Kids—The Howard Hughes Medical Institute invites curious kids to explore biology. Activities include dust exploration, classifying critters, microscopy, plant parts, and more.
http://www.hhmi.org/coolscience/

Discovery Channel School—This site offers multimedia, interactive video options to the classroom. The content is current and linked to the Discovery Channel and The Learning Channel programming, offering opportunities for teachers to tape the programming and use it interactively with TLC Elementary School lesson plans. Also provided for teachers and students on this site are previews of upcoming programs and "Bulletin Board" Discussion opportunities regarding lessons/program. For full audio effects, the plug-in RealAudio needs to be downloaded.
http://school.discovery.com/index.html

National Geographic Kids—The world of "National Geographic". Interactive games and explorations.
http://www.nationalgeographic.com/kids/

Bibliography

Compiled by LYNETTE J. FORD,
SHERRY NORFOLK *and* JANE STENSON

Books

Aardema, Verna. *Borreguita and the Coyote: A Tale from Ayutla, Mexico.* Illus. by Petra Mathers. New York: Knopf, 1991.
_____. *Bringing Rain to Kapiti Plain: a Nandi Tale.* Illus. by Beatriz Vidal. New York: Dial, 1981.
_____. *How the Ostrich Got Its Long Neck.* Illus. by Marcia Brown. New York: Scholastic, 1995.
_____. *Jackal's Flying Lesson.* Illus. by Dale Gottlieb. New York: Knopf, 1995.
_____. *Why Mosquitoes Buzz in People's Ears.* Illustrator Leo and Diane Dillon. New York: Dial Books for Young Readers, 1975.
"All Things are Connected." In Pleasant de Spain. *Eleven Nature Tales: A Multicultural Journey.* Little Rock, AR: August House, 1996.
"Anansi and Turtle." In Richard Young and Judy Dockrey. *African American Folktales for Young Readers.* Little Rock, AR: August House, 1993.
Andrews, Jan. *The Very Last First Time.* New York: Aladdin Paperbacks, 1985.
Anno, Mitsumasa. *Anno's Sundial.* New York: Philomel Books, 1985.
Arneach, Lloyd, and Lydia Halverson. *The Animals' Ballgame: A Cherokee Story from the Eastern Band of the Cherokee Nation.* (Adventures in Storytelling series). Chicago: Children's Press, 1992.
Asbjørnsen, Peter Christen, and Jorgen Moe. *The Three Billy Goats Gruff.* Boston, MA: Harcourt, 1991.
Asch, Frank. *Moonbear.* New York: Charles Scribner's Sons, 1978.
_____. *Mooncake.* New York: Aladdin, 1999.
_____. *Moon Game.* Englewood Cliffs, NJ: Prentice-Hall, 1984.
Bang, Betsy. *The Old Woman and the Red Pumpkin.* New York: Atheneum, 1975.
Bang, Molly, and Penny Chisholm. *Living Sunlight.* New York: Blue Sky Press, 2009.
Baylor, Byrd. *I'm in Charge of Celebrations.* New York: Charles Scribner's Sons, 1986.
Belle, Jennifer. *Animal Stackers.* New York: Hyperion Books for Children, 2005.
Brown, Peter. *The Curious Garden.* Boston: Little, Brown Books for Young Readers, 2009.
Bruchac, Joseph. *Heroes and Heroines, Monsters and Magic: Native American Legends and Folktales.* New York: Crossing Press, 2000

_____, and Gayle Ross. *The Story of the Milky Way: A Cherokee Tale*. New York: Dial, 1995.
Bruchac, Joseph, and James Bruchac. *How Chipmunk Got His Stripes*. New York: Dial, 2001.
_____. *Racoon's Last Race: A Traditional Abenaki Story*. New York: Dial, 2004.
_____. *Turtle's Race with Beaver: A Traditional Seneca Story*. New York: Dial, 2003.
Bruchac, Joseph, and Jonathon London. *Thirteen Moons on Turtle's Back*. New York: Philomel, 1992.
Bryan, Ashley. *Turtle Knows Your Name*. New York: Simon & Schuster, 1989.
Bunting, Eve. *Flower Garden*. New York: HMH Books for Young Children, 1994.
Burton, Virginia Lee. *The Little House*. New York: Houghton Mifflin, 1942.
Bushyhead, Robert H. *Yonder Mountain: A Cherokee Legend*. New York: Marshall Cavendish, 2002.
Caduto, Michael. *Earth Tales from Around the World*. Golden, CO: Fulcrum, 1997.
Canon, Jannell. *Stellaluna*. New York: Harcourt, 1993.
Carle, Eric. *Papa, Please Get the Moon for Me*. Saxonville, MA: Picture Book Studio, 1986.
_____. *The Tiny Seed*. New York: Simon & Schuster Books for Young Readers, 1987.
_____. *Very Busy Spider*. New York: Philomel, 1984.
_____. *Very Clumsy Click Beetle*. New York: Philomel, 1999.
_____. *The Very Grouchy Ladybug*. New York: HarperFestival, 1999 (1977).
_____. *The Very Hungry Caterpillar*. New York: Philomel, 1987.
Carlisi, Alison, and Teralene Foxx. *The Forest and the Fire*. Ills. by Teralene Foxx. Los Alamos, NM: Los Alamos Historical Society, 2005.
Chase, Richard. *Grandfather Tales*. Boston: Houghton Mifflin, 1948.
Conger, Leslie. *Tops and Bottoms*. New York: Four Winds Press, 1970.
Connelly, Bernardine. *Follow the Drinking Gourd: A Story of the Underground Railroad* (Rabbit Ears American Heroes & Legends). Chicago: Rabbit Ears Entertainment, 2013.
Cooney, Barbara. *Miss Rumphius*. New York: Puffin, 1982.
Cowcher, Helen. *Rain Forest*. New York: Farrar, Straus and Giroux, 1988.
Crews, Nina. *Jack and the Beanstalk*. New York: Henry Holt, 2011.
Darling, Kathy. *There's a Zoo on You*. Brookfield, CT: Millbrook Press, 2000.
Dayrell, Elphinstone. *Why the Sun and the Moon Live in the Sky*. Illus. by Blair Lent. Boston: Houghton Mifflin, 1968.
de Gerez, Toni. *When Bear Came Down from the Sky*. Illus. by Lisa Desimini. New York: Viking, 1994.
Del Negro, Janice. *Willa and the Wind*. Illus. by Heather Solomon. New York: Marshall Cavendish, 2005.
Demi. *The Empty Pot*. New York: Square Fish, 1990.
_____. *The Hungry Coat: A Tale from Turkey*. New York: Margaret K. McElderry Books, 2004.
_____. *The Stonecutter*. New York: Knopf, 1995.
Diakite, Baba Wague. *The Hunterman and the Crocodile: A West African Folktale*. New York: Scholastic, 1997.
Dorros, Arthur. *City Chicken*. New York: HarperCollins Publishers, 2003.
Duvall, Deborah. *How Rabbit Lost His Tail: A Traditional Cherokee Legend*. Albuquerque: University of New Mexico Press, 2003.
_____. *Rabbit Goes Duck Hunting: A Traditional Cherokee Legend*. Albuquerque: University of New Mexico Press, 2004.

Echewa, Obinkaram. *The Magic Tree: A Folktale from Nigeria.* Illus. by E.B. Lewis. New York: Morrow, 1999.
Edwards, Carolyn McVickar. *The Return of the Light: Twelve Tales from Around the World for the Winter Solstice.* Cambridge, MA: DeCapo, 2005.
Ehlert, Lois. *Cuckoo/Cucu: A Mexican Folktale.* San Diego, CA: Harcourt Brace Jovanovich, 2000.
_____. *Growing Vegetable Soup.* New York: HMH Books for Young Children, 1987.
_____. *Un Lazo a la Luna/Moon Rope.* New York: Harcourt Brace Jovanovich, 1992.
_____. *Planting a Rainbow.* New York: HMH Books for Young Children, 1988.
_____. *Waiting for Wings.* New York: HMH Books for Young Readers, 2001.
Emberley, Rebecca, and Ed Emberley. *Chicken Little.* New York: Roaring Book Press, 2009.
Farmer, Penelope. *Daedalus and Icarus.* Sand Diego, CA: Harcourt Brace, 1971.
Faulker, William J. *Br'er Tiger and the Big Wind.* New York: Morrow, 1995.
Feldmann, Susan. *The Storytelling Stone: Traditional Native American Myths and Tales.* McHenry, IL: Delta, 1999.
Freedman, Deborah. *Blue Chicken.* New York: Viking, 2011.
"The Frog." In George Shannon. *More Stories to Solve.* New York: Greenwillow Books, 1991.
Galdone, Paul. *The Three Little Pigs.* New York: Clarion Books, 1970.
Gershator, Phillis. *Tukama Tootles the Flute: A Tale from the Antilles.* New York: Orchard Books, 1994.
Gerson, Mary-Joan. *How Night Came from the Sea: A Story from Brazil.* Boston: Little, Brown, 1994.
_____. *Why the Sky Is Far Away: A Nigerian Folktale.* Illus. by Carla Golembe. Boston: Little, Brown, 1992.
Goble, Paul. *Iktomi and the Berries: A Plains Indian Story.* New York: Orchard Books, 1989.
_____. *Iktomi and the Boulder.* New York: Orchard Books, 1988.
_____. *Iktomi and the Ducks: A Plains Indian Story.* New York: Orchard Books, 1990.
Graves, Keith. *Chicken Big.* San Francisco: Chronicle Books, 2010.
Gregorowski, Christopher. *Fly, Eagle, Fly! An African Fable.* Illus. by Niki Daly. New York: Margaret K. McElderry Books, 2000.
Guiberson, Brenda Z. *Frog Song.* New York: Macmillan Children's/Henry Holt Books for Young Readers, 2013.
Haley, Gail. *Jack and the Bean Tree.* New York: Crown, 1986.
Hamilton, Martha, and Mitch Weiss. *How and Why Stories: World Tales Kids Can Read and Tell.* Little Rock, AR: August House, 2000.
Han, Suzanne Crowder. *The Rabbit's Escape.* Illus. by Yumi Heo. New York: Holt, 1995.
_____. *The Rabbit's Judgment.* Illus. by Yumi Heo. New York: Holt, 1994. (Told in English and Korean.)
Han, Soma, and John C. Stickler. *Maya and the Turtle: A Korean Fairy Tale.* North Clarendon, VT: Tuttle Publishing 2012.
Hayes, Joe. *A Heart Full of Turquoise: Pueblo Indian Tales.* Santa Fe, NM: Mariposa, 1988.
Hoberman, Mary Ann. *A House Is a House for Me.* New York: Viking Press, 1978.
Holt, David, and Bill Mooney, eds. *More Ready-to-Tell Tales from Around the World.* Little Rock, AR: August House, 2000.
Hook, Jason, and Richard Hook. *Where's the Dragon?* New York: Sterling, 2003.

Hooks, William H. *The Three Pigs and the Fox.* New York: Macmillan, 1989.
"How Dragon Lost His Tail." In Cora Cheney. *Tales from a Taiwan Kitchen.* New York: Dodd, Mead, 1976.
Howe, John. *Jack and the Beanstalk.* Boston: Little, Brown, 1989.
Hurston, Zora Neale. *Roy Makes a Car.* Adapted by Mary E. Lyons. New York: Atheneum, 2005.
Jamisch, Heinz. *The Fire: An Ethiopian Folktale.* Illus. by Fabrico VandenBroeck. Toronto: Groundwood Books, 2002.
Johnson, Paul Brett. *Bearhide and Crow.* New York: Holiday House, 2000.
Joyce, William. *The Leaf Men.* New York: HarperCollins, 1996.
Kellogg, Steven. *Chicken Little.* New York: William Morrow, 1985.
Ketterman, Helen. *Waynetta and the Cornstalk: A Texas Fairy Tale.* Morton Grove, IL: Albert Whitman, 2007.
Kimmel, Eric. *Anansi and the Moss-Covered Rock.* New York: Holiday House, 1988.
Knutson, Barbara. *Love and Roast Chicken: Trickster Tale from the Andes Mountains.* Minneapolis, MN: CarolRhoda, 2004.
Kurtz, Jane. *Fire on the Mountain.* Illus. by E.B Lewis. New York: Simon & Schuster, 1994.
Langton, Jane. *Salt: A Russian Folktale.* New York: Hyperion, 1992.
Larrañaga, Ana Martin. *The Big Wide-Mouthed Frog.* New York: Walker, 2003.
Litzinger, Rosanne. *The Old Woman and Her Pig: An Old English Tale.* San Diego: Harcourt, Brace, Jovanovich, 1993.
Lowell, Susan. *The Three Little Javalinas.* Flagstaff, AZ: Rising Moon, 1992.
McCully, Emily Arnold. *Mirette on the High Wire.* New York: Scholastic, 1993.
McDermott, Gerald. *Coyote: A Trickster Tale from the American Southwest.* San Diego, CA: Harcourt Brace, 1994.
_____. *The Magic Tree: A Tale from the Congo.* New York: Holt, 1994.
_____. *Raven: A Trickster Tale from the Pacific Northwest.* San Diego: Harcourt, Brace, Jovanovich, 1993.
_____. *Zomo the Rabbit: A Trickster Tale from West Africa.* San Diego: Harcourt, Brace, Jovanovich, 1992.
MacDonald, Margaret Read. *Conejito: A Folktale from Panama.* Little Rock, AR: August House, 2006.
_____. *Earth Care: World Folktales to Talk About.* Little Rock, AR: August House, 2005.
_____. *Old Woman and Her Pig: An Appalachian Folktale.* Illustrator John Kanzler. New York: HarperCollins, 2007.
_____. *Surf War!* Little Rock, AR: August House, 2009.
_____. *Twenty Tellable Tales: Audience Participation Folktales for the Beginning Storyteller.* New York: H.W. Wilson, 1986.
Maddern, Eric. *Rainbow Bier: An Aboriginal Folktale from Northern Australia.* Boston, MA: Little, Brown and Company, 1993.
Maggi, Maria Elena. *The Great Canoe: A Kariña Legend.* Toronto: Douglas & McIntyre, 2001.
Marshak, Samuel. *The Month Brothers: A Slavic Tale.* New York: Morrow, 1983.
Martin, Rafe. *Foolish Rabbit's Big Mistake.* Illustrator Ed Young. New York: G.P. Putnam, 1985.
_____. *The Language of Birds.* Ills. by Susan Gaber. New York: Putnam, 2000.
Mayo, Gretchen Will. *Earthmaker Tales.* New York: Walker, 1989.
McCarthy, Tara. *Multicultural Fables and Fairy Tales: Stories and Activities to Promote Literacy and Cultural Awareness.* New York: Scholastic, 1999.

Meister, Cari. *Follow the Drinking Gourd: An Underground Railroad Story* (Night Sky Stories). North Mankato, MN: Picture Window Books, 2012.
Milord, Susan. *Tales of the Shimmering Sky: Ten Global Folktales with Activities Retold by Susan Milord*. Charlotte, VA: Williamson Publishing, 1996.
Mitton, Jacqueline. *The Planet Gods: Myths and Facts About the Solar System*. Washington, D.C.: National Geographic Children's Books, 2008.
Mollel, Tolowa M. *The Flying Tortoise: An Igbo Tale*. Boston: Houghton Mifflin, 1994.
Momaday, N. Scott, and Charles Woodward. *Ancestral Voice: Conversations with N. Scott Momaday*. Lincoln: University of Nebraska Press, 1989.
"The Moon." In Robert Louis Stevenson. *A Child's Garden of Verses*. Chicago: Rand McNally, 1981.
"Moon Boon." In Douglas Florian. *Comets, Stars, the Moon, and Mars*. New York: Harcourt, 2007.
Moroney, Lynn. *Moontellers: Myths of the Moon from Around the World*. Flagstaff, AZ: Northland, 1995.
Munsch, Robert. *50 Below Zero*. Toronto: Annick Press Ltd., 1986.
Norfolk, Bobby and Sherry. *Anansi and the Tug O' War*. Little Rock, AR: Story Cove, 2006.
_____. *Anansi and Turtle Go to Dinner*. Little Rock, AR: Story Cove, 2006.
O'Callahan, Jay. *Herman and Marguerite: An Earth Story*. Atlanta: Peachtree Publishers, 1996.
Olaleye, Issac O. *In the Rainfield: Who Is the Greatest?* Illus. by Ann Grifalconi. New York: Blue Sky Press, 2000.
"Old Man Coyote and the Rock." In Joe Hayes. *Coyote &: Native American Folk Tales Retold by Joe Hayes*. Santa Fe, NM: Mariposa Books, 1983.
Palmer, William R. *Why the North Star Stands Still and other Indian Legends*. Englewood Cliffs, NJ: Prentice Hall, 1947.
Paye, Won-Ldy, and Margaret H. Lippert. *Head, Body, Legs: A Story from Liberia*. New York: Holt, 2002.
_____. *Talking Vegetables*. Ills. by Julie Paschkis. New York: Holt, 2006.
Pinkney, Jerry. *The Little Red Hen*. New York: Dial Books for Young Readers, 2006.
Pretor-Pinney, Gavin, ed. *Hot Pink Flying Saucers and Other Clouds*. New York: Penguin, 2007.
Quattlebaum, Mary. *Why Sparks Fly High at Dancing Point: A Colonial American Folktale*. New York: Farrar, Straus Giroux, 2006.
Reynolds, Aaron. *Chicks and Salsa*. New York: Bloomsbury Children's Books, 2005.
Ross, Gayle. *How Turtle's Back Was Cracked: A Traditional Cherokee Tale*. New York: Dial, 1995.
Rounds, Glen. *The Three Little Pigs and the Big Bad Wolf*. New York: Holiday House, 1992.
Schwartz, Amy. *The Lady Who Put Salt in Her Coffee: from the Peterkin Papers by Lucretia Hale*. San Diego: Harcourt, Brace, Jovanovich, 1989.
Scieszka, Jon and Smith, Lane. *Science Verse*. New York: Viking, 2004.
Seeger, Pete, and Michael Hayes. *Abiyoyo Returns*. New York: Aladdin Books, 2004.
Shannon, George. *Lizard's Song*. New York: HarperTrophy, 1992.
Sharmat, Mitchell. *Gregory, the Terrible Eater*. New York: Scholastic Trade, 2009.
Simms, Laura. *Moon and Otter and Frog*. New York: Disney-Hyperion, 1995.
Singh, Rina. *Moon Tales: Myths of the Moon from Around the World*. New York: Bloomsbury Publishing, Ltd., 2000.
Sloat, Teri. *Sody Sallyratus*. New York: Dutton Junior, 1997.

Snyder, Dianne. *The Boy of the Three Year Nap*. Illus. by Allen Say. Boston: Houghton Mifflin, 1993.
So, Meilo. *Gobble, Gobble, Slip, Slop: A Tale of a Very Greedy Cat*. New York: Knopf, 2004.
Spier, Peter. *Dreams*. Garden City, New York: Doubleday, 1986.
Stein, David Ezra. *Interrupting Chicken*. Somerville, MA: Candlewick Press, 2010.
Stevens, Janet. *Tops and Bottoms*. New York: Harcourt Brace, 1995.
Stewart, Sarah. *The Gardener*. New York: Square Fish, 1997.
Stileman, Kali. *Roly-poly Egg*. Wilton, CT: Tiger Tales, 2011.
"The Story of the Root Children." Sibylle von Oflers, retold by Jane Stenson in Norfolk, Sherry, Diane Williams and Jane Stenson. *Literacy Development in the Storytelling Classroom*. Santa Barbara, CA: Libraries Unlimited, 2009.
Tan, Amy. *The Moon Lady*. New York: Macmillan, 1992.
Taylor, Harriet Peck. *Coyote Places the Stars*. New York: Aladdin, 1997.
_____. *Secrets of the Stone*. New York: Farrar, Straus and Giroux, 2000.
_____. *When Bear Stole the Chinook*. New York: Farrar, Straus and Giroux, 1997.
Tolstoy, Aleksei. *The Great Big Enormous Turnip*. New York: Scholastic, 1969.
Tune, Suelynn Ching. *How Maui Slowed the Sun*. Honolulu: University of Hawaii Press, 1988.
Uchida, Yoshiko. *The Magic Listening Cap*. New York: Harcourt Brace, 1955.
Udry, Janice May. *The Moon Jumpers*. New York: Harper & Row, 1959.
Ungerer, Tomi. *Moonman*. New York: Harper & Row, 1967.
Van Allsburg, Chris. *Two Bad Ants*. Boston: Houghton Mifflin, 1988.
Ward, Helen. *The King of the Birds*. Ontario: Templar, 1997.
Ward, Jennifer. *What Will Hatch?* New York: Walker Books for Young Readers, 2013.
Whitman, Walt. *When I Heard the Learn'd Astronomer*. New York: Simon & Schuster, 2004.
Wiesner, David. *June 29, 1999*. New York: Clarion Books, 1992.
Williams, Carol Ann. *Tsuhu the Little Snail*. Illus. by Tatsuro Kiuchi. New York: Simon & Schuster, 1995.
Williamson, Ray A. and Jean Guard Monroe. *They Dance in the Sky: Native American Star Myths*. Boston: Houghton Mifflin, 2007.
Wilson, Barbara Ker. *Maui and the Big Fish*. London: Frances Lincoln Children's Books, 2004.
Wolkstein, Diane. *The Cool Ride in the Sky*. New York: Alfred A. Knopf, 1973.
_____. *Sun Mother Wakes the World: An Australian Creation Story*. New York: HarperCollins, 2004.
_____. *White Wave: A Chinese Tale*. Illus. by Ed Young. San Diego, CA: Harcourt Brace, 1996.
Yacowitz, Caryn. *The Jade Stone: A Chinese Folktale*. Illus. by Ju-Hong Chen. New York: Holiday House, 1992.
Zunshine, Tatiana. *A Little Story About a Big Turnip*. Columbus, OH: Pumpkin House, 2003.

Resources for Literature-Based Science Lessons

The following professional resources provide excellent literature-based science lesson plans along with cogent arguments for integrating language and literacy learning with science learning. We urge you to investigate these books, which include some stories that are perfect for use in the classroom.

Ansberry, Karen, and Emily Morgan. *Picture-Perfect Science Lessons Using Children's Books to Guide Inquiry, 3–6 (Expanded 2nd Edition)*. Arlington, VA: NSTA Press, 2010.
_____. *More Picture-Perfect Science Lessons Using Children's Books to Guide Inquiry, K–4*. Arlington, VA: NSTA Press, 2007.
_____. *Even More Picture-Perfect Science Lessons Using Children's Books to Guide Inquiry, K–5*. Arlington, VA: NSTA Press, 2013.
Butzow, Carol M., and John W. Butzow. *Exploring the Environment Through Children's Literature: An Integrated Approach*. Englewood, CO: Teacher Ideas Press, 1999. (Creative ideas for grade K–4.)
_____. *Science through Children's Literature: An Integrated Approach*. Englewood, CO: Teacher Ideas Press, 1989. (Very thorough and thoughtfully constructed lesson plans for grades K–5.)
Ellis, Brian "Fox." *Learning from the Land: Teaching Ecology through Stories and Activities*. Santa Barbara, CA: Libraries Unlimited, 2011.
Fredericks, Anthony D. *Investigating Natural Disasters Through Children's Literature: An Integrated Approach*. Englewood, CO: Teacher Ideas Press, 2001. (Grades 3–6; adaptable to K–2.)
Gertz, Susan E., Dwight J. Portman, and Mickey Sarquis. *Teaching Physical Science Through Children's Literature: 20 Complete Lessons for Elementary Grades*. New York: Learning Triangle Press, 1996.
Haven, Kendall. *100 Greatest Science Discoveries of All Time*. Santa Barbara, CA: Libraries Unlimited, 2007.
_____. *Stepping Stone to Science: True Tales and Awesome Activities*. Englewood, Co: Teacher Ideas Press, 1997.
Kraus, Anne Marie. *Folktale Themes and Activities for Children, Volume 1: Pourquoi Tales*. Santa Barbara, CA: Libraries Unlimited, 1998.
Lipke, Barbara. *Figures, Facts and Fables: Telling Tales in Science and Math*. Portsmouth, NH: Heinemann, 1996.
Norfolk, Sherry, Jane Stenson, and Diane Williams. *Storytelling Classroom: Applications across the Curriculum*. Santa Barbara, CA: Libraries Unlimited, 2006.
Royce, Christine Anne, Emily Morgan, and Karen Ansberry. *Teaching Science through Trade Books*. Arlington, VA: NSTA Press, 2012. (Most of the trade books are nonfiction, but there are several inventive lesson plans based on fiction books as well.)
Rubright, Lynn. *Beyond the Beanstalk: Interdisciplinary Learning through Storytelling*. Portsmouth, NH: Heinemann, 1996.
Staton, Hilarie N. *Science & Stories: Integrating Science and Literature, Grades 4–6*. Parsippany, NJ: Good Year Books, 1994.
Strauss, Kevin. *Tales with Tails: Storytelling the Wonders of the Natural World*. Santa Barbara, CA: Libraries Unlimited, 2006.
Wheeler-Tippen, Jodi, ed. *Science the "Write" Way*. Arlington, VA: NSTA Press, 2011. (In addition to the informational writing you would expect, collaborative writing of scientific stories, pourquoi stories, and imaginative writing are addressed. Includes assessment criteria.)

Professional Resources for Theory and Practice

Print Resources

Aston, Kevin. *How to Fly a Horse: the Secret History of Creation, Invention, and Discovery*. New York: Doubleday, 2015.

Bamford, Rosemary A., and Janice V. Kristo. *Making Facts Come Alive: Choosing and Using Nonfiction Literature.* Norwood, MA: Christopher-Gordon Publishers, Inc., 2003.

Blank Kelner, Lenore. *The Creative Classroom: A Guide for Using Creative Drama in the Classroom, PreK–6.* Portsmouth, NH: Heinemann, 1993.

Chancer, Joni and Gina Rester-Zodrow. *Moon Journals: Writing, Art, and Inquiry through Focused Nature Study.* Portsmouth, NH: Heinemann, 1997.

Cornett, Claudia. *Creating Meaning through Literature and the Arts: Arts Integration for Classroom Teachers* (4th ed.). New York: Pearson, 2010.

Donahue David. M., and Stuart, Jennifer, eds. *Artful Teaching: Integrating the Arts for Understanding across the Curriculum, K–8.* New York: Teachers College Press, 2010.

Gallas, Karen. *The Languages of Learning: How Children Talk, Write, Dance, Draw, and Sing Their Understanding of the World.* New York: Teachers' College Press, 1994.

_____. *Talking Their Way into Science: Hearing Children's Questions and Theories, Responding with Curriculum.* New York: Teachers' College Press, 1995.

Greene, Ellin, and Janice Del Negro. *Storytelling Art and Technique.* Santa Barbara, CA: Libraries Unlimited, 2010.

Hart, Betty, and T.R. Riesley. "The Early Catastrophe: The 30 Million Word Gap by Age 3." *American Educator*, Spring 2003, 4–9. http://www.aft.org//sites/default/files/periodicals/The Early Castrophe.pdf

Herndon, James. *How to Survive in Your Native Land.* Portsmouth, NH: Boynton/Cook Publishers, 1997.

Landay, Eileen, and Kurt Wootton. *Linking Literacy and the Arts: A Reason to Read.* Cambridge, MA: Harvard Education Press, 2012.

Lerman, Liz. *Liz Lerman's Critical Response Process.* Takoma Park, MD: Dance Exchange, Inc., 2003.

MacDonald, Margaret Read. *The Parent's Guide to Storytelling: How to Make Up New Stories and Retell Old Favorites.* New York: HarperCollins, 1995.

McCaslin, Nellie. *Creative Drama in the Classroom and Beyond.* White Plains, NY: Longman, 1996.

Richhardt, Ron, Mark Church, and Karin Morrison. *Making Thinking Visible: How to Promote Engagement, Understanding, and Independence for All Learners.* San Francisco: Jossey-Bass, 2011.

Sousa, David, and Tom Pilecki. *From STEM to STEAM: Using Brain-Compatible Strategies to Integrate the Arts.* Thousand Oaks, California: Corwin, 2013.

Spolin, Viola. *Theatre Games for the Classroom, A Teacher's Handbook.* Evanston, IL: Northwestern University Press, 1986.

Tatar, Maria. *Enchanted Hunters of the Power of Stories in Childhood.* London: W.W. Norton, 2009.

Online Resources

ArtsEdge website has lesson plans and tips for teachers
http://artsedge.kennedy-center.org/

Arts Education for Maryland Schools. Resources for arts education and evidence as to why it is important.
http://www.aems-edu.org/resources/index.html

Design for Accessibility: A Cultural Administrator's Handbook
http://arts.gov/sites/default/files/Design-for-Accessibility.pdf

Education Closet has lesson plans and tips for teachers.
http://www.educationcloset.com/arts-integration-links-and-resources/

Great Websites and Resources for Arts Integration
http://www.kutztown.edu/academics/visual_arts/arted/PDF/Book-bilbliography-for-Arts-Integration.pdf

Learner.org has lesson plans and tips for teachers.
http://www.learner.org/channel/libraries/connectarts68/library_w hat.html

Literatelearner.com has a clear explanation of the six traits of writing with sample rubrics.
http://www.literatelearner.com/6traits/page_template6t.php?f=main

About the Contributors

Tracy Drummer **Aiden** has been a teacher of young children for 14 years, 10 of which were teaching pre-kindergarten and kindergarten at Baker Demonstration School in Wilmette, Illinois. She received a Bachelor of Science degree from Western Illinois University and holds an M.S. from National-Louis University in counseling and an M.A.T. from National-Louis University in 2000.

Elizabeth **Barlock** holds a bachelor's degree from Illinois State University in elementary education and a master's degree in early childhood education. She has been teaching kindergarten for the past nine years at Baker Demonstration School in Wilmette, Illinois.

Judith **Black** creates programs that take new perspectives on our national history and help students generate enthusiasm for and explore all aspects of their world. She has been featured ten times at the National Storytelling Festival, and has won the Circle of Excellence Oracle Award, storytelling's most coveted laurel. Her website is www.judithblack.com.

Karen **Chace** is a teaching artist, storyteller, and author. She received the Brother Blue–Ruth Hill Award from LANES in 2009, and the National Storytelling Network's Oracle Service and Leadership Award in 2011. Her first book, *Story by Story: Creating a School Storytelling Troupe* was published in October 2014. www.storybug.net.

Lindsey **Cohn** grew up in the Blue Ridge Mountains of Virginia and moved to Knoxville, Tennessee, to go to Johnson Bible College. She finished her graduate work there and became a first-grade teacher at Mooreland Heights Elementary, in an arts integrated school and a tech 1:1 school. lindsey.cohn@knoxschools.org.

Vito M. **Dipinto** began his professional career as an organic chemist. Realizing later in life that he was really a performance artist he became an educator—a Montessori teacher, a science teacher, science curriculum designer and coordinator at the Baker Demonstration School, past chair of NLU's Science Education Department, and the senior science education faculty member at NLU.

Lynette J. **Ford** is a fourth-generation storyteller and the author of two collections from her family's heritage of tales, *Affrilachian Tales: Folktales from the African-American Appalachian Tradition*, and *Beyond the Briar Patch: Affrilachian Folktales,*

Food and Folklore. Both won the Anne Izard Storytellers' Choice Award. Her latest book is a collection of twisted folktale adaptations, resource information and creative-writing exercises for older students and adults. www.storytellerlynford.com.

Joyce H. **Geary** has taught at levels from preschool to college and seminary. She has taught in self-contained classrooms and as an English as a Second Language teacher. She uses stories to entertain, to bring students into a comfortable level of English language use and to help students understand the interconnection between story and other academic classes. She has taught workshops and classes on the use and value of story. jgeary@columbus.rr.com.

Jeff **Gere** is one of Hawai'i's most prolific and popular storytellers. He blends talents as a painter, puppeteer, mime, teacher, and director into a performance style that has electrified audiences of every age throughout Hawai'i and the mainland for two decades. His energy, range of voices, morphing elastic face and clear characterizations make his performances unforgettable events. www.jeffgere.com.

Mary **Hamilton** is a storyteller who combines her interests with those of her husband, Charles Wright. Mary tells the stories, and Charles collects the insects used in their collaborations. They share their Frankfort, Kentucky, home with nearly 10,000 insect specimens. Together, they present "Buggy Kentucky," a program of insect stories and facts. Alone, Mary tells many other stories and facilitates storytelling-related workshops. Learn more at www.maryhamilton.info.

Larry **Kinsella** is from Fairview Heights, Illinois, and together with his wife Marilyn has produced many "Stories 'n' Stones" programs. Marilyn, the storyteller, engages her listeners, while Larry demonstrates his expertise in the use of natural materials, ancient techniques for making tools, and how they were used. Their programs include hands-on activities for the students. His website is www.flintknapper.com.

Marilyn A. **Kinsella**, from Fairview Heights, Illinois, works with her husband Larry to produce their interactive "Stories 'n' Stones" programs, which combine storytelling with hands-on activities for students. Marilyn uses her skills as a storyteller to engage the imagination of her listeners, while her husband demonstrates his expertise in toolmaking and the use of tools made from natural materials. Her website is www.marilynkinsella.org.

Katie **Knutson**, a storyteller and teaching artist, spends most days in classrooms integrating storytelling and drama across the curriculum. She can also be found performing, writing for *Storytelling Magazine*, and leading workshops for teachers and tellers. Find out more at www.ripplingstories.com or stories2teach@gmail.com.

Sheri **Lucterhand** was a public school art teacher for fifteen years. She now runs her own art studio and teaches at the local art center. Her program focuses on connecting children's books and famous artists to basic art elements. lucterhand@gmail.com.

Jenny **McCrery** is a fifth-grade teacher at Bradley Academy, an Arts Integrated School in Murfreesboro, Tennessee. She lives in Murfreesboro with her husband of 16 years and their two children.

About the Contributors

Darlene J. **Neumann**, with partner Larry C. Neumann, performs as Two Voices, and share stories and songs from experience, history, science and folklore, telling tales individually or in tandem. She is the Library Media Specialist at the Science and Arts Academy, Des Plaines, Illinois. www.twovoicesstorytelling.com.

Larry C. **Neumann**, with Darlene J. Neumann, performs as Two Voices; individually or together, they share stories and songs from experience, history, science and folklore. While he is retired as a teacher, he directs middle school dramas and coaches for the Science Olympiad. www.twovoicesstorytelling.com.

Ingrid **Nixon** is a world-traveling storyteller who brings home tales for audiences of all ages. She lived in Alaska for over 20 years, working many of those years leading the naturalist programs in national parks. She's an award-winning reporter and film writer, and former public radio program host. www.IngridNixon.com.

Bobby **Norfolk** is a three-time Emmy winner and member of the NSN Oracle Circle of Excellence, a story-performer, recording artist, author, and teaching artist. His living history performances highlight the African American experience, bringing history to vivid life for audiences young and old. www.bobbynorfolk.com.

Sherry **Norfolk** is an award-winning storyteller, teaching artist, and author, performing and leading residencies and professional development workshops across the United States and Southeast Asia. The co-author of several books on storytelling in the classroom, she is an authority on integrating learning through storytelling. She serves as an adjunct professor of creative arts in learning at Lesley University and as storytelling adjunct at East Tennessee State University. www.sherrynorfolk.com.

Dana Allande **O'Brien** is a second-grade teacher at the Baker Demonstration School in Wilmette, Illinois, and has taught in Chicago and Los Angeles. She is interested in using improvisational games in the classroom for curricular and social/emotional purposes. She received an AB in psychology from the University of Chicago and a master's in teaching from DePaul University. dana.obrien@gmail.com.

Arianna **Ross** and her company Story Tapestries present programs that serve to develop the total person—social-emotional, intellectual and physical. She custom-designs her arts integration programs to better serve the needs of the community. For over 16 years, she has worked in K–12 schools and in colleges across the United States. www.storytapestries.com.

Lynn **Rubright** is an Emmy-award winning storyteller, as well as recipient of the National Storytelling Network's Lifetime Achievement Award and numerous other honors. She is co-founder of the St. Louis Storytelling Festival, and gives workshops for COCA (Center of Creative Arts, St. Louis). She is a professor emerita at Webster University in St. Louis. www.lynnrubright.com.

Anne **Shimojima**, a retired elementary library media specialist, performs historical pieces and folk tales from her Asian heritage and around the world. A frequent storyteller in festivals, schools, libraries, and museums, she also gives workshops on the use of storytelling in education and the creation of family history projects. www.anneshimojima.com.

About the Contributors

Fran **Stallings** is an internationally known storyteller, author, and recording artist. Retired from teaching university level biology, she now uses the traditional art of storytelling to impart modern science concepts while engendering respect for our planet's living things. She trains teachers, zoo docents, and park rangers nationwide and overseas. wwwfranstallings.com.

Geordan **Stenson** loves food. Along with storytelling, cooking and eating are two of his favorite pastimes. He has worked in multiple kitchens in Chicago and Europe, and is a sous chef at the Dana Hotel in Chicago, helping to create tasty delights including sausages, pickles, and balance in all things.

Jane **Stenson** is a storyteller, teaching artist, and educator. She has written and edited numerous works on the use of storytelling in the classroom, and is a leading authority on integrating learning through storytelling. She serves as co-chair of YES! (Youth, Educators, and Storytellers Alliance), a special interest group of the National Storytelling Network (NSN). www.janestenson.com stenson.stories@gmail.com.

Kevin **Strauss** has been telling stories since birth, according to his parents. He has been a professional storyteller for the last 15 years, and tells nature stories and folktales from around the world at schools, preschools and libraries across the Midwest. Visit him at www.naturestory.com and see him tell stories at www.StoryLibrary.org.

Julie **Tubbs** is director of community education at the Magic House, St. Louis Children's Museum, where she develops and implements hands-on programming for students, parents and educators. She holds a B.A. in elementary and special education, an M.A.T. in communications and is pursuing a degree in early childhood education.

Cy Ashley **Webb** spent the 1980s as a bench scientist, the tech boom doing intellectual property law, and the first decade of the millennium aspiring to be the world's oldest grad student at Stanford, where she is interested in political martyrdom. She writes for *Stark Insider* and the *San Francisco Examiner*.

Charles **Wright** works as a team with his wife, Mary Hamilton. Mary tells stories, and Charles collects insects. They share their Frankfort, Kentucky, home with nearly 10,000 insect specimens. Together, they present "Buggy Kentucky," a program of insect stories and facts. Learn more about "Buggy Kentucky" at www.maryhamilton.info.

Index

adaptations 1, 4, 69, 82, 83, 172, 191, 195, 196, 198, 201, 207
Alaska 206
alkaline 203
Amazonian rain forest 225, 228, 282
Anansi 20. 29–34, 281, 284, 285
Armstrong, Neil 267
asterisms 106, 108, 109, 111–113
atmosphere 227, 229, 243, 245

bacteria 202, 203
balance scale 123, 124
Big Dipper 106–110, 112–114; see Ursa Major
biodiversity 81, 85, 207
biosphere 227, 229, 243, 245; see also habitat
boll weevil 185, 188, 190
brachiopods 247
Brazil 225
brewing pan 199
buzzards 191–198

caldera 245
carnivores 178, 208–213
cells 69, 73, 145–147, 180–183, 202
Challenger 267–268
Chief Seattle 126
China 234–238
chlorophyll 143–147
chloroplasts 146, 147, 182
chrysalis 59–64, 67, 69, 72, 73
clay pot 242, 243, 245
climate change 198
coal canals 248
cocoon 62, 64, 69, 72, 167
color shadows 153–154
constellations 108, 110–113
coyote 107, 120–123, 281, 284–286
crop rotation 184, 185, 188
crystal and crystallization 254, 257–259
cyclone and cyclonic dust extraction 220, 222–223

decompose 158, 161, 203, 226
dehydration 204

density 35, 38, 39, 123
directionality 105
documentation 26, 28, 77, 78, 82, 83, 140
drinking gourd 106, 108, 113, 114, 282, 284
Dyson, James 223

ecology 68, 73, 172, 173, 174, 276, 287
ecosystem 42, 81, 157–159, 161, 166, 172, 185, 195, 197, 201, 213, 242
erosion 123, 197, 198, 237
ethnobotanist 145
eugenol 145–147
experiment 9, 12, 14, 16, 26–28, 23, 38, 41, 43, 87, 133, 140, 142, 145, 147, 152, 154, 185, 188, 189, 190, 202–204, 257, 258, 275

fairy loaves 247
faunal succession 249
food web 161, 164, 195, 208, 209, 212, 213
force 130, 131, 133, 137
fossils and fossil succession 124, 246–253
Fukushima 217–219

geological time scale 250–252
geosphere 227, 229, 243, 245
gravity 130, 131, 133
Great Basin Desert 103

habitat 53–55, 57, 60, 65, 78, 92, 159, 195, 196, 198, 207, 227, 228
Halite 258
Hawaii 239–245
herbivores 178, 208–213
High Eagle, J.C. 267, 269
Himalayas 236–236
hydrosphere 227, 229, 243, 245
hypothesis 9, 27, 139, 189, 237

igneous 124
Industrial Age 247
insects 13–15, 61, 67, 70, 87, 160, 161, 163–165, 167–169, 179, 208, 277, 292, 294

295

296 Index

interdependence 81, 126, 155, 157–159, 161, 166, 172, 197, 198, 202, 227, 229
Iroquois tribe 107

jackrabbits 103

Kamau, Abaya 193
Klondike Gold Rush 206

life cycle 4, 49, 60, 61, 64, 65, 74, 75, 77, 78, 79, 81, 83, 85–88, 163–165, 201, 206, 209, 244, 278

magnesium sulfate 259
McAuliffe, Christa 267, 269
measurement 104, 140, 144, 145, 189, 279
metamorphosis 59, 66, 67, 69, 124, 167, 277
Milky Way 103, 282
minerals 62, 123, 238, 258, 259
mitochondria 182
Mohs Scale of Hardness 123
moon 4, 98, 101, 105, 108, 116–119, 240, 261, 263, 265, 267–270, 275, 276, 280–283, 285, 286, 288
multicultural stories 21, 58, 106, 158, 281, 284
Musquakie tribe 107

NASA 260–271, 275
nebula 111
Next Generation Science Standards 158
nocturnal 102

Oklahoma Ag in the Classroom 189
organelle 181–183

Paiute Indians 102, 103
parasite 166, 167
patterns 106, 122, 137
Pawnee Indians 120
Pele 239–245
pH scale 203
plate tectonics 124, 237, 238, 239, 243, 244
Polaris 106, 114
polarity 144
pound stones 247
pourquoi stories 21, 52, 54–58, 84, 86, 87, 102, 103, 105, 132, 237, 238, 273, 277, 278, 287
prairie dogs 46–51
precipitation 258
predator 102, 104, 105, 164, 166, 167, 175, 177–179
preservation 199, 203–205
prey 102, 104, 164, 166, 167, 175, 178, 179, 193, 197
proboscis 61, 62, 64, 69, 71–73
pulleys 136–140

quartzite 254, 255, 258

rainbow 35, 37, 39, 83, 140, 283, 284
retina 154
Robertson, Ervin A. "Nimrod" 206
rock cycle 4, 74, 120, 123, 124, 239, 243, 244
rocks 4, 31–33, 123, 124, 132, 237, 238, 243, 244, 246–248, 259, 264; *see also* igneous; rock cycle; sedimentary
Rumpelstiltskin patterns 153

scientific method 5, 9, 10, 26–28, 187, 189, 190; *see also* documentation; experiment; hypothesis
scurvy 206
sedimentary 124
shadow puppets 151–153
shadows 102, 104, 148–154
Shaman 145
silhouette 150
skull 208, 209, 212, 214
social interaction 207
solvent 144, 146, 147
spiders 13–16, 18–21, 160, 161, 164, 166, 168, 282
Star 111
Stone 254–259
storyboard 39, 54
sun 3, 4, 18, 19, 35, 36, 66, 67, 69, 70–73, 85, 98–105, 108, 113, 114, 117, 120, 191, 192, 268, 271, 275, 276, 282, 286
supersaturation 258

tableaux 228, 230, 233
Taiwan 235–238
teeth 206–213
thinking routines 119
thrust 130
tornedo 19; *see* water spout; whirlwind
tsunami 215, 217–219
typhoon 234–237

Underground Railroad 113, 114

volcanoes 124, 239–245, 275
vortex 28; *see also* cyclone; tornado; water spout
Voyager 267, 268, 270, 271
vultures 193

Wasco tribe 107
wasps 13–16, 160, 161, 164, 165, 177
water cycle 60, 64, 74, 75, 81, 85–88, 278, 279
water spout 18–21; *see* tornado
wave 215–219
whirlwind 221

Yggdrasil 126
Yukon River 206

www.ingramcontent.com/pod-product-compliance
Lightning Source LLC
Chambersburg PA
CBHW051209300426
44116CB00006B/499